HENRY VAUGHAN

Jonathan F. S. Post

HENRY VAUGHAN

൞ The Unfolding Vision

PRINCETON UNIVERSITY PRESS
PRINCETON, NEW JERSEY

Copyright © 1982 by Princeton University Press

Published by Princeton University Press, 41 William Street,
Princeton, New Jersey
In the United Kingdom: Princeton University Press,
Guildford, Surrey

All Rights Reserved
Library of Congress Cataloging in Publication Data will be found
on the last printed page of this book
Publication of this book has been aided by the Whitney Darrow
Publication Reserve Fund of Princeton University Press

This book has been composed in Linotron Sabon type

Clothbound editions of Princeton University Press books are printed
on acid-free paper, and binding materials are chosen for strength
and durability

Printed in the United States of America by Princeton University
Press, Princeton, New Jersey

For Susan

For one throb of the artery,
While on that old grey stone I sat
Under the old wind-broken tree,
I knew that One is animate,
Mankind inanimate phantasy.

—W. B. Yeats, "A Meditation in Time of War"

Contents

ACKNOWLEDGMENTS	xi
ABBREVIATIONS	xiii
INTRODUCTION	xv

CHAPTER ONE
Vaughan In and Out of "the Shade of His Owne Bayes": *Poems* 1646 — 3

CHAPTER TWO
Olor Iscanus and the Disenchanted Muse — 25

CHAPTER THREE
Serious Play in Brecknock: Cavalier Fellowship and the Transmigration of Wit — 45

CHAPTER FOUR
Eminent Measure: The Poetics of Conversion — 70

CHAPTER FIVE
Making the Purchase Spread — 116

CHAPTER SIX
Spitting out the Phlegm: The Conflict of Voices in *Silex Scintillans* — 157

CHAPTER SEVEN
"The Night" and Vaughan's "Late and Dusky" Age — 186

CHAPTER EIGHT
Thalia Rediviva: Looking Backward and Forward — 212

INDEX OF VAUGHAN'S WORKS	235
GENERAL INDEX	238

Acknowledgments

IN THE COURSE of writing on Vaughan, I have acquired an embarrassing number of debts of which it is almost impossible to make a full disclosure. Joseph Summers first introduced me to serious study of the poet, and his patience and superb literary judgments have been continually invoked over the years. If my study falls short of the standards of scholarly and critical excellence he established in his own work on Herbert, it is not for want of trying on my part or for want of encouragement on his. The early stages of the project also received valuable support from former teachers and friends, George Ford, Anthony Hecht, Cyrus Hoy, and Stephen Wigler, all from the University of Rochester. I wish further to acknowledge my former colleagues at Yale: Louis Martz served as a generous scholarly resource on whom I happily drew, while Charles Berger, Richard Brodhead, Paula Johnson, and Michael Seidel allowed me to rely on them in various ways. I can only regret, with others, the loss of the opportunity to thank in person the late Richard Sylvester. Various portions of the manuscript in its early form received a vigorous scrubbing at the hands of Boyd Berry and Arthur Kinney, both of whom helped me to turn difficult corners, while Bruce Smith lent his fine touch to a number of rough spots that persisted into the final version. The longest sufferer, of course, has been my wife who, almost in spite of herself, has remained the most generous of critics and babysitters: it is to her that this book is dedicated.

Several institutions have aided significantly in the research and completion of this project. A dissertation fellowship from the Folger Shakespeare Library created a splendid opportunity to begin writing on Vaughan in 1974-1975, and if barely a sentence survives from this initial scholarly exploration, some of the ideas have proven neither so easy, nor perhaps so desirable, to remove. The study profited further from a week's research during the summer of 1977 at the University of Wales Library at Cardiff and the National Library at Aberystwyth; the excursion was sponsored in part by the Griswold Foundation of Yale. The major portion of the book, however, was written in 1979-1980, with the help of a year-long grant from the National Endowment for the Humanities, which the English Department of UCLA kindly allowed me to take in lieu of first-year teaching duties. Along with expressing my gratitude for the courtesies extended by the officers and staffs of the libraries already mentioned, I wish to thank the staffs of the Rush Rhees Memorial Library of the University of Rochester, the Beinecke and the Sterling Memorial Libraries of Yale University, the Henry E. Huntington Library in San Marino, and the University Research Library of UCLA. A grant from UCLA helped in the final preparation of the manuscript, which was typed by Jeanette Gilkison with pleasant expertise.

Earlier versions of chapters six and seven have appeared, respectively, in *Philological Quarterly* and *Studies in English Literature*; the material is reprinted here with kind permission of these journals. I would also like to express my appreciation to Mrs. Arthur Sherwood of Princeton University Press for the intelligent care she exercised in her capacity as Literature Editor; to Annabel Patterson, whose discerning reading of the manuscript for the Press served as a happy stimulus for revisions; and to Marilyn Campbell for her tactful preparation of the copy text. Beyond a general acknowledgment to Vaughan's editors, of whom Alan Rudrum deserves particular mention, and to others who have written on the Welsh poet, I have attempted in the notes to keep a more exact record of my scholarly debts.

Los Angeles
January, 1982

Abbreviations

CPHV	*Henry Vaughan: The Complete Poems*, ed. Alan Rudrum (Harmondsworth: Penguin Books Ltd., 1976)
JEGP	*Journal of English and Germanic Philology*
MLN	*Modern Language Notes*
MLQ	*Modern Language Quarterly*
MLR	*Modern Language Review*
PMLA	*Publications of the Modern Language Association*
RES	*Review of English Studies*
SEL	*Studies in English Literature*
SP	*Studies in Philology*
SPHV	*The Secular Poems of Henry Vaughan*, ed. E. L. Marilla (Uppsala: Lundequistska Bokhandeln, 1958)
Works	*The Works of Henry Vaughan*, ed. L. C. Martin, 2nd ed. (Oxford: Clarendon Press, 1957)

Introduction

WRITING in 1694 to his cousin, the antiquarian John Aubrey, Henry Vaughan concluded a brief account of the Welsh Bards with an extraordinary and not-so-brief description of one poet's sudden genesis:

> I was told by a very sober & knowing person (now dead) that in his time, there was a young lad father & motherless, & soe very poor that he was forced to beg; butt att last was taken up by a rich man, that kept a great stock of sheep upon the mountains not far from the place where I now dwell. who cloathed him & sent him into the mountains to keep his sheep. There in Summer time following the sheep & looking to their lambs, he fell into a deep sleep; In wch he dreamt, that he saw a beautifull young man with a garland of green leafs upon his head, & an hawk upon his fist: with a quiver full of Arrows att his back, coming towards him (whistling several measures or tunes all the way) & att last lett the hawk fly att him, w^ch (he dreamt) gott into his mouth & inward parts, & suddenly awaked in a great fear & consternation: butt possessed with such a vein, or gift of poetrie, that he left the sheep & went about the Countrey, making songs upon all occasions, and came to be the most famous Bard in all the Countrey in his time.[1]

It would be tempting to turn this romantic tale, composed in the fading hours of the author's life and the last of his writings to survive, into a poet's "final statement" about his own career; but I shall resist at the outset the double opportunity to be both synoptic and ingenious in favor of making a smaller point: after forty years of near-silence (most of his work was completed by 1655), Vaughan could still respond with obvious feeling to the myth of an abrupt, even brutal, and yet

---

[1] *Works*, p. 696. All references to and quotations from Vaughan's writings will be to this edition; hereafter, the page number(s) in parenthesis will follow the text reference.

miraculous transformation in which one poet is "created" by another and a garland is passed between them.

The myth of a dramatic rebirth is at the center of all critical interpretations of Vaughan, regardless of whether it is adopted or denied as a determining approach to the poetry. It has also been the source of considerable mischief. Critics valuing only the religious verse have used the "event" as evidence of a sharp break in the poet's consciousness and a reason to avoid discussing the considerable block of poetry that lies on the other side of this experience.[2] Those reacting against this "unrepresentative" view of the poet have sought to downplay the importance of a conversion of any kind in order to argue the distinctive merits of a secular Vaughan: his career, rather than being radically disjunctive, is interpreted as a continuous creative effort.[3] But the limitations of each approach are made

---

[2] Accounts of Vaughan's conversion date back to his nineteenth-century revival with H. F. Lyte's edition of the *Sacred Poems and Private Ejaculations by Henry Vaughan* (London: William Pickering, 1847). They are continued thereafter in that century by Alexander B. Grosart in the introduction to his edition of *The Works in Prose and Verse of Henry Vaughan*, 4 vols. (Lancashire: The Fuller Worthies Library, 1871) and in H. C. Beeching's introduction to *The Poems of Henry Vaughan*, ed. E. K. Chambers, 2 vols. (London: Lawrence & Bullen, Ltd., 1896). Modern scholars in the same tradition include F. E. Hutchinson, *Henry Vaughan: A Life and Interpretation* (Oxford: Clarendon Press, 1947); E. C. Pettet, *Of Paradise and Light: A Study of Vaughan's Silex Scintillans* (Cambridge: Cambridge Univ. Press, 1960); and R. A. Durr, *On the Mystical Poetry of Henry Vaughan* (Cambridge, Mass.: Harvard Univ. Press, 1962). Like the specialist studies provided by Elizabeth Holmes, *Henry Vaughan and the Hermetic Philosophy* (1932; rpt. New York: Russell & Russell, 1967), and Ross Garner, *Henry Vaughan: Experience and the Tradition* (Chicago: Univ. of Chicago Press, 1959) as well as the general overviews given by Joan Bennett, *Four Metaphysical Poets* (Cambridge: Cambridge Univ. Press, 1934) and M. M. Mahood, *Poetry and Humanism* (1950; rpt. New York: W. W. Norton & Co., 1970), all of the works in this group favor, almost to the complete exclusion of Vaughan's other writings, the religious verse of *Silex Scintillans*.

[3] Among the numerous attempts by E. L. Marilla to restore the secular poems to respectability, see "The Significance of Henry Vaughan's Literary Reputation," *MLQ* 5 (1944): 155-62; "The Religious Conversion of Henry Vaughan," *RES* 21 (1945): 15-22; "Henry Vaughan's Conversion: A Recent View," *MLN* 63 (1948): 394-97; "The Secular and Religious Poetry of Henry Vaughan," *MLQ* 9 (1948): 394-411; and especially his heavily annotated edition of the secular poems (*SPHV*). James D. Simmonds's *Masques of God:*

INTRODUCTION

bold in the light of the other. If enthusiasts of *Silex* are less than persuasive in painting a picture of a poet born willy-nilly from a single, powerful religious experience, secularists are unable to account for many of the impulses that went into the making of his finest verse. On the one hand, we find missing a framework that could deepen our understanding of the particular achievements of *Silex*; on the other, we have a mass of poetry without a strong center to it: and in both instances we come away with a partial view of Vaughan's accomplishments, secular and devotional alike.[4]

The following study attempts to respond to these deficiencies by presenting an integrating view of Vaughan that nonetheless respects the individual and, in many ways, independent achievements of each volume. Structured around the poet's and not the person's "conversion" to writing religious verse, it places Vaughan's relationship to Herbert at the center, since that experience was at the center of the Welsh author's poetic life. But since the event was also primarily and fundamentally a literary one—indeed, we have no way of understanding Vaughan's "conversion" except literarily—it begs to be put into a larger context, which is supplied partly by the poet's

---

Form and Theme in the Poetry of Henry Vaughan (Pittsburgh: Univ. of Pittsburgh Press, 1972), continues Marilla's work and provides, to date, the most sustained attack on the "conversionist" school as well as the most vigorous defense of the secular verse. Vaughan, it should be mentioned, is now at least partially represented in anthologies devoted to seventeenth-century "secular" poetry; see *Ben Jonson and the Cavalier Poets*, ed. Hugh Maclean (New York: W. W. Norton & Co., 1974), pp. 349-55.

[4] The latest book on Vaughan, Thomas O. Calhoun's *Henry Vaughan: The Achievement of Silex Scintillans* (Newark: Univ. of Delaware Press, 1981), includes a discussion of *Poems* (1646), but as the title indicates, the study is pitched toward interpreting the religious verse, whose distinctive merits Calhoun attributes to Vaughan's interests in hermeticism and his possible Rosicrucian affiliations. Although I am sympathetic with his attempt to understand Vaughan "historically," I remain unconvinced by his thesis. The biographical evidence is shaky at best; nor does it automatically follow that because Henry and Thomas were twins, they necessarily shared a similar interest in occult speculation, or if they did, that such speculation served as the cornerstone of Henry's poetry. For a discouraging word on this subject, see Eluned Crashaw, "The Relationship Between the Works of Thomas and Henry Vaughan," *Poetry Wales* 11 (1975): 73-97.

other writings and partly by the chaotic history of Civil War England, which significantly determined how Vaughan read his master. Accordingly, the major divisions of this book adhere to the order in which the works were published or, as in the case of *Olor Iscanus*, were intended to be published: the first three chapters focus on the early secular poetry (*Poems*, 1646, and *Olor*, 1651) and the subsequent four on the religious writings (*Silex Scintillans*, 1650 and 1655) with a concluding chapter on *Thalia Rediviva* (1678). Taken together, the arguments in each indicate the scope of the author's development, which was neither simply continuous nor radically disjunctive but involved, instead, a progressively deeper commitment to the offices of the poet during a time when everything else seemed to be falling apart. Always a revisionist, Vaughan expanded by contracting: he moved forward by seeming to repudiate what he had accomplished or was in the process of accomplishing; and his conversion to religious verse was only the most dramatic act, initiated in *Poems* and carried on in *Olor*, of continuing to question the appropriate direction for poetry in the midst of what the author came increasingly to view as "the last gasp of time."

In making a virtue out of a necessity, Vaughan most clearly resembles his contemporaries, Milton and Marvell, each of whom responded acutely to poetry and politics alike without slipping into battle cries or silence. And like them, the Welsh writer's accomplishments were peculiarly his own, finding in another poet a way to mediate the potentially awesome claims of the historical moment. Both more or less private than is usually supposed, Vaughan, in dialogue with Herbert, discovered a method to sustain a dialogue with a world beyond the self: the hawk "gott into his mouth." Or to alter the metaphor: in the shade of his master's bays, the younger man found a way to refashion the "Swan of the Usk"—the poet of his pastoral dreams—into the "hawkish" figure of a self-styled pastor-poet writing on behalf of a Church which had been driven underground. This figure, of course, was different from either the epic poet who could absorb his immediate culture into a myth of all mankind or the persona of Marvell's lyrics who judges human behavior with almost inhuman coolness, but it nonetheless took Vaughan into the heart of an action that was at once political and personal, immediate and yet rife with suggestions of eternal significance.

The succeeding pages are obviously tipped in favor of the religious poetry, a preference I have sought not to demonstrate through exhaustive arguments but to convey through the structure of the work itself. Vaughan's reputation for unevenness is so notorious that any defense of the usually maligned texts would be hobbled from the start and probably succeed in persuading only those already so inclined. Nonetheless, the secular verse plays a significant role here not only for the valuable light it sheds on Vaughan's entire poetic career but also for the strong poems, occasionally lost to criticism, whose merits are more easily glimpsed because of the positions they occupy in the collections themselves. This is especially true for *Olor Iscanus*, an ambitious misfire if there ever was one. But even a collection of literary remnants like *Thalia Rediviva* contains in the midst of mediocrity at least one poem of considerable distinction—"*To the pious memorie of* C. W. Esquire"—and a host of others that deserve interest if only because they are cousins to excellence. Vaughan's secular poetry is more often formidable than bad, and if readers are not instantly persuaded of its value, I hope that by mapping, or helping to map, the terrain I can create an easier passage through the volumes themselves. With this reason partly in mind, I have devoted a full chapter to *Thalia Rediviva*, a collection usually given only the briefest of notice in studies of Vaughan.

The four chapters on *Silex Scintillans* forming the heart of this study need less justification. In structuring them, I have sought to insure that the best poems receive considerable commentary and that, as one of its organizing principles, each chapter concludes with a detailed discussion of a superior Vaughan poem, one that epitomizes and encapsulates the special dimension of the poet being considered in that chapter. This cumulative design is then repeated at large when, in penultimate fashion, the portion of the book devoted to the religious verse closes with a single chapter on what I think is Vaughan's finest poem, "The Night."

If the general argument of the work serves to underscore the importance of Herbert to Vaughan, its overall strategy is nonetheless geared to freeing the younger poet from the shadow of his master. Herbert might have been the catalyst in Vaughan's poetic career, but as a pivotal force, he shaped rather than overwhelmed or displaced the Welsh poet's creative energies. The chapters concentrating on the religious verse thus describe various modes or phases—not stages—in Vaughan's imitation of his master: formalistic, figural, rhetorical, and prophetic or apocalyptic, with one chapter preparing the way for the next and the group as a whole defining the signal achievements of *Silex*. The first of these chapters, which is the only one to treat the authors in tandem, identifies the poetics of Vaughan's conversion. The second considers how Vaughan, in order to "match" his master, incorporated into his work the figure of a regenerated poet who was also an elected apologist of the Church of England. The next examines the rhetorical problems—the conflict of voices in *Silex*—that arose out of Vaughan's attempt to accommodate satire to an Herbertian posture of Anglican moderation. And the last focuses on prophetic or apocalyptic aspects of imitation as the younger author recognized, with increasing keenness, that he had inherited the invading darkness predicted by his master. All in all, these chapters seek to explore Vaughan's characteristic locutions and verbal effects while attempting to explain how a poet can be both worldly and ascetic, political and devotional, sure of his chosen status and yet uncertain about his election. Much in Vaughan remains paradoxical and problematic, but one paradox that is not a problem is that the Welsh poet, like Nicodemus, came to discover his light at the hour of his greatest darkness. *Silex Scintillans* is the living proof.

Beyond the particular contours of specialized studies of Vaughan, the portrait that emerges of him in these pages will perhaps further help to flesh out his place in the world of Cavalier and Metaphysical poets described recently by Earl Miner[5] and the even more recent account of him as a Protestant poet supplied by Barbara Lewalski.[6] In the first case, Vaughan is proof of how the "good" life and the "godly" impulse often coalesced in the same individual in the period. (Walton's remark of Sir George Hastings, "an excellent Angler, now with God," is one of the catch phrases Miner uses to define the Cavalier mode.) But Vaughan also, I believe, took this connection a step further than other mid-century writers by turning a Cavalier ideal of "friendship" into an extended conversation with his "dear friend," George Herbert, and produced a very different mode of verse: the humanized poetics associated with the Tribe of Ben are carried on in solitude by the heir of Herbert who rewrites and alters, revises and augments, the tradition bequeathed to him by his master. That tradition, admirably defined by Lewalski as being Biblically centered and Protestant-oriented, Vaughan also reshaped into a series of politically motivated poetic strategies as he confronted and negotiated, with even a little help from Counter Reformation tactics, some of the more radically Protestant elements of the 1640s and '50s. Forced to inhabit a narrower terrain than Herbert, he inevitably reduced the scope of *The Temple*, but the vision that he did present, focusing on the "story" of his regeneration, was nevertheless a vision that he represented as being of the Church of England and in true imitation of its truest defender. "Something happened,

---

[5] Miner, *The Metaphysical Mode from Donne to Cowley* (Princeton: Princeton Univ. Press, 1969) and *The Cavalier Mode from Jonson to Cotton* (Princeton: Princeton Univ. Press, 1971).

[6] Lewalski, *Protestant Poetics and the Seventeenth-Century Religious Lyric* (Princeton: Princeton Univ. Press, 1979), esp. pp. 317-51. The central points of difference in our approaches to Vaughan involve the transmission of ideas which she attributes to Protestant doctrine and I more to Herbert's poetry and to the immediate historical circumstance, although she does not entirely neglect these features. Our views of the religious verse, however, are basically more complementary than contradictory.

something to do with poetry, and not with prayer," wrote Frank Kermode in a seminal article on Vaughan some thirty years ago, "a trumpet sounded and the bones lived."[7] The present study attempts to determine the various sounds of the trumpet and to measure the life still in the bones.

[7] Kermode, "The Private Imagery of Henry Vaughan," *RES*, n.s. 1 (1950): 225.

HENRY VAUGHAN

CHAPTER ONE

Vaughan In and Out of "the Shade of His Owne Bayes": *Poems* 1646

> Piping on their reeds, the shepherds go,
> Nor fear an ambush, nor suspect a foe.
>
> —Homer *Iliad* (trans. Pope) 18. 525-26

"IT IS NOT ENOUGH for an ingenuous gentleman to behold these [ancient statues] with a vulgar eye, but he must be able to distinguish them and tell who and what they be," writes Henry Peacham.[1] Much the same could be said of the "gentleman" poets of the 1630s and '40s who moved among the statuesque figures of the Caroline court. It was important to be "in the know"—to praise the right women with the right phrase, to "tell who and what they be" in a manner that was at once distinct and poised yet not so "original" as to endanger the surface elegance of the tribute. When Lady Ventia Digby, wife to "that noble and absolutely complete gentleman, Sir Kenelm Digby,"[2] died, established authors as well as would-be wits quickly penned a book's worth of elegies. When natural, easy Suckling chose to outsmart his court rival, Thomas Carew, in "Upon my Lady Carlile's walking in Hampton-Court garden," he did so by glancing at this fabled beauty with an eye that certainly insinuated he was the more knowing of the two men.

Amatory opportunism had returned to the court, a court whose literary influence was felt by many, including the young Henry Vaughan. Under James I, Jonson had shrugged aside his predecessors' Petrarchisms and began a volume of verse

---

[1] Peacham, *The Complete Gentleman* (1622), ed. Virgil B. Heltzel (Ithaca: Cornell Univ. Press, 1962), p. 121.
[2] Ibid., p. 120.

by boldly announcing "Why I Write not of Love"; and for whatever reasons—the notorious boorishness of the king, the sense of a genre being exhausted—poets generally followed Ben in pursuing more "masculine" and classical forms of verse such as the epigram, epistle, ode, or satire. But with the arrival from France of Charles's Catholic bride, Henrietta Maria, "Cupid's Call," as Shirley later phrased it, came back in vogue. "The Court affords little News at present," writes James Howell in a letter of 1634 that surely deserves to be called familiar,

> but that there is a Love call'd Platonick Love, which much sways there of late; it is a Love abstracted from all corporeal gross Impressions and sensual Appetite, but consists in Contemplations and Ideas of the Mind, not in any carnal Fruition. This Love sets the Wits of the Town on work; and they say there will be a Mask shortly of it, whereof Her Majesty and her Maids of Honour will be part.[3]

Howell was documenting what later scholars have come to regard as the "*précieuse* fashions authorized by the queen,"[4] a system of etiquette popular in the French salons of the earlier seventeenth century that attempted to effect both "the purification of the language and of the relations between the sexes."[5] Particularly suited to the highly stylized form of the masque (Davenant's *Temple of Love* is the one alluded to by Howell), the cult of platonic love quickly found its way into the drama and poetry of the period. Besides inspiring Davenant's play entitled *The Platonic Lovers* (1636), the cult's influence is also present in some of the more celebrated drama of the period, such as Cartwright's *The Royal Slave* (1636) and Suckling's *Aglaura* (1636-37), both of which played at a private theater

---

[3] Howell, *Epistolae Ho-Eliane: The Familiar Letters of James Howell*, ed. Joseph Jacobs (London: David Nutt, 1890), pp. 317-18.

[4] Kathleen M. Lynch, *The Social Mode of Restoration Comedy* (1926; rpt. New York: Octagon Books, Inc., 1965), p. 43. See also, Alfred Harbage, *Cavalier Drama* (New York: Modern Language Association, 1936), chaps. 1-2.

[5] J. B. Fletcher, *The Religion of Beauty in Woman* (New York: Macmillan Co., 1911), p. 172; quoted by Lynch, *Social Mode of Restoration Comedy*.

as well as the court and reflect an extremely idealized and artificial view of the passions.

Poetry underwent a similar refinement in its expressions of love. Randolph's "An Elegy," written probably in the final years of the author's life (1634-35) and sometimes supplied with the adjective "Platonick" by his later editors,[6] revises and elevates a genre that had always been identified with the erotic, while Lord Herbert of Cherbury's "An Ode upon a Question moved" unties "that subtile knot" Donne had made between body and soul in "The Extasie" in order to celebrate the enduring permanence of spiritual union. It was left to the Jesuitical William Habington to string these sentiments into a sequence of lyrics, in sonnet fashion, which praised the virtues of a chaste love. His *Castara*, into its third edition by 1640 (the other two appeared in 1634 and 1635), was the work of someone who readily confessed to having "never felt a wanton heate,"[7] and the poetry reflects this pristine ardor in its theme (the couple marries), its imagery (filled with celibate overtones), and its diction (appropriately effete and sweet). In these lyrics love is carefully "abstracted from all corporeal gross Impressions and sensual Appetite"; the torment of passions—especially those arising from the conflicting values of honor and desire—that motivated Petrarchists a half-century earlier to woo in such fervent numbers had been effectively tamed. To a large degree, so was the poet's muse. Although Habington offered his lyrics as a corrective to the current fashions of verse clothed in "French garbe," his were not so free from the "effeminacy" that he accused others of possessing; instead of achieving his purpose of refining the licentious behavior of court wits, his poetry only further fostered

---

[6] Both W. Carew Hazlitt, *Poetical and Dramatic Works of Thomas Randolph* (London: n.p., 1875) and John Jay Parry, *The Poems and Amyntas of Thomas Randolph* (New Haven: Yale Univ. Press, 1917) prefer the expanded title, although it is dropped by G. Thorn-Drury, *The Poems of Thomas Randolph* (London: Etchells & Macdonald, 1929). For the possible date of the poem's composition, see Parry, *Poems and Amyntas*, p. 358.

[7] *The Poems of William Habington*, ed. Kenneth Allott (Liverpool: Univ. Press of Liverpool, 1948), p. 5.

a rarified atmosphere that helped to create a cynical Suckling or a carnal Carew. As the cast of characters to *Aglaura* indicates, for every "platonique," there was an "antiplatonique."

The *préciosité* of love in the Stuart court was perfectly in tune with its insular political attitudes. In Stephen Orgel's memorable phrase, Charles was more interested in the "illusion of power"[8] than in actual military conquests; his heroics were all staged, his victories imaginary. When Carew responded to Aurelian Townshend's request for an elegy on the death of the Swedish king, Gustavus Adolphus, his often-quoted answer betrays both a world on which actual political events had little bearing and a mode of poetry unwilling or unable to respond to the larger historical moment:

> Alas! how may
> My Lyrique feet, that of the smooth soft way
> Of Love, and Beautie, onely know the tread,
> In dancing paces celebrate the dead
> Victorious King, or his Majesticke Hearse
> Prophane with th'humble touch of their low verse. (ll. 5-10)[9]

It was hardly the time for a heroic poem, let alone an epic in the manner of a Virgil, Lucan, or Tasso (l. 11). Carew saw poets best serving the age by using "the benefit / Of peace and plenty" (ll. 46-47) to celebrate "our good King" (l. 48) in pastoral revels like Walter Montague's "*SHEPHERDS PARADISE*" (l. 54), a direct offspring of Henrietta Maria's interest in platonic love: "These harmelesse pastimes let my *Townsend* sing" (l. 89). Historians have rightly shuddered over the narrow and avowedly "escapist" vision expressed in Carew's poem and in others like it of the period:[10] a court in which

---

[8] Orgel, *The Illusion of Power: Political Theater in the English Renaissance* (Berkeley: Univ. of California Press, 1975).

[9] References to and quotations from Carew's works are from *The Poems of Thomas Carew*, ed. Rhodes Dunlap (Oxford: Clarendon Press, 1949). The full title of his poem to Townshend reads, "*In answer of an Elegiacall Letter upon the death of the King of Sweden from Aurelian Townsend*" (pp. 74-77).

[10] See, for instance, the remarks by C. V. Wedgwood, *Poetry and Politics*

one of its leading poets could urge others to discover their artistic models in Montague's tedious and prolix "salon" pastoral had certainly lost its sense of perspective.

Henry Vaughan "Gent.," as the author identified himself on the title page to his first volume of verse, *Poems* (1646), never held a position at court and perhaps was never there in attendance, but he was certainly not immune from its influence. The young author wrote of "Les Amours," commended "*Monsieur Gombauld*" for his *L'Endymion*, and was current with some of the fashionable theater of the day; he might even have been in the audience at Oxford that included the king and queen for a celebrated performance of Cartwright's *Royal Slave*. Moreover, the simple title of *Poems*, along with the allusion to his present station in life, was strongly reminiscent of Carew's *Poems* (1640, 2nd ed., 1642) in which the author is described as "One of the Gentleman of the / Privie-chamber, and Sewer in / Ordinary to his Majesty."[11] But it is Vaughan's

---

under the Stuarts (1960; rpt. Ann Arbor: Univ. of Michigan Press, 1964), chap. 2; Christopher Hill, *The Century of Revolution, 1603-1714* (Edinburgh: Thomas Nelson and Sons Ltd., 1961), pp. 96-100; and Perez Zagorin, *The Court and the Country: The Beginnings of the English Revolution* (London: Routledge & Kegan Paul, 1969), pp. 70-73.

[11] As French Fogle points out in his edition of *The Complete Poetry of Henry Vaughan* (1964; rpt. New York: W. W. Norton & Co., 1969), p. 2, Vaughan's title was "honorary": it signaled his membership in a social elite whose privileges derived from either ancestral or economic status or a combination of the two; in Vaughan's case, the distinction was more the former than the latter (F. E. Hutchinson, *Henry Vaughan: A Life and Interpretation* [Oxford: Clarendon Press, 1947], chaps. 1 and 2). For a broad discussion of the Welsh social structure and the gentry's place in it, see A. H. Dodd, *Studies in Stuart Wales* (Cardiff: Univ. of Wales Press, 1952), chap. 1, which one should supplement with Howell A. Lloyd's *The Gentry of Southwest Wales, 1540-1640* (Cardiff: Univ. of Wales Press, 1968), pp. 15-21. Considering Vaughan's attendance at Oxford and his probable intention to pursue a career in law, the best gloss on the "Gent." of *Poems* is very likely still Sir Thomas Smith's description, quoted frequently in the seventeenth century, that "as for gentlemen, they be made good cheape in England. For whosoever studieth the lawes of the realme, who studieth in the Universities, who professeth liberal Sciences: and to be short, who can live idely, and without manual labour, and will beare the port, charge and countenance of a Gentleman, he shall bee called maister, for that is the title which men give to esquires and other Gentlemen"; *The Common-Wealth of England* (London, 1594), p. 37.

preface "To all Ingenious Lovers of Poesie" that best establishes, via Habington, his allegiance to some of the *précieuse* fashions of the day; chastity reigns supreme:

> *You have here a* Flame, *bright only in its owne* Innocence, *that kindles nothing but a generous* Thought; *which though it may warme the Bloud, the fire at highest is but* Platonick, *and the* Commotion, *within these limits, excludes* Danger. (p. 2)

Along with including the author among the "Platonicks," the preface, in which one "Gent." addresses other "gentlemen," is a study in courtly nonchalance. Affectation is mimicked, a touch of decadence savored: "*If any shall question that* Courage *that durst send me abroad so late, and revell it thus in the* Dregs *of an Age, they have my silence: only,* Languescente seculo, liceat aegrotari" (when the age is languishing, one is permitted to be sick). Even the poet's translation of Juvenal's Tenth Satire is reported to have been undertaken not in a spirit of moral fervor but in order "*to feather some slower Houres,*" while the quip from Persius planted on the title page—"*Tam nil, nulla tibi vendo / Illiade*" (I will not sell [my book] for all your *Iliads*)—seems to make the possibility of heroic action as out of place in this volume as it was in Carew's poem to Townshend. Preciosity is doubly underlined by an author who, in prizing a book so slight in its original edition that the lines had to be double-spaced, would not part with his "achievement" for all the great books in literature.

The verse itself readily reveals its affinity with the effete fashions of the day. When Shirley, man about London and friend to Habington, writes in "Love for Enjoying" of the poet's art as being parallel to the "lapidary's" (l. 18), with the two contributing "here and there a star" (l. 19) that affords "flame" and "lustre"[12] to a lady, he describes exactly the poet's casual attitude toward his muse which, almost two centuries later, led Hazlitt to describe Caroline verse as a poetry of "fancy" rather than of "imagination"—the latter a

---

[12] *The Dramatic Works and Poems of James Shirley*, ed. Alexander Dyce, 6 vols. (1833; rpt. New York: Russell & Russell, 1966), 6: 422-23.

term of praise he reserved for the Elizabethans.[13] Regardless of whether we agree with Hazlitt's neat discriminations, or even the language in which they are expressed, court poetry in Charles's day was basically fanciful and decorative. Argumentation was limited, rhetorical strength rare. Although poets frequently borrowed their matter from Donne, they never attempted to overwhelm a woman by imitating his masculine, persuasive force; and though they might reveal a Jonsonian concern with a lady's appearance, they rarely showed his penetrating moral vision. The "lapidary's art" was not meant to be "original"—to create *ex nihilo*—but to cut, polish, and refine what had already been made available to him by the tradition. Rather than dazzling his audience, he settled for one or two flashes. In its most positive light, these methods have been seen as analogous to mannerism in painting, with its supreme attention to "restyling"; viewed negatively, they betrayed a sign of the failure of love to inspire anything new.[14] But in either instance the mode was what gentlemen of the court practiced and the mode in which Vaughan began his career as a poet, even if he was not of the court.

The derivative nature of *Poems* is suggested immediately by the name of the woman wooed and eventually won in the course of the thirteen poems that make up the lyric half of the collection. Amoret, one of Spenser's heroines in *The Faerie Queene*, was to be later pursued by William Browne and still later by Edmund Waller in 1645, the year before *Poems* was published. If not quite a household word, she was certainly familiar fare to "all Ingenious Lovers of Poesie," and this was the audience the Welsh author was attempting to reach. A diminutive *Amoretti*, a collection with an already diminished scope (the title means "little loves"), Vaughan's sequence, like

---

[13] *The Complete Works of William Hazlitt*, ed. P. P. Howe, 21 vols. (London: J. M. Dent and Sons Ltd., 1930), 5: 82.

[14] See, respectively, Louis L. Martz, *The Wit of Love* (Notre Dame, Ind.: Univ. of Notre Dame Press, 1969), pp. 93-94; and A. J. Smith, "The Failure of Love: Love Lyrics after Donne," in *Metaphysical Poetry*, ed. Malcolm Bradbury and David Palmer (London: Edward Arnold Ltd., 1970), pp. 41-71.

Spenser's, concludes with a similar intention of betrothal between poet and mistress, a minor variation on the courtly love scheme recently reintroduced by Habington, who celebrates his marriage at the beginning of the second part of *Castara*. And like both of these earlier collections, Vaughan's possesses little formal inventiveness. Most of his poems are in couplets, either pentameter or octosyllabics; a few make tentative experiments with stanzas of varying line lengths, and several more use conventional song forms. Instead of striking out in new directions, Vaughan works studiously within the existing traditions as he shows his familiarity with the popular modes of wooing—both Renaissance and Cavalier—to which he adds a touch of the classics. The poet writes on the recognized Petrarchan themes of absence ("To Amoret gone from him") and of night ("To Amoret, Walking in a Starry Evening"); he descends briefly into an underworld littered with Cupid's victims ("To my Ingenuous Friend, R. W."); and he signals an awareness of his contemporaries in works such as "Amyntas *goe, thou art undone*" (after Randolph), "To Amoret. The Sigh" (Carew), and "To his Friend Being in Love" (Suckling). Although hardly an ambitious collection of lyrics, it nonetheless covers a number of amatory possibilities without being repetitious: all thirteen poems are written in decidedly different moods. Less interested in perfecting a single stance—as both Suckling and Lovelace were—the young author explored a variety of poses; and though anyone familiar with Vaughan's later works can find his signature in these, the poetry is hardly so individual that it could not have come from the hand of any number of gentleman writers. On this score, it seems significant that the lyric sometimes thought to be the best of the amatory poems—"A Song to Amoret"—is also the quintessence of that noble and slightly self-indulgent mode which, through the efforts of a Lovelace or a Marquis of Montrose, has come to be identified as the special trademark of the "Cavalier" poem. For all of its grace, Vaughan's poem has the anonymity of an anthology piece:

> Fortune and beauty thou mightst finde,
>   And greater men then I:
> But my true resolved minde,
>   They never shall come nigh.
>
> For I not for an houre did love,
>   Or for a day desire,
> But with my soule had from above,
>   This endles holy fire.   (p. 9, ll. 17-24)

The Cavalier poet's attitude toward his "lapidary" art also influenced both how he intepreted the amatory tradition and the diction he chose in order to express his love. "*To Amoret, of the difference 'twixt him, and other Lovers, and what true Love is*" belongs to a subgenre of love poetry extremely popular in the seventeenth century which includes such chestnuts as Donne's "A Valediction: forbidding mourning" and Marvell's "The Definition of Love";[15] both evoke Samuel Johnson's famous description of a "metaphysical" poem as one in which "the most heterogeneous ideas are yoked by violence together [while] nature and art are ransacked for illustrations, comparisons, and allusions."[16] Vaughan's poem is clearly "late" Donne. The echo in lines 15-28 of the fourth and fifth stanzas of "A Valediction" is sufficiently pronounced to have attracted the notice of most readers, an effect the young poet surely intended. But what is striking about the poem is not just that Vaughan fails to reproduce his predecessor's conceits—the witty connections that keep spirit and flesh bound together as part of a single vision—but how, in unwinding these conceits, the younger author refines and rarifies the imagery of the phenomenal world. He makes the imagery precious rather than precise. Donne's opening simile ("As virtuous men passe mildly away") possesses a certain, immediate delicacy quickly interrupted by the drama of people attempting to determine the exact moment when the soul departs ("The breath goes

---

[15] Rosalie Colie, *"My Ecchoing Song": Andrew Marvell's Poetry of Criticism* (Princeton: Princeton Univ. Press, 1970), pp. 43-51, esp. p. 45.

[16] Johnson, *Lives of the English Poets*, ed. G. B. Hill, 3 vols. (Oxford: Clarendon Press, 1905), 1: 20 (Life of Cowley).

now, and some say, no"). Vaughan's, on the other hand, lingers over the notion of evaporation, of a slightly occult and decadent setting of the sun: "the Evenings cooler wings / Fanne the afflicted ayre"; the "faint Sunne" does not complete a revolution but "leav[es] undone, / What he begunne"—something that rarely happens in Donne's poetry. The natural world, in fact, is in the process of disappearing from sight, and lover and reader are placed in the same, basically nondramatic, position of witnessing a sublunary life already false to the eye:

> They shoot their tinsill beames, and vanities,
>   Thredding with those false fires their way;
>   But as you stay
>   And see them stray,
> You loose the flaming track, and subt'ly they
>   Languish away,
>   And cheate your Eyes. (p. 12, ll. 8-14)

In Marjorie Nicholson's terms,[17] the circle has been broken, but not necessarily just because of the Copernican revolution. Vaughan's "*fire at highest is but* Platonick": it purposefully discounts one-half of Donne's vision, and his choice of diction leads inevitably away from a firm representation of the sensuous world. Like the lapidary artist, he contributes here and there a jeweled line, but he does not attempt a major reworking of the raw material already before him in the tradition. As the Preface states, "*the* Commotion, *within these limits, excludes* Danger."

Probably the best known and most elegant of the love poems is "To Amoret gone from him." Included in Grierson's legendary anthology of *Metaphysical Lyrics and Poems of the Seventeenth Century* (1921) as the sole representative of Vaughan's secular output, the lyric cultivates even more carefully an attitude of precious evanescence. No urgent "Platonick" operating within firmly held cosmic principles, the rec-

[17] Nicholson, *The Breaking of the Circle: Studies in the Effect of the "New Science" on Seventeenth-Century Poetry*, rev. ed. (New York: Columbia Univ. Press, 1960), chap. 4.

ollective speaker now keeps company mainly with his "fancy." The "loose tye of influence" he witnesses in Nature has its analogues in the attenuated appeals he makes to Amoret. Languishing and saddened although not quite elegiac, he describes a mannered, cosmetic nature acting a part in a slightly coquettish "salon" courtship:

> Fancy and I, last Evening walkt,
> And, *Amoret*, of thee we talkt;
> The West just then had stolne the Sun,
> And his last blushes were begun:
> We sate, and markt how every thing
> Did mourne his absence; How the Spring
> That smil'd, and curl'd about his beames,
> Whilst he was here, now check'd her streames:
> The wanton Eddies of her face
> Were taught lesse noise, and smoother grace;
> And in a slow, sad channell went,
> Whisp'ring the banks their discontent.   (p. 8, ll. 1-12)

The moment is caught in its precious decline: the sun has blushed its last, and the sounds of nature are becoming faint to the ear; even the narrative has a studied fragility. Presented with equal timidity, the persuasion to love at the end of the poem reveals a plaintive delicacy more along the lines of the epigraph to *Howard's End*—"only connect"—than of the ardent appeals one might normally expect from a wooer who, in the next poem, refers to himself as "The mighty Amorist":

> If Creatures then that have no sence,
> But the loose tye of influence,
> (Though fate, and time each day remove
> Those things that element their love)
> At such vast distance can agree,
>   Why, *Amoret*, why should not wee.   (ll. 19-24)

Warm sighs and faint whispers, images of fading light, languid deaths, and soft souls, sickly over the pale cast of thought in many of these lyrics. This is not "a poetry of cool, deliberate statement and reasoned argument"[18]—especially if this critic's description is meant to suggest an urbane sophistication on Vaughan's part. If nothing else, the author's frequent borrowings from Habington prevent him from venturing very far in the direction of either "The Torrid, or the frozen Zone," as Carew was to define the amatory alternatives in "Mediocritie in love rejected." In "To Amoret. The Sigh" (pp. 5-6), for instance, Vaughan certainly remembered Carew's sensuous "A Prayer to the Wind," but he also had not forgotten some of Habington's more delicate trifles such as "To Castara." Like Carew's poem, which begins "Goe thou gentle whispering wind, / Beare this sigh," Vaughan's gets off to a similar airborne start: "Nimble Sigh on thy warme wings, / Take this Message, and depart"; but the presence of the first word, "Nimble," also one of Habington's favorite expressions, indicates the true course of the poem. While Carew moves quickly in the direction of the torrid zone, Vaughan hovers about in an "airie voyage," and the descent he charts to Amoret's "white bosome" resembles a pilgrimage to a holy shrine, not the erotic pillaging the other poet had imagined. Although the basic arguments of the two poems are the same—a plea for action—the precious tone of Vaughan's is clearly more in keeping with Habington's "Forsake with me the earth, my faire, / And travell nimbly through the aire, / Till we have reacht th' admiring skies" (ll. 1-3).[19] Mediocrity in love seems acceptable as the fire of platonic love in the poem burns just warm enough to support Helen Gardner's conception of Vaughan as something of a "tepid wooer."[20]

Since the women of love poetry—whether Sidney's imaginary Stella or Jonson's Lady Digby—were frequently surrogates for the muse, it is hardly surprising that Vaughan should intersperse among his wooing activities poems that have a

---

[18] James D. Simmonds, *Masques of God: Form and Theme in the Poetry of Henry Vaughan* (Pittsburgh: Univ. of Pittsburgh Press, 1972), p. 82.
[19] *The Poems of William Habington*, p. 63.
[20] Gardner, *The Metaphysical Poets* (Baltimore: Penguin Books, Inc., 1959), p. 319.

direct bearing on his place in a community of poets. Winning a spot in Amoret's heart was important; so was winning a position among his fellow writers. "To my Ingenuous Friend, R. W." (pp. 3-4) and "A Rhapsodie" (pp. 10-12) are the only poems in the collection in which Amoret has no place; their relevance to the sequence (with special reference to the second verse) has been argued either on the grounds of dramatic verisimilitude (a fatigued wooer needs time out for a drink and some male companionship) or because Vaughan was following Habington's warning that a man "wholly employed in the soft strains of love" risks his masculinity.[21] It seems equally certain that the author was using these occasions as a double opportunity to flesh out a self-portrait of the artist as a young man which would "endear" him to other coterie poets whose own insularity matches the *préciosité* of his love for Amoret. These occasional poems differ more in scenario than in attitude from the amatory verse; like the love poems, they focus on the element of fancy, especially as it is suggested in the title of each. The word "ingenuous" (meaning generous) in "To my Ingenuous Friend, *R. W.*," for instance, was often conflated with "ingenious" (witty) in the seventeenth century (Vaughan uses both versions in back-to-back headings),[22] and the combination of the two helps to underscore the salient features of the "gentleman" writer who should be congenial as well as witty. Playful, fanciful, even "modish," this poem mixes familiar allusions to local detail—especially taverns—with a dream of the Elysian Fields where the two men will be fully able to satisfy their thirst. Vaughan also uses the occasion to pay his respects to Jonson, in many ways the father of seventeenth-century coterie poetry, by placing "Great *B E N*" in prime view to all, with his adopted son, Thomas Randolph, standing nearby. But while acknowledging his associations with them, the young poet also keeps his distance: unlike Herrick, whose descent into the underworld concludes with

---

[21] These positions have been stated, respectively, by Marilla, *SPHV*, p.127 and Rudrum, *CPHV*, p. 449.
[22] Rudrum, *CPHV*, p. 442.

an apotheosis of "Father *Johnson*" ("The Apparition of his Mistresse calling him to Elizium"),[23] Vaughan, in an action prophetic of his career as a whole, passes by Jonson and his tribe, although in this case only to continue on a tour of the underworld until he arrives at a flowery bank to "drinke all sense, and cares away" (l. 56).

"A Rhapsodie" is even more clubby. The poet is now within an actual tavern where, for a few moments at least, he is the center of attention and enjoys the ecstasy anticipated at the end of the first poem but not then experienced. As the title also indicates (the etymology of rhapsody derives from the Greek meaning to stitch songs together),[24] the piece is a bit of whimsical pandemonium made up of a variety of exaggerated gestures which combine together to say "this is a poet": a pseudo-invocation to the muse of "royall, witty Sacke"; a little high-spirited banter in which Vaughan plays with some of the conventions of *ut pictura poesis* popular in his day to show, in Jonson's words, that "the Pen is more noble, than the Pencill";[25] a short encounter with "realistic" satire; a few political asides "dark" enough not to have their message easily decoded by anyone on the outside; and a brief concluding Bacchic song. The medley of forms is all part of a "dream Poeticall" (l. 70), a rhapsody, deliberately slight and occasional, whose title was perhaps meant to recall, parodically, a third use of the word in the seventeenth century: an epic or book from an epic usually associated with Homer.[26] The gentleman writer who would not sell his book for all the *Iliads* continues to live idly.

The final lyric in this brief sequence of poems blends the author's double pursuit of his mistress and his muse into a

[23] *The Complete Poetry of Robert Herrick*, ed. J. Max Patrick (1963; rpt. New York: W. W. Norton & Co., 1968), pp. 273-74.

[24] OED, "rhapsode"; cf. also "rhapsodize," s.v. 1.

[25] Jonson quoted in Annabel M. Patterson, *Marvell and the Civic Crown* (Princeton: Princeton Univ. Press, 1978), p. 134; in a passage relevant to Vaughan, Patterson traces the connections between the Stuart courts and contemporary interest among royalist writers in the doctrines of *ut pictura poesis* (pp. 133-36).

[26] OED, "rhapsody," s.v. 1.

single, triumphant celebration—a homecoming in which he weaves a victory crown for his amatory and verbal achievements, slight though the latter might seem. "Upon the Priorie Grove, His usuall Retyrement" takes us full circle: the Elysian Fields that figured in the opening verse are now realized in the vision of the Priory Grove, a landscape otherwise dull to the eye but deliberately sweetened and transformed by the poet's imagination so that, for a time at least, nothing separates it from its final, perfected shape in eternity. Vaughan also shows himself realizing his poetic inheritance, especially as it has been defined by a code of gentlemanly behavior: the allusion to the Priory Grove as the place of "His usuall Retyrement"—argued unpersuasively by Marilla to be an editorial addition[27]—firmly identifies the poet as a member of the gentry, that conspicuous albeit vaguely defined class of people who could be recognized by their recreative if not creative habits. Idleness is finely tuned, a clear indication of a way of life, a form of behavior that both enhances and is enhanced by the art of composing retirement verse; and it seems especially appropriate that the reflective status of poetry and life, a "kind" of poetry associated with a particular station in life, should be significantly in evidence at the scene in which Amoret is finally won: they form together a composite measure of the man.

But the victory is not limited to wooing. The opening lines of the poem "discover" Vaughan "in the shade of his owne bayes," saluting his accomplishments and, by implication at least, suggesting himself as in some respects the equal of Jonson, whom Vaughan depicted in the first poem of the collection as resting in the comfort of his own literary achievements. To announce his arrival, the gentleman poet begins with a version of "the muse's looking glass" all his own:

> Haile sacred shades! coole, leavie House!
> Chaste Treasurer of all my vowes,
> And wealth! on whose soft bosome layd
> My loves faire steps I first betrayd.   (p. 15, ll. 1-4)

[27] *SPHV*, p. 148.

If we think of these lines as a statement about the poet's own art in which the traditional pun on "leaves" is exploited, we can avoid the awkward possibilities encouraged by too literal a reading.[28] Vaughan is not lying on the lawn where he surprises an ambling Amoret; the opening salute is to his verse—"Chaste Treasurer of all my vowes" (a phrase that certainly evokes the poet's debt to both "platonick" love and Habington's *Castara*)—and the recognition that follows refers to the course of his love as it has been revealed ("betrayd") in the previous poems, either with or without Amoret's knowledge.[29] The remainder of the lyric is a further celebration or a final incarnation of the chaste vision. In a passage strongly reminiscent of the beginning of "L'Allegro," Vaughan banishes all melancholic sounds from his province, and in place of the "hoarse bird of Night" (l. 6), he lets dwell "Within these leaves" only the voice of "*Philomel*," a traditional symbol of innocence and a figure for the youthful amatory poet.[30] The pastoral vision that emerges is one of sheer, uncorrupted "fancy":

> The poisonous Ivie here no more
> His false twists on the Oke shall score,
> Only the Woodbine here may twine,
> As th' Emblem of her Love, and mine;
> The Amorous Sunne shall here convey
> His best beames, in thy shades to play;

---

[28] Hutchinson, *Life*, p. 52.

[29] One advantage of this reading is that it avoids some editorial hairsplitting over the usage of "betrayed." Rudrum (*CPHV*, p. 455, ll. 3-4n) is undoubtedly right to correct Marilla (*SPHV*, p. 148), who misappropriates *OED* 6 ("betray" meaning to disclose something against one's will) for his own purposes; but Vaughan could also simply have been using the word as a synonym for "disclose" (*OED*, 7) without necessarily suggesting any breach of secrecy on his part.

[30] See Milton's sonnet, "O Nightingale, that on yon bloomy Spray," published in *Poems* (1645), the year before Vaughan's collection appeared; its significance as a self-conscious piece of juvenilia is admirably argued by William McCarthy, "The Continuity of Milton's Sonnets," *PMLA* 92 (1977): 96-109. That Vaughan associated his early career as an amatory poet with the nightingale is obvious from his later remarks in "Idle Verse" (p. 446), esp. ll. 21-24.

> The active ayre, the gentlest show'rs,
> Shall from his wings raine on thy flowers;
> And the Moone from her dewie lockes
> Shall decke thee with her brightest drops:
> What ever can a fancie move,
> Or feed the eye; Be on this Grove.   (ll. 11-22)

Summing up love poetry written after Donne, A. J. Smith has remarked how the "Caroline Mode" enacts "a celebration of a love in the midst of questioning the point and dignity of life altogther, and . . . let[s] the contrary motives stand as balancing opposites, gracefully posing a basic human question."[31] This description might indicate a level of self-consciousness to which Vaughan's amatory verse can hardly be said to aspire, but *Poems* contains not just a sequence of love lyrics; it also includes a translation of Juvenal's Tenth Satire, a poem that certainly questions, with a thoroughness rarely equaled in literature, "the point and dignity of life altogether." The 551 lines, replete with their own title page, stand in a nearly exact balance with the amatory sequence, whose poems in the first edition are accorded approximately the same amount of space as the satire; their line total also falls only slightly less than one hundred short of the translation. More starkly dramatic than graceful, the division of the collection into two balancing parts reflects attitudes toward life diametrically opposed to each other. Thematically, stylistically, and generically, they explore altogether different realms of human behavior and in very different voices: the vanity of wooing has become the vanity of human wishes.

The overwhelming impression created by the translation is that the "hoarse bird of Night," so carefully restrained in "Upon the Priorie Grove," has escaped and suddenly begun its dirge. Although several lyrics in the first part of *Poems* have their satirical moments ("A Rhapsodie" and "To Amoret Weeping"), neither attempts the epic scope for which Juvenal was famous, nor does either achieve the "kind of lofty and

---

[31] Smith, "The Failure of Love," p. 48.

sublime speech" that Isaac Causabon, quoting Longinus, responded to in the Roman satirist.[32] The first six words in Juvenal open to a world beyond the court—"In all the parts of Earth"—and they continue in their outward motion:

> ... from farthest West,
> And the Atlanticke Isles, unto the East
> And famous Ganges; Few there be that know
> What's truly good, and what is good in show
> Without mistake.　　　　　　　　(p. 18, ll. 1-5)

In contrast to the lapidary's art, with its concern for a delicate reordering of form, the strategy of the satirist is to make all form seem trivial—a specious concern with exteriors, a supervaluation of the letter over the spirit: "satire is conditioned to be out of shape,"[33] writes Michael Seidel; and Juvenal's Tenth, expanded by Vaughan from 366 lines in the Latin original to 551 in the English, sprawls over the page with a wearying indifference to narrative continuity. The discrete, fully delineated shifts in the speaker's stance, recorded in the movement from lyric to lyric, have been collapsed and amalgamated into a single point of view that moves randomly over the earth's terrain, always discovering the same thing: the brutalizing folly of human ambition. Sejanus, Pompey, Alexander, the famous and the infamous, the named and the unnamed, are leveled all alike by the double action of satire—"a regress in the form of a progress, a presentation in the form of a violation."[34]

In its fidelity to the original, Vaughan's rendition stands midway between Robert Stapleton's sober, scholarly translation of Juvenal published the year after Vaughan's (and certainly one of the most popular of its day)[35] and Samuel

---

[32] Peter E. Medine, "*Isaac Casaubon's* Prolegomena *to the* Satires *of Persius: An Introduction, Text, and Translation*," ELR 6 (1976): 294.

[33] Seidel, *Satiric Inheritance, Rabelais to Sterne* (Princeton: Princeton Univ. Press, 1979), p. 9.

[34] Ibid., p. 23.

[35] Stapleton's early work on Juvenal, published in 1644, was restricted to a translation of the first six satires which he later expanded to include all

Johnson's "Vanity of Human Wishes"—subtitled "The Tenth Satire of Juvenal Imitated."—and unquestionably the most powerful reworking of Juvenal's poem in English. Stapleton's version attempts to preserve Juvenal's antiquity: original place names are glossed in the notes, the pagan deities retained, and local detail faithfully recorded. Except for a brief allusion in the general preface to England as a "*Kingdome* as eminent in *knowledge* as in *Luxury*," the translator scrupulously resists any desire to modernize the text. Johnson, on the other hand, gives a fully modernized "imitation" of the original. Although his poem follows the basic argument in Juvenal, it erases all of Juvenal's contemporary reporting in favor of taking examples from British history, past and present, that only further illustrate the "general truth" of the Roman account; they also help to make the later work a fully independent creation that can be read profitably on its own.

Vaughan's "translation" or "paraphrase" is updated in certain places but not modernized throughout. He looks at Juvenal from both sides of the Channel, stressing points of continuity between the two worlds but also leaving room for slight differences to emerge. When he supplies the name of "*Licinius*" (l. 365) to an unnamed barber in the original, he seems to be peering over Juvenal's shoulder, yet his rendering of "Festino ad nostros" (I hasten to our own countrymen [l. 273]) as "I haste to Rome" (l. 426) clearly identifies him as something of an outsider. Vaughan could also show an Englishman's concern for his native reader by trimming away a number of the pagan gods and place names from the Latin original, a naturalizing touch quickly countered by his adding some exotic details not in Juvenal that demonstrate his affinity with the Roman satirist's world. In this respect, his most adept act of blending the two cultures is in his allusion to the "Gemonian doome" (l. 139), an "outlandish" reference to the Scala Gemoniae (steps overlooking the Tiber from which criminals were thrown) missing in Juvenal and which the later poet

---

sixteen poems in 1647. An elaborate folio edition was brought out in 1660 entitled *Mores hominum*.

was undoubtedly able to "recover" because of its frequent use in English drama of the period.[36] The implied motto of this poem would seem to be: "when in Rome do as the Romans do, but not always." The actual motto taken from Horace involves a similar question-begging freedom: "*Nec verbum verbo curabi[s] reddere fidus / Interpres*" (if you do not seek to render word for word as a slavish translator). Indeed, Horace's "curabis" has become "curabit" in Vaughan.

The most obvious effect of Vaughan's method of translating is the difficulty it poses in determining his share in the poem. Sometimes lines that seem to be clear additions to the original turn out upon close inspection to be only loose paraphrases;[37] at other points, Vaughan can nearly bury from sight a particular attitude of his own in a section of the poem that seems otherwise faithful to Juvenal. The "Tenth Satyre" is modernized, but the question is by just how much and for what precise historical purpose? Hutchinson for one is doubtful about whether the poet intended any parallels to be drawn between the fall of Sejanus and the demise of the Earl of Strafford in 1641,[38] but it is difficult to overlook this possibility, especially since the poem has been updated in a number of other ways that obviously reflect upon the present confusion. The Soldier (l. 36), for instance, who threatens the wealthy, is not in the original; nor is there (or could there be) any mention "Of some torne Brittish Galley" (l. 223) in Juvenal, an anachronism undoubtedly intended to call to mind the perilous conditions of England. On a more subtle note Vaughan could add to the original a remark, spotted recently by Alan Rudrum,[39] that certainly sounds like a reference to the parts played by the king and the populace in the execution of Strafford,

---

[36] The phrase appears in both Jonson's *Sejanus*, 5.1.61 (where Vaughan most likely came upon it) and in Massinger's *The Roman Actor*, 1.1. 95.

[37] Following Guiney and Morgan, Martin, for instance, lists ll. 141-43 and ll. 173-74 as Vaughan's additions; but they are, in fact, contained in the original. See, ll. 79-80 and l. 100, respectively, in the Loeb *Juvenal*, trans. G. G. Ramsay, rev. ed. (Cambridge, Mass.: Harvard Univ. Press, 1940).

[38] Hutchinson, *Life*, pp. 42-43.

[39] Rudrum, *CPHV*, p. 463, ll. 440-41n.

actions whose arbitrary nature is perhaps more severely criticized in another statement Vaughan added to the original: "The least pretence will hit, / When Princes feare, or hate a Favourite" (ll. 117-18). And finally, if we take a step backwards it seems difficult not to see these interpolations in conjunction with the personalities of the two men which, for instance, allowed Jonson to interpret Sejanus as a tragic character and a recent historian to say of Strafford that he "was the greatest tragic figure among the revolution's victims."[40] As both a distant "Son of Ben" and a royalist sympathizer, Vaughan would not have missed this association.

And yet the satire is not a piece of straightforward political propaganda. Vaughan's implied indictment of Strafford's ambition, his brief, critical asides about the king, his indignant condemnation of the populace: all of these attitudes flicker in and out of a narrative whose concerns are wide (and sometimes vague) enough to absorb effectively these local reflections and make it as difficult for his later readers to determine a single "party" attitude in the translation as it would have been for contemporaries who might have wished to decode the work for its immediate political message. Vaughan's primary affiliation throughout is with Juvenal; his partially modernized text never strays very far from its ancient model: "*Honest (I am sure) it is, and offensive cannot be,*" the poet innocently remarks of his translation, "*except it meet with such* Spirits *that will quarrell with* Antiquitie, *or purposely* Arraigne *themselves*" (p. 2). Whatever Vaughan's precise attitude is toward the present turmoil involving Strafford, Parliament, Charles, and the possibility of a rebellion, he is not willing to reveal it in any clear-cut, incriminating fashion. Antiquity offers both a possible commentary on and a handy shelter from an unruly present: any attempt to "Arraigne" this poet is likely to reflect more on the accuser than on the accused.

But for readers of the whole collection, one thing can be said with certainty about Juvenal's appearance in it: his pres-

---

[40] Zagorin, *The Court and the Country*, p. 224.

ence disturbs—even throws out of shape—the quiet attitudinizing of the gentlemanly mode of poetry. The preciosity of the amatory sequence, including "A Rhapsodie," is balanced perilously against the dark possibilities uttered by a "hoarse bird of Night," a voice not necessarily prophesying doom but clearly responsive to a reality greater and more threatening than that usually encountered in the "Lyric feet" of Caroline verse. Juvenal might be considered fit reading for gentlemen, as Henry Peacham argued,[41] but the Roman satirist was definitely a foreign presence among poets of the court or those otherwise influenced by its "smooth soft way / Of Love, and Beauty." There is nothing in the works of Randolph, Waller, Suckling, or Lovelace even remotely akin to the Tenth Satire, whose concluding position at the end of Vaughan's collection seems, in effect, to usurp the office allotted to *Coelem Britannicum*—that elaborate mask in which the Caroline "code is written large"[42] that concluded Carew's volume of poems published six years earlier. Archaic anyway, Carew's mask was a creaking anachronism by 1646. Under pressure from Parliament and its army, the king had been forced from his court, taken refuge at Oxford, and was approaching his dismal end in 1649. Juvenal's world had clearly impinged on Charles's, and if the Roman satirist does not, in fact, predict the fate of the English prince, his intractable presence in Vaughan certainly signals an end to a kind of poetry precious in its conception and self-consciously narrow in its response to human experience. The young poet who began his career by mapping out a place for himself among other gentleman writers closes his first volume by questioning the very stability of that context.

[41] Peacham, *The Complete Gentleman*, p. 101.
[42] Smith, "The Failure of Love," p. 53.

CHAPTER TWO

Olor Iscanus and the Disenchanted Muse

> I may be wrong, but, Tityrus, to me
> The times seem revolutionary bad.
>
> The question is whether they've reached a depth
> Of desperation that would warrant poetry's
> Leaving love's alternations, joy and grief,
> The weather's alternations, summer and winter,
> Our age-long theme for the uncertainty
> Of judging who is a contemporary liar—
> Who in particular, when all alike
> Get called as much in clashes of ambition.
>
> —Robert Frost, "Build Soil, *A Political Pastoral*"

SOMETIME in the early 1640s Vaughan was chased back to his native Brecknockshire by the outbreak of the English Civil War. It is impossible to date his return with any precision, but in all likelihood it was in late 1642 or early 1643. London was in the hands of Parliament, men were rapidly choosing sides, and on August 22, 1642 Charles raised his standard in Nottingham and began preparations for an assault on London. Except for what can be gleaned from the translation of Juvenal's Tenth, none of the lyrics in *Poems* 1646 describe in any detail the events of these days; but the collection as a whole certainly reflects an understanding of the threat posed to the muse during these years, a threat perhaps avoided or at least minimized if a poet with court leanings escaped to the country where he might warble his native woodnotes wild. "Upon the Priorie Grove," regardless of when it was actually written, certainly indicates in its celebration of "*Philomel*" a possible habitat where the muse might not only survive but also receive nourishment from its surroundings. Indeed, such is the conclusion reached by Anthony à Wood in describing the poet's return to Wales: in "wholly devoting himself to poetry and humane studies, [Vaughan] ultimately showed that those hours passed in the gardens of the Muses were not utterly wasted, since he was able to show his poetic faculty in certain specimens, one of which is called *Olor Iscanus.*"[1]

Wood's blithe attitude toward Vaughan's rustication is matched only by his chariness in praising the poet's hortulan literary activities. The sole flower he picks as deserving any mention at all is *Olor Iscanus*, the work Vaughan began composing immediately after *Poems* and in some ways the most "regional" of his writings. A "strange case"—to use Harold Walley's phrase[2]—not least of all because it was the poet's one offspring to receive an early favorable notice, it is also the most heterogeneous collection of material ever printed with Vaughan's name attached to it. Seventeen original poems in English, five in Latin, twenty translations in verse and four in prose, all out of Latin into English, the volume, moreover, has proven to be stubbornly resistant to critical interpretation largely because of its perplexing bibliographical history. Apparently ready for the press by December 17, 1647 (the date of the dedicatory epistle to Lord Kildare Digby), *Olor* did not, in fact, appear in print until some three and a half years later. When it did, it was accompanied by the mysterious note on the title page, "Published by a Friend," and the even more mysterious publisher's note to the reader that treats the recovery of the collection, like one of Browne's urns, as a thing surfacing from the depths of an archaic past:

> *Here is no* Royall Rescue, *but here is a* Muse *that* deserves *it. The* Author *had long agoe condemn'd these* Poems *to* Obscuritie, *and the* Consumption *of that* Further Fate, *which* attends *it. This* Censure *gave them a* Gust *of* Death, *and they have* partly *known that*

---

[1] Quoted in F. E. Hutchinson, *Henry Vaughan: A Life and Interpretation* (Oxford: Clarendon Press, 1947), p. 49.
[2] Harold R. Walley, "The Strange Case of *Olor Iscanus*," *RES* 18 (1942): 27-37.

Oblivion, *which our* Best Labours *must* come to *at* Last. *I present thee then not onely with a* Book, *but with a* Prey, *and in this* kind *the first* Recoveries *from* Corruption. (p. 36)

William R. Parker has identified the "Friend" as almost surely Thomas Powell, a sequestered Anglican minister and royalist neighbor of Vaughan's who composed several commendatory poems for *Olor*.[3] (Only one poem was actually included in the volume; the other was printed along with the verse in *Thalia Rediviva* in 1678.) But neither the three-and-a-half year gap nor the author's alleged decision to condemn these poems "*to* Obscuritie" has ever been explained satisfactorily. Moreover, there is a lingering suspicion among critics that the "ur" *Olor* dedicated to Lord Digby was markedly different from the volume we now possess. Perhaps containing more amatory verse (the "Etesia" poems in *Thalia* are the usual candidates) and even some political poetry (now destroyed), it was, so the arguments go, pruned and reshaped either because of the author's newly acquired piety (*Silex* was published in 1650) or because of possible reprisals that might be brought against a fervent royalist poet.[4] Whichever is the case (and there are problems with both), the end result of this approach seems clear: *Olor Iscanus* is something less than complete or "finished," perhaps published without the author's knowledge, and a possible victim of some protective but distorting editorial work.

If bibliographical problems have made *Olor* into something of a dark wood for criticism, commentary on the verse itself has not cleared any secure pathways through its maze of material. In the nineteenth century, the volume was almost invariably looked at through the lens of the opening poem,"To the River *Isca*," which was assumed to celebrate the rural

---

[3] Parker, "Henry Vaughan and his Publishers," *The Library*, 4th ser., 20 (1939-40): 408-11.

[4] Walley, "Strange Case," pp. 33-34; Marilla, "The Religious Conversion of Henry Vaughan," *RES* 21 (1945): 15-22; Hutchinson, *Life*, pp. 73-77; and Alan Rudrum, "Some Remarks on Henry Vaughan's Secular Poems," *Poetry Wales* 11 (1975): 40-41.

beauties of Vaughan's native region of Brecknockshire. H. C. Beeching, parroting a half-century of casual commentary on the collection, remarked that "the poem that gives its title to the volume, *Olor Iscanus*, is also the first in merit";[5] but otherwise he found little to like in the rough, Donne-like verse that makes up the "bulk of the book." In the twentieth century, the collection has been glimpsed through another glass. More recent commentators, especially Marilla and Simmonds, admire a political Vaughan committed to a world of the present; they prize the poet's satiric edge, his modernity, the cutting quality of his pentameter couplets. For Marilla, the touchstone poem for testing Vaughan's mettle as an artist is not "To the River *Isca*" but the lyric that immediately follows entitled "The Charnel-house." Vigorous and intense, the poem "is quite demonstrably one of the most skillful of Vaughan's compositions."[6] To a modern reader what is immediately apparent in the responses to these two "opening" poems is a difference between a vision of poetry influenced largely by the presence of Wordsworth and a later corrective determined essentially by the tastes of Eliot. Though the gap is considerable, the two views do share at least one thing in common: the part of *Olor* that least conforms to the critic's particular standard is inevitably judged a poetic failure.

It is possible, however, that Vaughan knew what he was up to in *Olor* and that by filtering these later opinions through an eyewitness of sorts, by merging bibliographical considerations with criticism, we can sharpen our focus on what is happening in the poetry before us. The "note" from the publisher to the reader, whether it was composed by the bookseller, Humphrey Mosely, or by Vaughan's friend, Thomas Powell, offers just such a perspective. With its emphasis on authorial uncertainty ("*the* Author *had long agoe condemn'd these* Poems *to* Obscuritie"), its description of the chastening process that poetry must sometimes undergo as it passes through

[5] *The Poems of Henry Vaughan*, ed. E. K. Chambers, 2 vols. (London: Lawrence & Bullen, Ltd., 1896), 1: xxvi.
[6] Marilla, *SPHV*, p. 172.

a charnel-house of its own ("*and they have* partly *known that* Oblivion, *which our* Best Labours *must* come to *at* Last"), and its warning about the toll taken on art along the way ("*Here is a* Flame [that] *hath been sometimes* extinguished"), the note functions less as an apology for the author than a directive to the reader alerting him, in good book-jacket fashion, to the central issue of the collection: the uncertain fate of poetry- and fiction-making during a period of history decidedly hostile to art.

"Lift not thy spear against the Muse's Bower"[7] is Milton's slightly grandiloquent way of describing the perilous balance that existed in the middle years of the century between the sanctuary of the poetic imagination and the forces of history, between lyric preciosity and the demands of reality. The warning voice sounded in this sonnet, probably raised in 1642 in response to Charles's planned invasion of London, was not alone; it would be reiterated later in a different key at the end of the decade in Marvell's description in "An Horatian Ode" of the forward youth who could no longer "in the Shadows sing / His Numbers languishing."[8] But the difference of a few years was also the difference between Milton's miniature defense of poetry in which the writer could still attempt to preserve a careful distance from events and Marvell's subsequent acknowledgment that a defense was no longer possible. The sanctuary had been raided and the price exacted by history was increased pressure on the poet to "forsake his muses dear."[9]

Milton, of course, like the forward youth, willingly, if only temporarily, gave up the bower for the more immediate and

---

[7] John Milton: *Complete Poems and Major Prose*, ed. Merritt Y. Hughes (Indianapolis: The Odyssey Press, 1957), p. 140.

[8] *The Poems and Letters of Andrew Marvell*, ed. H. M. Margoliouth, 2 vols., 3rd ed. (Oxford: Clarendon Press, 1971), 1: 91, ll. 3-4.

[9] For an elaborate examination of Marvell's response to apocalyptic history and the fate of pastoral poetry in mid-century England, see Geoffrey H. Hartman, " 'The Nymph Complaining for the Death of Her Faun': A Brief Allegory," in *Beyond Formalism: Literary Essays, 1958-1970* (New Haven: Yale Univ. Press, 1970), pp. 173-92, esp. pp. 190-91.

perhaps grander claims of his country's destiny, but for Vaughan, whom political history had not favored, his only alternative could be poetry. Although notoriously and to some critics annoyingly vague about his actual military experience,[10] the poet nevertheless left a record of his battles in the form that mattered most to him: in *Olor Iscanus*, Vaughan describes the casualties suffered by the muse once the spear had, in fact, been lifted against the bower. The gap between "*Philomel*" and the "hoarse bird of Night" in *Poems*, between amatory pursuits and the satiric perspective, widens into a gulf in *Olor* between pastoral and elegy itself. Furthermore, what has taken the shape of a debate over the last two centuries for liking either "To the River *Isca*" or "The Charnelhouse" but rarely both is symptomatic of a more fundamental rift embracing moral, political, and poetic choices that Vaughan responded to in *Poems* and now develops into an "argument" that he "forces" his readers to share. That critics have readily divided over these two poems attests to the poet's partial success in this matter; but the demand of the underlying design in *Olor*, a ground bass perhaps cumulatively more powerful than the merits of any individual verse, can only be felt in its fullness by attending more closely to these opening poems and their relationship to the collection at large.

"To the River *Isca*" describes Vaughan's literary utopia. Thematically and verbally, the poem recollects his earlier celebration of the Priory Grove, itself a celebration of the poet's coming of age that closes off his first volume of verse written under the rubric of Henry Vaughan "Gent." The connection is purposeful because it asks us, in this later poem, to focus on the poet's desire to stretch his wings, to perform his own

---

[10] In addition to E. L. Marilla, "Henry Vaughan and the Civil War," *JEGP* 41 (1942): 514-26, and the chapter in Hutchinson's *Life* (pp. 55-71), the most recent discussions of local political turbulence and its possible effects on the poet are Sir Frederick Rees, "Breconshire During the Civil War," *Brycheiniog* 8 (1962): 1-9; Roland Matthias, "In Search of The Silurist," *Poetry Wales* 11 (1975): 6-35; and Thomas O. Calhoun, *Henry Vaughan: The Achievement of Silex Scintillans* (Newark: Univ. of Delaware Press, 1981), pp. 37-57.

Ovidian transformation from the cooing nightingale of the first collection to the Swan of the Usk of the second. With Apollo and Orpheus instead of Ben Jonson at the head, "*Isca*" solemnly describes a *translatio studii* of poetry as it has flowed from its original springs in Greece to its present source in the nearby Severn River. Vaughan desires to bring the waters of creation into his native Brecknockshire:

> When *Daphne's* Lover here first wore the *Bayes*,
> *Eurotas* secret streams heard all his *Layes*.
> And holy *Orpheus*, Natures *busie* Child
> By headlong *Hebrus* his deep *Hymns* Compil'd.
> Soft *Petrarch* (thaw'd by *Laura's* flames) did weep
> On *Tybers* banks, when she (*proud fair!*) cou'd sleep;
> *Mosella* boasts *Ausonius*, and the *Thames*
> Doth murmure SIDNEYS *Stella* to her *streams*,
> While *Severn* swoln with *Joy* and *sorrow*, wears
> *Castara's* smiles mixt with fair *Sabrin's* tears.   (p. 39, ll. 1-10)

In his description of this westering migration of the muse, if the ordering is a bit precious that is part of the point, since Vaughan is emphasizing the preciousness of order. Repetition, continuity, the presence of verbal echo, all contribute to the pastoral dream here, a dream of uninterrupted communication in which the hallowing process of poetry transforms reality into myth and smoothes the passage from this life to the Elysian Fields. Death is perceived as only a slight exchange of geographic locations, one that does not interrupt the poet's musing, either in this verse or in his next life:

> Poets (like *Angels*) where they once appear
> *Hallow* the *place*, and each succeeding year
> Adds *rev'rence* to't, such as at length doth give
> This aged faith, *That there their Genii live.*
> Hence th'*Auncients* say, That, from this *sickly aire*
> They passe to *Regions* more *refin'd* and *faire*,
> To *Meadows* strow'd with *Lillies* and the *Rose*,
> And *shades* whose *youthfull green* no *old age* knowes,
> Where all in *white* they walk, discourse, and Sing
> Like Bees *soft murmurs*, or a *Chiding Spring*.   (ll. 15-24)

Vaughan's fantasy in this pastoral is not the shepherd's usual amorous desire; it turns instead on the wish to see himself as a *genius loci* whose powers, as one critic has argued, are "intrinsically related to vision and prophecy: to determining the destiny of an individual or a nation."[11] In Vaughan's case, the destiny he wishes to shape is that of the Usk, a surrogate for the spirit of poetry in which "*Vocall Groves* [may] grow there, and all / The *shades* in them *Propheticall*" (ll. 39-40). Near the center of the poem, Vaughan, at the mediating point between past and future, begins a Yeatsian incantation to "all Bards born after me," and he fittingly performs a protective, ritualistic tightening of the verse into octosyllables, which he eventually pares down to dimeter as he distills the pastoral features of the Usk into their essential virtues:

> *Honour, Beautie,*
> *Faith* and *Dutie,*
> *Delight* and *Truth,*
> With *Love,* and *Youth.* (ll. 73-76)

These, in turn, yield the perfect royalist symbol of closure—the crown. In that symbol, the pastoral and the political, poetry and history, seem momentarily adjudicated, but the balance is a nervous achievement and easily imperiled, especially since "Crown," the first word in a swelling pentameter, is set against the last word "*Fate*" without an end stop to the line: "Crown all about thee! And what ever *Fate* / Impose elsewhere" (ll. 77-78). The poem concludes by carefully measuring the peace of the Usk, "*the Land redeem'd from all disorders!*", against the "graver state" of a world that seems safely over the horizon. In the context of the complete poem, the closing gesture makes it clear that Vaughan associates the future survival of poetry, at least poetry in its purest, most original condition extending back to Apollo, with the pastoral

---

[11] Hartman, "Romantic Poetry and the Genius Loci," in *Beyond Formalism*, p. 314.

world, and that to break the peace of the Usk is to violate the sacred ordering powers of the muse.

It comes as a considerable shock therefore to discover that the next poem, "The Charnel-house," is literally the "graver state" which Vaughan had sought to dismiss from "*Isca*" and which we, as readers, had not been led to expect in a collection of verse composed by "The Swan of the Usk." The opening words, "Blesse me! what damps are here?", implicate the reader further in the poet's surprise over his sudden fall into the underworld. In this hazardous domain, Vaughan's language, as Simmonds points out, "consistently emphasizes the shocking irreducible immediacy of death";[12] but whereas this critic focuses on the central, unifying features of the poem, I would argue its opposite effects: the shifting nature of experience all but circumvents the poet's abilities to shape and organize. From the opening lines to the end, the excitement of the verse is in Vaughan's attempt to describe and catalogue the invading materialism discovered in his "fall": "How thou arrests my sense," he gasps after his initial glimpse of the "Fragments of men, [the] Rags of Anatomie" (l. 6), where the "eloquent silence" of the scene threatens to overwhelm the poet's tongue. In the face of the surrounding vanities, Vaughan assumes many masks, chiding, mocking, stretching himself, as he says of the dead, to excess (l. 19). There is much wit and some forced urbanity to his gestures, but the protean reality of corruption eventually works its effects on the poet. Nearing the end, and apparently nearing exhaustion, Vaughan mutters: "Thus could I run o'r all the pitteous score / Of erring men, and having done meet more" (ll. 49-50), and he concludes with a pun on "blind Conceit" (l. 54) that, in identifying the method of his verse with the other vanities of man, confesses to a partial failure of vision. When the poet emerges from "The Charnel-house," he is a different person: chastened and subdued, he has been educated in the "vast tenter'd hope[s]" (l. 17) of man, hopes that seem specifically to recollect the shoreless

[12] James D. Simmonds, *Masques of God: Form and Theme in the Poetry of Henry Vaughan* (Pittsburgh: Univ. of Pittsburgh Press, 1972), p. 93.

thoughts and ambitious dreams of the previous poem, and now rendered as a handful of dust. In the context of this diminished reality, it is no wonder that, upon going outside, the poet should think of himself as a note-taker leaving his "sad library" (l. 60), as a scribe recording the fragmented details of human history: the *genius loci* of the previous poem has been dispossessed of his comfortable heritage, his mythic companions, his ability to create the landscape in his image.

The gap between these two poems is great, the action of crossing over disturbing, and it seems only natural that for two centuries critics have found one side more comfortable to be on than the other. Were it the only instance of such a juxtaposition, it could easily be ignored, but Vaughan has taken care, as he does in both *Poems* and the devotional verse, to structure his poetry around a few central experiences, where the repetition of an idea deepens and expands meaning while it lends unity to the collection at large. In *Olor*, the pattern that keeps presenting itself to the reader is the experience that pressed down on Vaughan: the sudden, violent transition between innocence and experience, between the valley of the Usk and the battle of Routon Heath, between the pastoral and elegiac worlds that stubbornly refuse to blend even into the mellowing mead of pastoral elegy. At nearly regular intervals in the collection (the second, seventh, twelfth, and sixteenth poems), Vaughan punctuates the seventeen original poems with specific versions of the charnel house in the elegies on the victims of the Civil War. The elegies naturally center on the violations caused by time and history, but in *Olor* they assume a larger, deconstructive purpose, for in each case, they follow immediately after the only poems in the volume that lay claim to being called pastorals—indeed even ask us to recall specific motifs from "To the River *Isca*." Amid the other commendatory poems and verse epistles, Vaughan keeps rehearsing the powerful reality of his expulsion from the Usk to the charnel house. With each "pairing," moreover, the thematic connections and reversals are sufficient to show Vaughan deliberately undermining the preciousness of the first by the ravagings of the second. The spear is set against the bower, and to pass from one mode to the other is to experience a fall into history that serves to waken both poet and reader to the limitations of art.

It is only natural that the first puncturing of the pastoral myth in *Olor* by the actual facts of history should also be the most violent. The poem to "*Monsieur Gombauld*," followed by "An Elegie on the death of Mr. R. W. slain in the late unfortunate differences at *Routon* Heath, neer *Chester*, 1645," push the imagination to opposite poles in the forms of experience they recount. The poem on the pastoral-romance *Endimion* is deliberately "escapist," with Vaughan less concerned with commending the artist than with reproducing the steps of the shepherd's exotic, nocturnal pilgrimage until both eventually recover the imaginative regions of the Usk in the bower "exempt / From Common frailtie" (l. 20). Vaughan stops here, even though there are still two books in the original to go, and he turns to praise Gombauld's art which, like the foliage of the bower, is "so neatly [woven]" (l. 45) as to admit no gap between fiction and reality, or, as Vaughan says, between fable and truth, fancy and history (l. 46). As pastoral-romance, the work establishes its own conventions of verisimilitude apart from reality; these celebrate the fictive powers of the human mind

> Which shall these Contemplations render far
> Lesse mutable, and lasting as their star,
> And while there is a *People*, or a *Sunne*,
> *Endymions* storie with the *Moon* shall runne.   (p. 49, ll. 49-52)

These final lines, however, seem deliberately proleptic since the next poem chips away at their sentiments and thereby challenges the conventional conclusion rung on the immortality of art. The Civil War has claimed one more person; the blithely confident assertion that Endimion's story will continue until a solar disorder should occur is exactly what happens on a symbolic level in the following poem when Vaughan describes R. W.'s disappearance as simply "*There was a Sun*"

(l. 95). The elegy records an historical fact, and Vaughan's insistence on including, in the title alone, the initials of the victim, the exact location of the battle, and the date on which it took place, drives a wedge between the pleasant fancy of Endimion and the immediate demands of reality.[13]

The elegy possesses an eerie power achieved in part from the way Vaughan sublimates his shock over R. W.'s death into a criticism of his own inability to perform properly the task of mourning the dead man. At best, the poem is a self-confessed failure, a belated offering to a lost opportunity, and, fittingly, the quotation from Virgil appended to the lament calls attention to the piety of Vaughan's actions, not the power of the poet's vision. "*Nomen & arma locum servant, te, amice, nequivi / Conspicere—*" ("Thy name and arms guard the place; thee, my friend, I could not see"). Vaughan plays Aeneas to the fallen Deiphobus, the Trojan warrior whose slaughter the leader did not actually witness but whose mangled body he discovers in his reluctant descent into the underworld. Equally reluctant, Vaughan reiterates his ambivalence in his dutiful deliverance of his task. At the outset, he acknowledges that to begin writing the elegy is to cross over a threshold of sorts where it is no longer possible for him to deny the reality of history.

> I am Confirm'd, and so much wing is given
> To my wild thoughts, that they dare strike at heav'n.
> A full years griefe I struggled with, and stood
> Still on my sandy hopes uncertain good,
> So loth was I to yeeld, to all those fears

[13] Writing from Horton probably in 1633 to his former tutor and friend Thomas Young, Milton meditates on whether "I have given up my selfe to dreame away my Yeares in the armes of studious retirement like Endymion wth the Moone as the tale of Latmus goes." The letter, containing the sonnet "How soon hath time," is only one of many significant documents in which Milton considers the question of poetic vocation, but his leisurely juxtaposition of Endimion's world of fantasy with a life of "credible employment" serves as a suggestive anticipation of Vaughan's predicament in *Olor*, one, however, in which leisure is now interpreted as an obvious luxury. See *The Complete Prose Works of John Milton*, ed. Don M. Wolfe et al., 8 vols. to date (New Haven: Yale Univ. Press, 1953-), 1: 319-21.

I still oppos'd thee, and denyed my tears.
But thou art gone! and the untimely losse
Like that one day, hath made all others Crosse. (p. 49, ll. 1-8)

In the fashion of classical laments, Vaughan succeeds at giving the "*Arithmetick*" (l. 30) of the occasion—R. W.'s nobility, honor, and martial prowess—but even during these moments the poet's inadequacy surfaces. The highest praise, for example, that he bestows on his young friend also identifies the poet's shortcomings. The image Vaughan chooses to illustrate the soldier's speed and dexterity (the quickness with which the eye records sensory impressions) does not, he admits, apply equally to himself. Despite the importance of vision to the commemorative task, Vaughan emphasizes how his light failed just at the crucial time of death:

Just so mov'd he: like *shott* his active hand
Drew bloud, e'r well the foe could understand.
But here I lost him. Whether the last turn
Of thy few sands call'd on thy hastie urn,
Or some fierce rapid fate (hid from the Eye)
Hath hurl'd thee Pris'ner to some distant skye
I cannot tell, but that I doe believe
Thy Courage such as scorn'd a base Reprieve. (ll. 59-66)

The uncertainty and possible guilt here deepens into a clear expression of the limits of his present role: "I have / Fail'd in the *glories* of so known a grave" (ll. 69-70) Vaughan confesses, as the "*sad delight*" (l. 74), the poem that might have been possible for him to write in the past—containing all the sweet and sour of proximity—is now the property of someone else. Like Aeneas, whose actions are so pitiable because forced upon him, the manner in which Vaughan submits himself to his task lends a note of distinction to this lament that befits the heroic attitudes it celebrates. The poem refuses to steal any of the glory from its subject; even the commemorative functions of elegy are privileges that Vaughan sees as belonging more readily to the "pious hand" (l. 75) of another. Coming fast on the heels of Endimion's dream where fiction is all, this poem shocks in its pointed resistance to the solace found in the forms of art.

The next pairing seems designed to assure us that the sudden intrusion of history into the world of innocence was no accident; the experience is becoming as predictable to the reader as it apparently was to Vaughan, and the opening line of the second elegy, "I knew it would be thus," answers the suspicions of both. Like the previous lament, this one, "An Elegie on the death of Mr. R. *Hall*, slain at *Pontefract*, 1648," appears immediately after the pastoral myth of the Usk has been recollected once more—this time in the brief epithalamion, "To the best, and most accomplish'd Couple——." The epithalamion is the most idyllic and carefully crafted of the poems in *Olor*; its separation from the actual events of history is not spoiled by Vaughan's letting out the identity of the couple. His secrecy in this has annoyed some, but his purpose is clear: reality cannot touch this most perfect of couples; and for his pair Vaughan, like Prospero, rounds all the edges.

> Blessings as rich and fragrant crown your heads
>   As the mild heav'n on *Roses* sheds,
>   When at their Cheeks (like Pearls) they weare
>   The Clouds that court them in a teare,
>   And may they be fed from above
> By him which first ordain'd your love!   (p. 57, ll. 1-6)

Like the movement in this stanza, the overall movement of the poem endorses the continuity and protection found in a circle. The blessings that rain from heaven in the first two lines are returned at the end of the poem when the couple evaporates into the sky with the delicacy of Marvell's drop of dew: "So you to both worlds shall *rich presents* bring, / And *gather'd* up to heav'n, leave here a *Spring*" (ll. 37-38). At every turn, the poem indulges itself in the pastoral climate, sometimes almost to the point of suffocation, as Vaughan reproduces nearly image for image the flora of the Usk: the "*unseen spreadings* of the Rose," the sunshine days free from the "*tyrant-heat*," and the rich odors of spring all about. In both poems "crowning" is the central activity, while in the epithalamion at least, Vaughan seems deliberately to step forward and play the part of the god of order, Apollo. Not only does he smooth transitions, as the mode demands, through a variety of lotuslike effects with language—rich aspirates, assonance, and sibilants—but he even images his role in the figure of the sun whose "*parcell'd glories* he doth shed [that] / Are the *faire Issues* of his head" (ll. 25-26). Like the sun's "*heat* and *lustre*," Vaughan's poem bears the distinctive stamp of his style, for which he will be remembered to the couple, just as they will leave copies of themselves in the offspring they bear. Once more, as in Endimion's fancy, the dallying of fiction-making comes to the fore, and we have, again, a people and a sun.

But in the face of the next poem, the events of this one seem to vanish like threads of gossamer blown by the wind. The opening of the elegy, "I knew it would be thus!", robs the pastoral of its authority even while it prepares the reader for the report to come. Significantly, the victim, R. Hall, differs from R. W. as the best and most accomplished is distinguished from youthful courage and loyalty. It is for him that Vaughan reserves the role of Pallas by bestowing upon him Aeneas's famous "——*Salve aeternum mihi maxime Palla! / Æternumque vale!*——" ("hail thou for evermore, noblest Pallas, and for evermore farewell"); and like Aeneas at the time of Pallas's death, the poet seems to have a sure sense of his destiny. Steeled to his task, Vaughan refuses to be shadowed by the failure of an earlier missed performance. He challenges both the rights of others to mourn in his place and also his previously timid lament:

> But I past such dimme Mourners can descrie
> Thy fame above all Clouds of obloquie,
> And like the Sun with his victorious rayes
> Charge through that darkness to the last of dayes.
>
> (p. 58, ll. 9-12)

Initially a visionary Apollo of the underworld, Vaughan illuminates his suffering by keeping his eyes on the end of time, "the last of dayes." From this transcendent perspective, Hall's death can be interpreted as a casual "fall," a mere "blott unto thy *Martyrdome*" (l. 18), that teaches us to scorn our weakness. Vaughan's boldness here matches the victim's valor, but along the way the two men separate, and the poet's Apollonian behavior becomes more humanized, frail, and limited. Hall's wisdom seems to absorb, rather than to reflect, the poet's, for

> Those richer graces that adorn'd thy mind
> Like stars of the *first magnitude*, so shin'd,
> That if oppos'd unto these lesser lights
> All we can say, is this, *They were fair nights*. (ll. 51-54)

By the poem's conclusion, the gap between the two has expanded, the thread that connects the living with the dead drawn out to thinness. The general loss of light brought about by Hall's death has infiltrated the poet's own vision to the point where Vaughan blends his reference to this world's "*dark and narrow glasse*" (l. 71) into an image of the poem itself. In the final lines, the earlier Apollo has become Icarus. Vaughan marks his path of descent whereby the poet, now a "dimme Mourner" himself, prepares to fade altogether into the voice of a Virgil, whose hail and farewell echoes with a double purpose:

> Since then (thus flown) thou art so much refin'd,
> That we can only reach thee with the mind,
> [I] will not in this *dark* and *narrow glasse*
> Let thy scant *shadow for Perfections* passe,
> But leave thee to be read more high, more queint,
> In thy own bloud a *Souldier* and a *Saint*.
> —*Salve aeternum mihi maxime Palla!*
> *Æternumque vale!*— (ll. 69-76)

Vaughan's final pairing of pastoral and elegy gives a conclusion of sorts while it resists, more stringently than ever, a resolution between these modes. The poems to Katherine Philips and the dead Elizabeth, second daughter of Charles, appear side by side, and with these two poems to women of nearly the same age, Vaughan seems to bore into the fundamental experience in *Olor*—the repeated violation of innocence. In this case the violation centers even more markedly on art itself, as Vaughan sculpts into its essential poetic features the meaning of the sharp disjunction between pastoral and elegy. Vaughan addresses each woman as if she were the spirit, the apotheosis, of her respective genre. Katherine Philips, regardless of where she actually lived in Wales, belongs to the valley of the Usk. Another example, this time identifiable, of "the best, and most accomplish'd," she is the shrine to which poets flock, like sheep, in the hope of receiving inspiration. Her verse, Vaughan tells us, performs "new miracles in Poetrie" (l. 16), and in his description of it as an incantation, we hear once again the rhythms of a potentially hallowing tradition:

> Say wittie fair one, from what Sphere
> Flow these rich numbers you shed here?
> For sure such *Incantations* come
> From thence, which strike your Readers dumbe.
>
> (pp. 61-62, ll. 1-4)

Like the "*Vocall Groves*" of the Usk, her incantations call for others to surround her and "Sweetly spend their *Youthfull houres*" ("*Isca*," l. 44) imitating her innocent poems in which "no Coorse trifles blot the page" (l. 11). Despite Vaughan's own reluctance in the poem to come into her fold, a reluctance that perhaps signals his disenchantment with a vision of nature unmediated by God, Katherine Philips, as a poet, is nevertheless at the absolute center of the pastoral vision in which imagination and art radiate outward, creating a ceremony of innocence and order.

The poem to Elizabeth diminishes this security at once, and the grim predictability of the elegy itself is nearly as powerful as the actual suffering it describes: there is no levity in this vision of the charnel house. Potential royalist martyr and daughter to the dead king, she appears in the collection at this moment also as a belated response to the perilous balance between "crown" and "fate" described in "To the River *Isca*." Her death, in effect, is a final breaking of the circle; the "crown" she comes to possess at the end of the elegy belongs to another realm altogether. The essential virtues of the pastoral, "*Honour, Beautie, / Faith* and *Dutie, / Delight* and *Truth, /* With *Love,* and *Youth*," reappear once again, but as genii who preside only over a desolate shrine in order to protect a casket whose soul has flown away; they are the guardians of emptiness, of absence:

> Youth, Beauty, Vertue, Innocence
> Heav'ns royall, and select Expence,
> With Virgin-tears, and sighs divine,
> Sit here the *Genii* of this shrine,
> Where now (thy fair soule wing'd away,)
> They guard the *Casket* where she lay.   (p. 63, ll. 1-6)

The vision of innocence which she represents has vanished and her death, interpreted as a ravaging of the pastoral (ll. 15-18), seems to deny altogether the world of the Usk as a source for imaginative strength. Vaughan's focus, moreover, on Elizabeth's suffering in this life (to a degree unusual even in elegy) transforms her into a spirit of lament, a surrogate voice of woe who has, from the moment of her birth, been continually rehearsing her funeral rites. Nurtured for sorrow, Elizabeth figures as a tutelary voice of elegy: she possesses a sound, like Cassandra's, that can move people to pity, but her message has no power over time and circumstance. Amid her lament of "Tears without noise, but (understood) / As lowd, and shrill as any bloud" (ll. 13-14), the identification between poet and victim is also completed on another level, for in her cries we hear the voice of the poet of the collection who claims in his autobiographical poem, "*Ad Posteros*," a power "to give innocent blood a voice" in order to alleviate "the burden of his destiny." But the destiny no longer has much to do with the shaping power of the muse and its noble Apollonian heritage: the tears rendered in this elegy and in

"*Ad Posteros*" are for poetry itself. Significantly, Vaughan's final address to the Usk in *Olor* ("*Ad fluvium Iscam*") contains no swans or swains, not even Apollo—only a description of the river's murmuring whispers and the sounding complaints of the dismembered Thracian, Orpheus.

Writing of the "happy man" tradition in the seventeenth century, Maren-Sofie Røstvig has pointed to the importance of Virgil, with particular reference to two lines from the Second Georgic quoted by Abraham Cowley in his *Ode on Solitude* and adapted by Vaughan as a motto to *Olor*: "*O quis me gelidis sub montibus Æmi / Sistat, & ingenti ramorum protegat umbra?*" ("O who will set me down in the cool glade of Haemus, and protect me with the ample shadow of his branches" [ll. 488-89]).[14] Vaughan simply changed "*sub montibus Æmi*" to "*in vallibus ISCÆ*" in order to make the quotation geographically immediate; but the difference between his and Cowley's use of Virgil is also the difference between emphasizing a question rather than an answer, a means rather than an end, an agent instead of an idea. Cowley celebrated solitude with such unhesitating fervor that he even used its sentiments to form the substance of his own epitaph—much to the amusement of Samuel Johnson.[15] Vaughan's adaptation, in conjunction with the epitaphs included in the collection, however, clearly underscores the gap between the poet and the pastoral ideal even though the author was actually living in the region of the Usk itself. "O who will set me down in the cool valleys" points to an action not yet accomplished, and the question echoes the length of *Olor* as beginnings suddenly become endings, pastoral empties into elegy, and the poet is robbed continually of the opportunity to "muse" at ease. He inhabits the solitary extremes of the imagination rather than a world in which solitude prevails.

Furthermore, if we remember the Virgilian context of these

---

[14] Røstvig, *The Happy Man: Studies in the Metamorphoses of a Classical Ideal*, 2 vols., 2nd ed. (Trondheim: Norwegian Universities Press, 1962), 1: 217.

[15] Ibid., p. 213.

lines, in which pastoral contentment appears as only a pleasant alternative for the aspiring poet not favored by a greater destiny, we also glimpse the predicament of the poet as it is repeatedly presented in *Olor*. Uncertain of his own chosen status, he is even less certain of the security associated with the pastoral itself. Aspiration seems, once again, delimited by context even though not altogether limited by it. The poet of *Olor*—the "Swan of the Usk"—exists in a limbo somewhere between Spenser's Colin Clout, who hangs up his pipe at the end of *The Shepheardes Calender*, and the "uncouth swain" of "Lycidas" who closes his monody by setting out for "fresh Woods, and Pastures new." In "*Ad fluvium Iscam*," Vaughan represents his situation precisely in the figure of the archetypal poet Orpheus who perseveres, albeit in a state of dismemberment. He continues to sing yet with little promise of triumph, and in this ambivalent portrait is a further reflection of the collection at large. Delayed in its publication, the volume nonetheless survives, even perhaps in slightly mutilated form, as a testimony to ambition—ambition "refigured" in the light of *Silex Scintillans* (1650) and by a poet who at this point was writing in the shade of *The Temple*. Almost thirty years later when *Olor* was reissued (1679) and Vaughan had altogether "retired" from writing poetry, the volume appeared with only one change: the motto from Virgil had been erased. The heat of the times as well as the heat of inspiration had long since passed.

CHAPTER THREE

Serious Play in Brecknock: Cavalier Fellowship and the Transmigration of Wit

> Is't not Even
> Whether wee dye by peecemeale, or at once
> Since both but ruine?
> —Henry Vaughan, "Upon a Cloke lent him by Mr. J. Ridsley"

"THE MAN who has fallen," writes Paul de Man, "is somewhat wiser than the fool who walks around oblivious of the crack in the pavement about to trip him up."[1] Vaughan is both fool and wise man in *Olor*. The meticulous pairings of pastoral and elegy keep repeating the plummet from innocence to experience as the poet penetrates more deeply into the disturbing, and in some cases, paralyzing effects of the fall on the speaker's consciousness. In these pairings, Vaughan reveals his continued preoccupation with the contrasting voices of "*Philomel*" and the "hoarse bird of Night," but the volume would risk being uniform to the point of monotony if the poet simply set up a version of Van der Noot's *Theater for Worldings* and punctured pastoral dream after dream in order to demonstrate the mutability of all things.

Along with the pastoral and elegiac voices in *Olor*, there is another voice variously described by critics as ironic, satiric, or "Democritean." Whatever name we choose, the wisdom of this "stance" arises not just from Vaughan's accepting his fall but from his willingness to share with others his exploration of the zany, vertiginous confusion that frequently ac-

---

[1] De Man, "The Rhetoric of Temporality," in *Interpretation: Theory and Practice*, ed. Charles S. Singleton (Baltimore: Johns Hopkins Univ. Press, 1969), p. 196.

companies this experience. Neither entirely helpless as in his elegies nor especially hallowed as in his pastorals, the writer fends for himself in a brazen and corrupt world. Vaughan wittily renders this impoverished condition in his allusion to the poet's "thredbare, goldless genealogie" ("To his friend———," p. 44, l. 13). At least twice fallen, he is without God or gold, divinity or money, and the pun, condensing the poet's once-sacred connections, seems literally to muffle the idea of a noble heritage in a background echo. As the wordplay also indicates, this voice originates not at the solitary extremes of the imagination, as do those of pastoral and elegy, but near the center of society. It intrudes, reproves, jokes, and judges; *it can be both impudent and affectionate within the space of a single line:* it can also slide into self-pity. But whether spinning out trivial anecdotes or ringing the praises of another writer, it attempts a powerful blend of play with a strong desire to discover a sense of ballast in shared human experience. It is the voice of a distant "Son of Ben" attempting to provide a center for another circle of friends to replace the one whose demise the young author had recorded in *Poems 1646*.

Broadly speaking, all of the poems in this mode are epistolary or quasi-epistolary in form. Some are addressed simply to a "friend"; others name people who, if it were not for Vaughan's poem, would be lost to posterity. Still others are written in complimentary fashion to eminent literary figures of the day, such as Cartwright, Davenant, and Fletcher. For the more ambitious author of *Olor*, the form was well-suited to the dual purpose of social commentary and self-promotion, to creating a space for himself in a contemporary literary setting even if the "scene" was far from the center in London. "The verse epistle openly declares its basis in actual experience, and reveals the poet in his own person," writes D. J. Palmer.[2] Compared to pictures that " 'only refresh the memory and lighten our longing by a solace that is unreal,' " argues

[2] Palmer, "The Verse Epistle," in *Metaphysical Poetry*, ed. Malcolm Bradbury and David Palmer (London: Edward Arnold Ltd., 1970), p. 73.

Seneca, " 'how much more pleasant is a letter, which brings us real traces, real evidences, of an absent friend.' "[3] Less restrictive in style, diction, and subject matter than the courtly lyrics of Vaughan's first volume, its principal obligation (and appeal) is to reflect the nuances of thought in which the author seems most characteristically himself: in a world of continuous movement, his shifting presence is the one constant. Indeed, in "Upon a Cloke lent him by Mr. *J. Ridsley*"—a poem whose "fantasticality of invention," in Rudrum's apt phrase,[4] works to test the limits of the epistolary form itself—Vaughan provides a humorous twist on the mode as preeminently a place for self-revelation when, at the exact center of the poem, he literally invites us to imagine him naked:

> I have since known more
> And worser pranks: One night (as heretofore
> Th' hast known) for want of change (a thing which I
> And *Bias* us'd before me) I did lye
> Pure *Adamite*, and simply for that end
> Resolv'd, and made this for my bosome-*friend*.
> O that thou hadst been there next morn, that I
> Might teach thee new *Micro-cosmo-graphie!*
> Thou wouldst have ta'ne me, as I naked stood,
> For one of th' *seven pillars* before the floud.
>
> (pp. 52-53, ll. 37-46)

This close-up view of the speaker, moreover, is also the moment when the "absent friend" seems most verbally immediate to the imagined recipient: the double parenthetical asides allude to previous episodes outside the frame of the poem that Vaughan and his friend shared and to which we, as readers, are not privy. At the end of the poem, however, we are all invited to approve of the author's freedom of wit. If we have been put through some anecdotal hurdles in this epistle, it is all part of a game whose amusement has been to use the muse to trace the protean character of a poet's self:

[3] Ibid., p. 83.
[4] Rudrum, "Some Remarks on Henry Vaughan's Secular Poems," *Poetry Wales* 11 (1975): 45.

> But I have done. And think not, friend, that I
> This freedome took to Jeere thy Courtesie,
> I thank thee for't, and I believe my Muse
> So known to thee, thou'lt not suspect abuse;
> She did this, 'cause (perhaps) thy *love* paid thus
> Might with my *thanks* out-live thy *Cloke*, and *Us*. (ll. 93-98)

Given the mediating function of the verse epistle in general, it is not surprising that the first one in *Olor* should appear immediately after the opening fall sustained in "The Charnel-house." The process of reification, begun in that poem, is both denied and continued in the splendid irony of "*In Amicum fœneratorem*" (to his friend, the moneylender, p. 43), where it is not even certain just how we are meant to take the meaning of "*amicum*" in the title. The poet's cunning is apparent throughout but nowhere more than in his ruthless handling of the underlying myth of *Olor*: the pastoral conventions themselves. The speaker does not want to deliver a golden world; he wants only to be delivered his gold, and he images the sign of his greed in the parodic, twisted figure of an Orpheus "forcing" money from his stony patrons, a neat reversal of "Natures *busie* Child" who sings inspired by his surroundings in "*Isca*." Vaughan also insures that poetry has abandoned its associations with the lyre. Instead of vocal music, he describes other strange noises: "a crying summe" of money, messages dressed in "*chink*" (slang usage in the seventeenth century for the sound of coins hitting together), the ringing peal of coins in a chest, and even the threat of "a Poets curse," to name but a few. Vaughan, wonderfully indifferent to his own corruptibility and corruption as a poet, indulges in some barely human grunting—"But wilt have money *Og*?" (l. 19)—and guttural gestures—"I have no land to glutt / Thy durty appetite, and make thee strutt / *Nimrod* of acres" (ll. 25-26).

The progress of the verse marks the regressive, decaying effects of "*Decoy* gold" on the speaker. He shifts his interest from simply inverting individual symbols of the golden world to presenting a full-scale, perverted picture of the easy life. Suiting the description to his listener, Vaughan attempts to bribe the moneylender with a pastoral kingdom in which the natural, idyllic pleasures of Parnassus turn into a merry-go-round of sensual offerings. For his moneylending friend, the poet pours on the riches, loading every rift with too much ore: "Wee'l suck the *Corall* of their lips" (l. 39), he says of the nymphs, in a phrase whose greedy ardor destroys the platonic enterprise of pastoral love and also plays on the usurer's lack of taste in anything but money. The reduction is furthered in this instance if we know that coral was given to infants in Vaughan's day to aid them in cutting teeth (*OED*, s.v. 3). But even without this reference, the vision of a Tantalus roving in a forest of "*Amber-tresses*" feasting upon the nymphs's "spicie breath, a meale at need" (ll. 40) makes it clear that human action is approaching a primal, if not bestial, level. In a final consumptive gesture that fuses the rival oral claims of speaking and supping the poet gives a bearlike nod to his "friend": "Thou must then (if live thus) my neast of honey, / Cancell old bonds, and beg to lend more money" (ll. 51-52). The act of eating, Freud suggests, is a "destruction of the object with the final aim of incorporating it":[5] Vaughan's irony, here and throughout, is aimed at engulfing the engulfer and at establishing a view of the poet too wise to be dizzied by the charms of the pastoral world. He will not trip on any cracks because he knows that the whole sidewalk is in need of repair.

The ironic consciousness, however, could easily collapse into a scene of bedlam. As de Man again has argued: "irony possesses an inherent tendency to gain momentum and not to stop until it has run its full course.... It may start as a casual bit of play with a stray loose end of the fabric, but before long the entire texture of the self is unraveled and comes apart. The whole process happens at an unsettling speed."[6] This could serve as a good gloss on what happens to those master ironists, Hamlet and Democritus Junior, each of whom plays

---

[5] Freud, *An Outline of Psychoanalysis*, trans. James Strachey (New York: W. W. Norton & Co., 1949), p. 21.
[6] De Man, "The Rhetoric of Temporality," p. 197.

with more than a single loose end and finds his freedom to mask and parody, cavil and subvert, sometimes tethered by the mind bending back on itself. In Hamlet's words, "I could be bounded in a nutshell and count myself a king of infinite space, were it not that I have bad dreams" (2. 2. 58-60).

The poem that follows, entitled simply "To his friend———," is Vaughan's version of the poet's bad dream. It starts as a bit of casual play, the fragility of which is felt in three slightly defensive, parenthetical asides in the first seven lines, and it moves jokingly through a description of the poet's "thredbare, goldless genealogie." But the superior and knowing stance of the previous verse begins to crumble when the speaker says he can look back

> Into the wombe of time, and see the Rack
> Stand useless there, untill we are produc'd
> Unto the torture, and our soules infus'd
> To learn afflictions, I begin to doubt
> That as some tyrants use from their chain'd rout
> Of slaves to pick out one whom for their sport
> They keep afflicted by some lingring art,
> So wee are meerly thrown upon the stage
> The mirth of fooles, and Legend of the age.   (pp. 44-45, ll. 20-28)

In the preceding poem the muse was inviolable if only because it assumed its fallenness. Now, the poet's poverty becomes a trope for his powerlessness, and, pointedly, the prison which he had managed earlier to evade by avoiding all mention of it ("Talk not of *Shreeves*, or gaole," l. 24) seems to loom all the larger in his mind. Vaughan's reflection on the "wombe of time," his dream, summons up an image of the poet bound in a smaller compass than Hamlet's nutshell: an image figured in the progressively shriller and more heated language of the verse, "I'm mad at Fate, and angry ev'n to sinne, / To see deserts and learning clad so thinne" (ll. 39-40), which boils into a Timon-like fever of curses (ll. 41-58), before the poet literally burns himself out in his final indictment: " 'Las! They're but quibbles, things we Poets feign, / The short-liv'd Squibs and Crackers of the brain" (ll. 59-60). Crackbrained, the poet escapes his madness only by feigning "Crackers of the brain," which is to say he does not escape at all. As Hamlet knew, there is more freedom in being bound in a nutshell, and the attempt by Vaughan to escape through a final posture of wisdom is singularly unconvincing. The closing eight lines simply give too many exceptions to prove the rule of a cool intelligence:

> But wee'l be wiser, knowing 'tis not they
> That must redeem the hardship of our way,
> Whether a Higher Power, or that starre
> Which neerest heav'n, is from the earth most far
> Oppresses us thus, or angel'd from that Sphere
> By our strict Guardians are kept luckless here,
> It matters not, wee shall one day obtain
> Our native and Celestiall scope again.   (ll. 61-68)

Either above or below, superior or inferior to his environment, Vaughan oscillates in these two poems between victor and victim. The third poem in this brief sequence, "To his retired friend, an Invitation to *Brecknock*" attempts to fuse the garrulous wit of the first epistle with the simpering yet irascible figure of the poet in the second. More settled than either of the previous speakers, this persona "reports" on his immediate surroundings; and the new touch of realism testifies both to his advancing wisdom—his knowledge of the world—and to his practical concern with the survival of poetry. The friend addressed is, among other things, a vestige of the poet in the previous verse, now looked at with amusement. His harassed and badgered condition is humorously represented in the badgerlike image of a monk whipping himself:

> But thou may'st prove devout, and love a Cell,
> And (like a Badger) with attentive looks
> In the dark hole sit rooting up of books.
> Quick Hermit! what a peacefull Change hadst thou
> Without the noise of *haire-cloth*, *Whip*, or *Vow*?
>   (pp. 46-47, ll. 38-42)

Together, the poet and his friend share a vocabulary—a literary subtext that exists largely underground, or at least in competition with, the local noise and civil outrage of the times—to be recovered occasionally with something like its old, full force with the lifting of a wineglass.

Besides its sheer verbal exuberance, much of the poem's mastery lies in how the poet keeps his friend and the hostile environment in a remarkably stable equilibrium. Of the first twenty-six lines, for example, he spends thirteen chiding his friend with gentle, academic irony and another thirteen battering the newfangledness of Brecknock. There is glee in both of these gestures, one performing a check on the other: Vaughan plays Pythagoras's ox off against Brecon's pigs, and his friend's possible illness against the justices "vext with the *Cough*, and *flegme*" (l. 20). Nearly each line adds a new point of difference between the "orthodox" companion, whom the poet beckons in leisurely, often Latinate phrases, and the heterodox surroundings Vaughan crushes with choppy, Saxon thrusts. The contest between culture and anarchy persists, even down to differences in alcoholic beverages and their effects, while along the way the poet figures as a purveyor of wisdom, an isolated and belated classicist, who thinks of his town's connections to Rome, of his friend's Greek habits, and who looks for wit in the enthusiastic extremes of religious behavior. " 'Midst noise and War" (l. 76), he is the keeper of sanity and civilization. The philosophic mean, defined at the end of "The Charnel-house" and sought in the closing moments of "To his friend," is the substance from which this, Vaughan's most Cavalier poem, is woven.

Significantly, the centering process, itself central to the "Cavalier mode," is reflected in the poem's geography as well as in the poet's balancing gestures. Beginning on the outskirts of town, Vaughan's description carries the reader into the middle of Brecknock, before the poet draws a circle around himself and his friend in the town tavern.[7] At this point, the

[7] Kenneth Friedenreich, *Henry Vaughan* (Boston: G. K. Hall, 1978), p. 95, makes a similar observation in pointing out the Puritan allusions in the poem.

centering action is repeated in the round figure of the cup of wine, which, like the crown in "To the river *Isca*," is intimately associated with the survival of poetry:

> Here lives that *Chimick*, quick fire which betrayes
> Fresh Spirits to the bloud, and warms our layes,
> I have reserv'd 'gainst thy approach a Cup
> That were thy Muse stark dead, shall raise her up,
> And teach her yet more Charming words and skill
> Than ever *Cælia, Chloris, Astrophil*,
> Or any of the Thredbare names Inspir'd
> Poore riming lovers with a *Mistris* fir'd. (ll. 65-72)

Less concerned than "*Isca*" with prophecy, Vaughan's "Charming words" at this moment suddenly insist on their own powers of recovery. "Here" is coyly evasive and inclusive, referring simultaneously to the tavern, the glass of wine, and the text of the poem itself, while the sense of rebirth is literally imaged in the toast. (Because of the syntax, the cup and the hypothetically dead muse are fused in a single gesture of salute.) But the "charm" of language is also strictly contained within the commodious social vision; Vaughan only plays slightly with the thaumaturgic meanings of the word and its connection to the magic of poetry which Milton, for example, more thoroughly explores in his masque at nearby Ludlow Castle. The multiple use of spondees ("Here lives," "quick fire," and "Fresh Spirits") picks up and mimics the italicized, stressed, disyllables of "*Chimick*," and together they certainly invigorate lines 65-66; but the chiasmic structure of the verse militates against these accented cadences being transformed into the sounds of a Bacchic revelry. Indeed, by the second half of line 66, they have already begun to cool into the more routine iambic of "and warms our layes."

Despite its message, the celebration is finally a sobering one. If we do hear a Cavalier Vaughan, we must also listen to a voice easily disturbed by its surroundings.[8] "Why should wee /

---

[8] Simmonds, *Masques of God: Form and Theme in the Poetry of Henry Vaughan* (Pittsburgh: Univ. of Pittsburgh Press, 1972), pp. 122-26, Frieden-

Vex at the times ridiculous miserie?" (ll. 77-78) is exactly the question that keeps cutting through the jolly notes "blith (as of old)" (l. 75) and makes, for instance, the closing effort to tighten the circle into a comfortably secure knot so problematic. Near the end, when Vaughan recounts his decision to steal a revel in the town, he does so only after describing the refusal of others to take him seriously: "An age that thus hath fool'd it selfe, and will / (Spite of thy teeth and mine) persist so still" (ll. 79-80). Besides the issue of whether Vaughan senses his own lack of moral bite here—and hence his authority as a Jonsonian poet—there is the more immediate question of whether his "jests" are self-generated fun and a sign of his independence, or whether he has been forced to sublimate his anger and contempt until even his "good" humor seems only a reflex. The poet does not stay to give his answer but goes out to play in a grimly apocalyptic company of cheaters who will revel "Till those black deeds bring on the darksome day" (l. 84).

With this poem, particularly, it has become canonical in Vaughan criticism to defend the poet from Whittier's charge that the "Swan of the Usk" was basically insensitive to "England's civil strife." Seeking relief, of course, is not necessarily political indifference, as Hutchinson points out,[9] while it is also possible to elevate and dignify the poet's mirth through a connection with stoicism.[10] But if temporary withdrawal or transcendence represent two sides of the same coin, a more

---

reich, *Henry Vaughan*, pp. 95-98, and less so Earl Miner, *The Cavalier Mode from Jonson to Cotton* (Princeton: Princeton Univ. Press, 1971), pp. 299-300, notice certain tremors in the verse, but nevertheless interpret the poem as if its author had been Jonson rather than a late imitator of Jonson as much at variance with the father as potentially comparable to him. Miner is more scrupulous in this respect, but the lack of conviction that belies his final assessment of the verse ("There seems to be real confidence in the conclusion of the poem," p. 300) indicates that he perhaps recognizes more in the poem than he is willing to let on.

[9] F. E. Hutchinson, *Henry Vaughan: A Life and Interpretation* (Oxford: Clarendon Press, 1947), pp. 59-60.

[10] Simmonds, *Masques of God*, p. 122. Friedenreich, *Henry Vaughan*, pp. 98-99, repeats both of these positions.

embracing alternative has already, I think, been supplied by Vaughan: it involves not dissolution through alcohol, but dismissing the casual and careless gesture itself. In "An Invitation" Vaughan raises his cup to poetry, yet he never seems altogether certain that the glass will not shatter. Compared to other mid-century Cavalier lyrics such as Lovelace's Grasshopper Ode, Vaughan's poem easily resists the luscious interior comforts found in a "genuine summer" of friendship and song. Nor does it settle into a comfortable note of celebrating itself. To set his Bacchic revelry alongside of the *locus classicus* in this mode—a stanza from Jonson's Pindaric Ode to Cary and Morrison[11]—helps to measure the distance between the Welsh poet's methods and the Cavalier mood evoked by Ben. Blending elegiac and Dionysian modes, the relevant section from Jonson's poem reads:

> Call, noble *Lucius*, then for Wine,
> And let thy lookes with gladnesse shine:
> Accept this garland, plant it on thy head,
> And thinke, nay know, thy *Morison*'s not dead.
> Hee leap'd the present age,
> Possest with holy rage,
> To see that bright eternall Day:
> Of which we *Priests*, and *Poets* say
> Such truths, as we expect for happy men,
> And there he lives with memorie; and *Ben*   (ll. 75-84)[12]

Both poems are concerned with invocations, poetic inspiration, and friendship; both are concerned with defining the good life. Beyond these similarities, however, the younger poet's lyric is meager in many of its offerings. There is no naming and, of course, no recognition of nobility which that act confers. Nor does it seem feasible for the little-known Vaughan to emerge suddenly as an anchoring presence, a cornerstone,

---

[11] Miner, *Cavalier Mode*, pp. 51-52 and pp. 71-74, defines the characteristic Cavalier *topoi* in this poem; on the important issue of naming in Cavalier poetry in general, I am indebted to his discussion on pp. 3-15.

[12] *Ben Jonson*, ed. C. H. Herford and Percy and Evelyn Simpson, 11 vols. (Oxford: Clarendon Press, 1925-1952), 8 (1947): 245-46.

to his fiction, as Jonson actually does in the stanza above. And with the mention of "Thredbare names" amid a supposedly "vatic" or inflationary gesture, the occasion sufficiently collapses so that the Cavalier pose is reinterpreted for what, in fact, it could sometimes become: a muse of "Charming words" with precious little else to sustain it. Caelia, Chloris, and Astrophil appear in Vaughan merely as figures of inspiration cut loose from everything but their rhetorical associations. Geographically and imaginatively a long way from the court, Vaughan's poem discovers some of the weaker seams of Cavalier sentiment: the game of amatory verse continues in Brecknock but only as a faint echo of the dignified roll call of lovers' names that hallows the opening of "To the river *Isca*" and on whose banks Whittier, among others, assumes Vaughan is always to be found.

In the other Cavalier lyric in the collection to which "An Invitation" is often compared, our suspicions are confirmed about Vaughan's ambivalence toward a muse of charming words. "To my worthy friend Master *T. Lewes*" (p. 61) thins out jollity to the point of nonexistence. As an echo of an echo, the poem is interesting for what it omits as well as includes. It begins where "Appleton House" ends: with a description of nature, thick and viscous, whose slow movement Vaughan sets forth as a *"key"* (l. 9) for personal behavior.

> Sees not my friend, what a deep snow
> *Candies* our Countries wooddy brow?
> The yeelding branch his load scarse bears
> Opprest with snow, and *frozen tears*,
> While the *dumb* rivers slowly float,
> All bound up in an *Icie Coat*.   (p. 61, ll. 1-6)

In poeticizing "oppression," Vaughan plays with some verbal burying of his own. The load of the "yeelding branch" he doubly weights with the internal slant rhyme of "scarse bears," while he further retards the river's movement by repeating the long vowel sound of "slow" in "float." Such measurable hesitations, richly sensuous in the lingering detail of the account, are set against the wilder motions of the "world" at large, a word that has its inevitable rhyme—inevitable, that is, in Cavalier and Neoplatonic poetry—in "hurld." In apparent contrast to the cold temperature outside, Vaughan issues his invitation to his friend with enthusiastic warmth: "Let us meet then!" But after this gesture, even the reputedly chilly Milton can offer a cozier interior in a poem like "Lawrence of Virtuous Father" than Vaughan gives here. With methodical regularity, imitative of the surrounding nature but without its descriptive richness, the poet slowly seals off himself (and presumably his friend) from the hostile outside, as they put on the "*Icie Coat*" reserved earlier for the cold landscape. The two disappear partially from sight when Vaughan refers to the need to "walk in our forefathers way" (l. 10); they slip further away with each separate question about what they should not do (ll. 11-14); and, except for the implied contrast, they are altogether missing in his description of the individual who "looks oft beyond his terme set here" (l. 16). When we learn at the end that the poem has been arguing for "discreet Joyes" (l. 21), we also see that Vaughan's discretion in presenting so little evidence of joy has all but beaten this experience into airy thinness. The point is not so much that Vaughan is teaching a kind of stoicism by negative example as that he is emptying the Cavalier gesture of most of its grace: the snow falls and the river freezes, the times are bad; let us meet then and . . . ? Vaughan is more Burton's than Lovelace's grasshopper-poet: "sing they must in Summer, and pine in the Winter, for there is no preferment for them."[13]

All of these poems show Vaughan attempting to use the epistolary form as a way to mediate between himself and a particular audience and to seal up the gap between pastoral and elegy, but the poet never seems altogether comfortable in his relationship to the disturbing events around him or to those whom he addresses. He plays, but he plays seriously.

---

[13] Robert Burton, *The Anatomy of Melancholy*, ed. A. R. Shilleto, 3 vols. (London: George Bell and Sons, 1896), 1:356 (Pt. 1, Sec. 2, Memb. 3, Subs. 15).

Irony keeps giving way to bitterness or self-pity; the commodious voice slips too easily into formulaic doctrine where, instead of filling the page or the ear of his listener with warmth, his utterances move either toward archness or anonymity. The presentation of the self rarely seems, as it does with Donne, a carefully controlled portion of the ego, nor does it assume the aura of stability central to Jonson's ethical view of poetry. Referred to by his cousin, Aubrey, as "Ingeniose, but prowd and humorous,"[14] Vaughan remains in these occasional poems slightly aloof from his immediate audience, as if he does not trust entirely in the Cavalier ideal of friendship with its desire to sustain and continue "the little society of the good few."[15] Indeed, his poem to Katherine Philips—that choreographer of masquerades celebrating the virtues of platonic friendship—is noteworthy for insisting on a space between the poet and the object of his praise: "So I concluded, It was true / I might at distance worship you / A *Persian* Votarie, and say / *It was your light shew'd me the way*" (ll. 27-30).[16]

The verbal uncertainties and hesitations in these poems form slight ripples in the Cavalier seam of friendship. When *Olor* finally reached the press in 1651, however, it also included a number of verse and prose translations which, in the manner of his translation of Juvenal in *Poems*, challenge, qualify, and even undermine attitudes central to the preceding verse. For each group of translations, Vaughan creates an obvious arc in the ordering of material that carries the reader chronologically forward from the initial works of pagan authors to those of writers who are increasingly more Christian in focus. Thus we move from Ovid to the Polish Jesuit, Casimire, in the poetry, and in the prose from Plutarch to the Spanish bishop,

---

[14] *Aubrey's Brief Lives*, ed. Oliver Lawson Dick (1949; rpt. Ann Arbor: Univ. of Michigan Press, 1962), p. 303.

[15] Miner, *Cavalier Mode*, p. 275.

[16] Patrick Thomas, "Orinda, Vaughan and Watkyns: Anglo-Welsh Literary Relationships During the Interregnum," *The Anglo-Welsh Review* 26 (1976): 96-102, concludes in the most recent discussion of their relationship that "there is no concrete evidence that Vaughan's friendship wth Orinda was transferred from London to Wales" (p. 99).

Don Antonio de Guevara. In each case, Vaughan begins with a classical work whose author does more than simply prefigure the pious writers at the end; rather, these initial translations serve as wedges that cause attitudes previously expressed in the original poetry to topple before the reader: they turn the partial dissolution of the Cavalier mode into something like a full-scale demolition, with the attack centered on friendship itself. In doing so, Vaughan insures that the "proces of time (which corrupts all things)" (p. 97) is felt both in the poet's own "retreat" into translation and in the decomposition of beliefs central to sustaining a vision of social poetry altogether.

The crack is certainly in evidence in Vaughan's rendering into English of Plutarch's *Of the Benefit we may get by our Enemies*, the second longest of the prose translations in *Olor*. The title might well have been "Of the Frailty of Friendship," for at many points in the treatise friendship is put as much to the test as the individual who endures a hostile and cruel world, and it is frequently found to be wanting. Indeed, the homiletic nature of the translation keeps pushing into tight juxtaposition the seemingly opposed concepts of friends and enemies, playing one off against the other, until it is no longer possible to make any safe distinctions between the two. Friends exist only in name; the blurring of meaning is meant to insure that the individual who reads this discourse on self-reliance will come to trust in only himself. Thus Plutarch reports, and Vaughan translates, how Chilo the Wise "when hearing one affirme That he had not an Enemy in the World . . . return'd upon him this Quere, *If he had ever a Friend?*" (p. 97), while later we learn that the enemy looks "through the Bosomes and inward parts of thy Friend, thy Servant, and thy Familiar" (p. 99). Indeed, the tongue of loyalty is "too short to speak home, too long when [it] smooth[es] us, and quite dumb to admonish; it followes that wee can only heare the truth from our Enemies" (p. 103). By the end of the treatise, the reversal between the two has been wittily effected: Plutarch and Vaughan would have their respective readers more dependent on their enemies than their friends, "*Lest... being rid of our Enemies, wee begin to fall out with our friends*" (p. 107).

Typically, Vaughan reserves his more important statements for verse, and in his four translations from Ovid he reworks Plutarch's witty, final formulation into the most wholesale assault on loyalty in *Olor*. Banished to Tomis, Ovid was free from his enemies in Rome, but his newly acquired distance also brought a recognition of the even greater treachery that existed among his friends. His *Tristia* and *Epistulae ex Ponto* record the pain of his fall and his subsequent embittering enlightenment; and if the story was familiar lore to every English schoolboy in Vaughan's day,[17] the possible parallels between Vaughan, living in a self-imposed exile, and Ovid are equally obvious. Yet Vaughan is doing more than striking a plaintive, autobiographical note: he rearranges the order of the poems in the original to telescope the sudden dissolution of Ovid's circle of Bacchic poet-friends in Rome and adds subtitles that serve as stage directions to mark the widening gyre of distrust. The first in appearance, *Tristium*, 5.3, for example, is happily called "To his fellow-Poets at *Rome*, upon the birth-day of *Bacchus*" (p. 65), while Vaughan's next (*De Ponto* 3.7), "To his friends (after his many sollicitations) refusing to petition *Cæsar* for his releasement," strikes a more caustic note. The third (*De Ponto* 4.3) is utterly inconsolable, "To his Inconstant friend, translated for the use of all the *Judases* of this touch-stone-Age," and the final one (*Tristium*, 3.3), "To his Wife at *Rome*, when he was sick" is Ovid's epitaph to himself. For a poet who is sometimes thought of as "content in a circle of country friends,"[18] Vaughan's poison-pen letters, though appearing under the guise of Ovid, come as a shock, particularly when they dig with such bitterness into the kind of experience celebrated in "An Invitation":

---

[17] Davis P. Harding, *Milton and the Renaissance Ovid*, University of Illinois Studies in Lang. and Lit., vol. 30, no. 4 (Urbana: Univ. of Illinois Press, 1946), pp. 29-31.
[18] Miner, *Cavalier Mode*, p. 300.

> Yet know (though deafe to this) that I am he
> Whose *years* and *love* had the same *Infancie*
> With thine, Thy *deep familiar*, that did share
> *Soules* with thee, and partake thy *Joyes* or *Care*,
> Whom the same *Roofe* lodg'd, and my *Muse* those nights
> So solemnly endear'd to her delights;
> But now, perfidious traitour, I am grown
> The *Abject* of thy brest, not to be known
> In that *false Closet* more.
>   ("To his Inconstant Friend," pp. 68-69, ll. 21-29)

The point here, and in this sequence in general, is not that Vaughan has anyone specifically in mind, or that his translations are directed against the iniquities of the city and, thus, serve as covert encomia of the country life; but, rather, appearing immediately after the original poetry, they systematically rechannel the social ebullience of the Jonsonian mode of poetry—its blitheness—into the narrower straits of self-indulgence: jollity and callousness are two aspects of the same character, and, together, they yield the figure of Janus. Furthermore, by beginning the sequence with Bacchus and ending with Judas, Vaughan slyly insinuates that we see the camaraderie of the former occasion, which once included himself, as, in fact, a Last Supper of sorts: a circle of friends is no more immutable than the individuals who make it up, and, hence, the poet includes the fourth epistle to place a gravestone on the whole experience.

Such attention, of course, to the vanities of fellowship only argues more strongly Vaughan's desire for companionship and recognition on another level. For if the Welsh poet was not exactly a noble Palemon fit for the company of a "Matchless Orinda," neither was he a connoisseur of loneliness for its own sake. "A natural and secret hatred and aversation towards society in any man," wrote Bacon in his essay "Of Friendship," "hath somewhat of the savage beast; but it is most untrue that it should have any character at all of the divine nature; except it proceed, not out of a pleasure in solitude, but out of a love and desire to sequester a man's self for a higher conversation."[19] Unable to find "true" literary companions among the living in *Olor*, Vaughan, nevertheless, did begin to explore the possibilities of a "higher conversation" in the only place where mutability was no longer an issue and yet his own ambitious desires for poetry might still find fulfillment: to the writers of the immediate past. Partially protected by the shade of other authors, he could turn a series of political and imaginative defeats into a moment of poetic triumph.

Vaughan's poems to Cartwright and Fletcher (Davenant was still alive) are more than simply exercises in a conventional, commendatory mode. They attempt to effect what the Welsh poet describes explicitly in the poem to Fletcher as a transmigration of wit from the dead to the living (ll. 17-20), an "aesthetics" of borrowing particularly common among Cavalier writers.[20] (Surpassing his contemporaries, Vaughan will eventually extend this aesthetic into a method of creating not just a verse or two but an entire collection of poetry.) Sheer tours de force, these poems bring together the vigorous display of self, as witnessed in "Upon a Cloke," with a keen desire to find transcendence in the act of poetry that develops from a mutual identification of celebrator and celebrated and leads ultimately to the enshrinement of both writers. In doing so, the poems also move beyond the idea of the literary circle itself, for the sustenance Vaughan has sought to provide for his "friends" he now seeks in solitary fashion from the poetry of other poets. " 'More than kisses, letters mingle Soules,' "

---

[19] *The Works of Francis Bacon*, ed. James Spedding, Robert Ellis, and Douglas Heath, 14 vols. (London: Longman and Co., Ltd., 1857-1874), 6 (1858): 437.

[20] Miner, *Cavalier Mode*, pp. 268-69. Discussing Randolph's "A gratulatory to Mr. Ben Jonson for his adopting of him to be his Son," Miner sums up one-half of the poet's argument by remarking that "surely a son may steal Promethean fire from his father" (p. 268). The image is Randolph's and, for my purpose, a felicitous one since his acknowledged thievery as well as his desire to pay back the loan is relevant to Vaughan both in his commendatory poems to Cartwright and Fletcher and in the making of *Silex Scintillans*. See below, chapter 5.

Donne has said,[21] and these verse epistles to the dead, commemorating achievements that are past, touch elegiac notes and strains of ambition that run deep in *Olor Iscanus*.

No other poems in the collection are so agile in balancing the praise of one with the dispraise of others and demonstrating along the way the meaning, if not the intent, of Plutarch's phrase "of the benefit we may get by our enemies." "Upon the *Poems* and *Playes* of the ever memorable Mr. *William Cartwright*" correctly anticipated the sea of commendatory verse that threatened to swamp Cartwright's achievement and also Vaughan's. At the time of the volume's publication in 1651, the tide had reached a near-record high of fifty-four poems, with Vaughan's managing to float to the top only because it accounts so fully for the lambent dullness that plays around this mode. Securing his own privileged position among the celebrity's admirers, the Welsh poet throughout claims to give the inside view of Cartwright. In the opening lines, he wades into the stream, shouting, while pretending not to shout, as he delivers several of his most brutally endstopped couplets that simultaneously close off his associations with the others and begin to forge the seal between the honored writer and himself:

> I did but *see* thee! and how *vain* it is
> To *vex* thee for it with *Remonstrances*,
> Though *things* in fashion, let those *Judge*, who sit
> Their *twelve-pence* out, to *clap* their *hands* at *wit*;
> I fear to *Sinne* thus *neer* thee; for (*great Saint!*)
> 'Tis known, *true beauty* hath no need of *paint*.   (p. 55, ll. 1-6)

The only writer of the fifty-four to begin with such fanfare, Vaughan recedes slightly in the next few lines, but even in retreat he continues to promote his advantage: the common habits of the playgoers who, for twelvepence, clapped their hands like mannequins at Cartwright's wit are refigured in the current bevy of versifiers who, for fashion's sake, fix a "*Labell*

---

[21] Quoted by Palmer, "The Verse Epistle," p. 83; letter to Sir Henry Wotton.

... to thy fair *Hearse*" (l. 7). Neither group has much vision and even less taste, while Vaughan disparages the verse of his rivals as only scratching the surface. Their role as funeral mourners is like his own in the epitaph to Elizabeth: they "Can teach *Posterity* our present *griefe* / And their own *losse*, but never give *reliefe*" (ll. 9-10). Vaughan's greatest act of differentiation from them, however, is to give his rivals a version of the "*Labell*" that they are themselves supposedly in the process of composing. In lines that do not so much parody the others—and thus damage the object of praise—Vaughan delivers with irony a standard encomium that he prefaces with an announcement that casually proclaims he has the power to turn it on and off when he wishes. Matching the images of "*force*" he assigns to Cartwright, his earlier trumpeting becomes now a minor triumph:

> I'le tell them (and a *truth* which needs no *passe*,)
> That *wit* in *Cartwright* at her *Zenith* was,
> *Arts*, *Fancy*, *Language*, all *Conven'd* in thee,
> With those *grand Miracles* which *deifie*
> The old worlds *Writings*, kept yet from the *fire*,
> Because they *force* these worst times to *admire*.
> Thy matchless *Genius*, in all thou didst write,
> Like the *Sun*, wrought with such *stayd heat*, and *light*,
> That not a *line* (to the most *Critick* he)
> Offends with *flashes*, or *obscurtie*.   (ll. 11-20)

Playing in front of a crowd, Vaughan presses his identification with Cartwright further through a series of slightly dizzying analogies. The imitations Cartwright has discovered in the "*Motley stock* in men" (ll. 21-22) and rendered into print Vaughan has copied in his own copy of the motley crowd of mourners. Both poets play as if they had "in all their *bosomes* been, / And seen those *Leopards* that lurk within" (ll. 23-24), while the effect of the analogies is to show Vaughan boring through the exterior of the hearse, "fixt" with the labels of others, in order to establish a common ground of personal intimacy with Cartwright. Moreover, as a prelude to singing

Cartwright's own monarchical status, Vaughan wittily uses the playwright's work as a means to establish his own credentials as Cartwright's best reader and judge. Describing the effects of various scenes from the drama, Vaughan speaks of

> . . . those *soft beauteous Readers* whose *looks* can
> Make some men *Poets*, and make any man
> A *Lover*, when thy *Slave* but *seems* to dye,
> Turn all his *Mourners*, and melt at the *Eye*. (ll. 27-30)

The distinction between making some men poets and any man a lover returns us, of course, to the beginning of the verse and the tears of loss that many (lovers) offer but with no relief: excessive sympathy works to deny their poetic roles as Vaughan, who has shed only a few tears, reaffirms his place as Cartwright's poet. Furthermore, as Marilla has scrupulously observed,[22] the lines about the melting lover are stolen from Herrick's poem on Fletcher (1645) and now used metonymically by Vaughan to claim even more distance between himself and those (like Herrick) who cannot see clearly because they are all tears.

This difference of vision is played out to the end and is finally attributed by Vaughan as the source of his power. Cartwright's language, if properly perceived, will make "*Souls* shine at the *Eyes* [not tears], and *Pearls* display / Through the *loose-Chrystal-streams* a *glaunce of day*" (ll. 37-38). The dead poet should, in effect, be kept visible in the living one, and Vaughan's earlier imitation of Cartwright is therefore not only the greatest honor done to him, but it assures the younger writer of his own poetic importance. It is also the surest sign of relief. Wit "transmigrates": it shines in the younger author and enshrines the two of them together. Neatly enough, the closing couplet is a double, or perhaps triple, blast that unites Charles's royal commendation and Cartwright's "*force*" with Vaughan's voice and situation as a royalist poet who hushes the hum of others:

[22] Marilla, *SPHV*, p. 224, ll. 25-30n.

> But what's all this unto a *Royall Test?*
> Thou art the *Man*, whom great *Charles* so exprest!
> Then let the *Crowd* refrain their *needless humme,*
> When *Thunder* speaks, then *Squibs* and *Winds* are *dumb.*
>
> (ll. 39-42)

On the grounds of ingenuity alone, it would be hard to outdo the poem to Cartwright. The more modestly titled "Upon Mr. *Fletchers* Playes, published, 1647" (p. 54) focuses, in fact, on the exhaustion of wit, on the loss of imaginative play that has occurred with the schisms of Civil War. Signaling this concern, Vaughan's remark, "Wits last *Edition* is now i' th' *Presse*" (l. 26) is perhaps a bit of hyperbole frequently uttered to commend a poet's inimitable genius,[23] but, as happens often in *Olor*, Vaughan can make the commonplace interesting because of the context he supplies. Like the poem to Cartwright, this one begins with heavy criticism of the mode itself. Vaughan runs through all the scandalous ways one might use the commendatory occasion to "*Inch* low fame [and] / Stretch in the *glories* of a strangers name" (ll. 9-10). Such shows of ambition, naturally, throw more praise on the celebrator than on the celebrated—"This speaks thee not" (l. 5)—but if we are expecting Vaughan to assert (conventionally) his modesty, we are, as he says of himself later, "*richly* Cosen'd" (l. 19). He is annoyed at the other versifiers mainly because they threaten to tarnish the image of Fletcher, reduce the spoils, and thus "Clip those *Bayes* I Court, weak *striver* I, / But a faint *Echo* unto *Poetrie*" (ll. 11-12). Since he is without "Titles to *swell* the *reare* of *Verse* with lord" (l. 8), Vaughan argues his more desperate need of recognition than the others: "I have not *Clothes* t'adopt me" (l. 13); the twist is even wittier if we remember that in the previous poem, "Upon a Cloke," Vaughan was down to his last outfit. In all, this figure of the loud "*Verser remonstrative*" is denied, parodied, turned inside out, and then put on again by the poet himself. Mocking the parvenu who publishes in "some *Suburb-page*" (l. 3) is this even

[23] Marilla, *SPHV*, p. 218, l. 26n.

more ambitious Johnny-come-lately from Wales. The masking is deliciously insouciant and Vaughan, bending to the occasion, recognizes the need for a new route: "Yet *Modestie* these *Crosses* would improve, / and *Rags* neer thee, some *Reverence* may move" (ll. 15-16). Wit's last edition seems in the press, indeed.

But there is a more serious side to the poem, and it hinges, as it did in the poem to Cartwright, on the transmigration of wit—on the continuation of the dead author in the living and on the rekindling of a flame that will illuminate the surrounding darkness. The central paragraph of the poem (ll. 17-42) concentrates on two ideas: the continuation of Beaumont's spirit in Fletcher's lines and the double advantage it gives to them; and the difference between illusion and reality developing out of the pun on dramatic versus political "*plotts*," a difference between "*kill*[ing] and *Circumvent*[ing] in *Jest*" (l. 36) and the actual "*abominable policie*" of the Scots (l. 32). Vaughan, who has already done much playing, continues the line of wit whose origin lies (at least in this poem) with Beaumont, while his earlier aggressive acts upon rival poets are now reinterpreted as harmless tropes for war. He "*Circumvent*[s] in *Jest*." Like Fletcher, whose "anger'd Muse" literally only plays with disaster, Vaughan stages a brief tragicomedy, one in which art eventually triumphs over the political reality even though, with the closing of the theaters, it looks initially as if the Puritans are to be the victors. Plotting drama instead of "*abominable policie*," Fletcher appears as an "archpacifist" of sorts, as Vaughan walks along by his side conscious of the fragile bonds that keep the two men together.

The closing lines, with their pun on "lines" and their summarizing view of the poet's situation in *Olor*, seem to me among the most moving in the entire collection:

> But (happy thou!) ne'r saw'st these *stormes*, our *aire*
> *Teem'd* with even in thy time, though *seeming faire*;
> Thy gentle *Soule* meant for the *shade*, and *ease*
> Withdrew betimes into the *Land* of *Peace*;

> So *neasted* in some Hospitable shore
> The *Hermit-angler*, when the *mid-Seas* roare
> Packs up his *lines*, and (ere the tempest *raves*,)
> Retyres, and leaves his *station* to the *waves*.
> Thus thou diedst almost with our *peace*, and wee
> This *breathing time* thy last fair *Issue* see,
> Which I think such (if *needless Ink* not soyle
> So *Choice a Muse*,) others are but thy *foile*;
> This, or that *age* may write, but never see
> A *Wit* that dares run *Paralell* with thee.
> True, B E N must live! but bate *him*, and thou hast
> Undone all *future wits*, and match'd the *past*.   (ll. 43-58)

There is, first of all, Vaughan's impish denial that any age will see a wit who dares run parallel with Fletcher when, of course, he has been attempting to do exactly that for much of the poem. Touched with humor, this small self-referential flash hits surely on the same note of bravado that energizes so much of the verse in *Olor*, and must have been involved in the salvation of the collection itself. The closing also registers Vaughan's belief in the power of art to survive its immediate environment, despite the diminished role it is sometimes forced to play. Fletcher, who died "almost with our *peace*," has left a "last fair *Issue*" in his work; and the "breathing time" it affords and which Vaughan commemorates, while perhaps a reference to the political quiet,[24] is certainly the Welsh poet's recognition of the older writer's legacy now carried on briefly in the playful wit of the commendatory occasion. "Such *remnants* from thy *peece* Intreat their date" (l. 6), Vaughan had mentioned earlier in a statement that doubly acknowledges his debt to the original in the pun on "*peece*." But Vaughan

---

[24] I am less sure than Marilla (*SPHV*, p. 216) that this reference can be used to give a posterior date of April 1648—the beginning of the "Second Civil War"—for the composition of the poem simply because I do not see how it is possible for Vaughan to have known at the time that he was living between the two Civil Wars. The poem was not included in the folio volume of the works of Beaumont and Fletcher, published in 1647, and attempts to provide an exact date of composition must rely on circumstantial evidence at best.

also admits that Fletcher now moves in a twilight of his own—a "gentle *Soule* meant for the *shade*, and *ease*"—whose reflection aptly appears in the smaller poet-figure of the "*Hermit-angler*" who "packs up his *lines* . . . and leaves his *station* to the *waves*" in order to follow the departing shadow of the dead. If it were possible to choose the moment when Vaughan put down his secular pen, in spirit if not in fact, it would have to be this one. In this light, it is also perhaps more than coincidence that the final lines, in the tribute they pay to Fletcher, explicitly deny for the first and only time in Vaughan's poetry, Jonson's absolute authority. Vaughan, of course, did not follow Fletcher, but the poem to the dramatist traces the way to Herbert.

CHAPTER FOUR

Eminent Measure: The Poetics of Conversion

> We say that an author is *original* when we cannot trace the hidden transformations that others underwent in his mind; we mean to say that the dependence of *what he does* on *what others have done* is excessively complex and irregular. There are works in the likeness of others, and works that are the reverse of others, but there are also works of which the relation with earlier productions is so intricate that we become confused and attribute them to the direct intervention of the gods.
>
> —Paul Valéry, "Letter About Mallarmé"

VAUGHAN'S "conversion" to writing religious poetry in *Silex Scintillans* can be misleading only if valued for the wrong reasons. When his first editor, the Reverend H. F. Lyte, interpreted *Silex* as the response of a man on "the brink of the grave" brought to the "high and holy claims of God,"[1] he initiated, in favorite nineteenth-century fashion, one of the biographical heresies which twentieth-century criticism has been generally so good at exposing. In this case, however, the situation has been different. Confusion about the poet's "conversion" continues to persist largely because critics, in either denying or defending the event, have at some level offered a counterversion to Lyte's pleasing fiction that Vaughan's transition must necessarily represent a profound personal change in the poet's spiritual life. Thus, R. A. Durr, though cautious of accepting other sentimental accounts of Vaughan's "regeneration," nevertheless develops his own in the commentary he supplies on Vaughan's gropings for the mystic way: " 'Men wondered at the sudden alteration that had come over him.

---

[1] Lyte, *The Sacred Poems and Private Ejaculations of Henry Vaughan* (Boston: Little, Brown and Co., 1856), p. 16.

One said this and another said that, but what had really happened to him no one imagined. For God had secretly drawn him to Him in divine light, and this brought about a sudden conversion.' "[2] E. C. Pettet, with more apology but equal certainty, is also tempted by biographical explanations when he exhumes details of Vaughan's life in order to confute Frank Kermode's suggestion that the "conversion [was] rather a poetic than a religious experience."[3] For both Durr and Pettet, the theory has the added advantage of minimizing the need to examine in any detail the writing of Vaughan's "unregenerate" years.

Those who might have gained most from Kermode's advice have, on the other hand, borrowed his support but resisted his counsel. This group wishes to value only the "poetic experience," which they see threatened by any discussion of a suddenly enlightened Vaughan. Objecting to the way biographical speculation has muddied the waters for literary interpretation, they opt for discarding the issue altogether: "as a biographical concept, [the conversion] is unfounded," admonishes James Simmonds, "and as a critical concept, an exegetical tool, it is misleading."[4] Thus, the dismissal begins. But the actual rebuttal, which also lays some of the theoretical

---

[2] Durr, *On the Mystical Poetry of Henry Vaughan* (Cambridge, Mass.: Harvard Univ. Press, 1962), p. 9. The quotation in Durr comes from the fourteenth-century German mystic, Heinrich Suso's *Life of the Servant*, trans. James M. Clark (London, 1952), p. 16.

[3] Pettet, *Of Paradise and Light: A Study of Vaughan's Silex Scintillans* (Cambridge: Cambridge Univ. Press, 1960, p. 17); Kermode's essay, "The Private Imagery of Henry Vaughan," appears in *RES*, n.s. 1 (1950): 206-25.

[4] Simmonds, *Masques of God: Form and Theme in the Poetry of Henry Vaughan* (Pittsburgh: Univ. of Pittsburgh Press, 1972), p. 5; see also his appendix, "Immorality and Profane Literature," pp. 208-17. In denying both the fact of an actual, sudden conversion and the relevance of the concept to an understanding of Vaughan's poetry, Simmonds follows E. L. Marilla's many attempts to disprove the traditional view that *Silex Scintillans* represents a complete break with the secular verse. See especially, "The Religious Conversion of Henry Vaughan," *RES* 21 (1945): 15-22, "Henry Vaughan's Conversion: A Recent View," *MLN* 63 (1948): 394-97, and "The Secular and Religious Poetry of Henry Vaughan," *MLQ* 9 (1948): 394-411. Kenneth Friedenreich, *Henry Vaughan* (Boston: Twayne Publishers, 1978) sidesteps the issue altogether but like Simmonds (p. 4) asserts Kermode's caveat that Vaughan's poetry should not be treated as prayer (pp. 31 and 171).

groundwork for smoothing the transition between a secular and a devotional Vaughan, has a familiar ring to it. The argument runs that since Vaughan was still engaged in writing some secular verse at the time when he was supposed to have "converted," the experience cannot have been either immediate, deep, or overwhelming, and therefore it is better to view the poet's career as "continuous" and "organic" rather than as "radically disjunctive." But even this correction smacks slightly of out-Heroding Herod, for once again, the poet's biography is used to ignore the possibility that Vaughan's "regeneration," whatever else it contained, represents fundamentally a verbal and poetic experience.

If two centuries of criticism have played rather freely with Vaughan's "conversion," the poet has shown himself to be notably reticent in his use of the actual word. The only time he refers explicitly to the experience—choosing a variant noun form—is in the 1654 Preface to the completed *Silex Scintillans* when he records his debt to "Mr. *George Herbert*, whose holy *life* and *verse* gained many pious *Converts*, (of whom I am the least)" (p. 391, ll. 23-25). Whatever specialized meaning the word can have for the Christian tradition, Vaughan's use of it here suggests essentially a general enthusiasm, not necessarily just for the religious way itself, but for a writer of the religious way, George Herbert. In this context, Vaughan's confession to being a "pious *Convert*" seems basically honorific in intent. Like his reference, for instance, to being a "weak Eccho" of Katherine Philips, it proclaims his admiration for the verse of another, now in a vocabulary proper to the subject matter at hand, and it establishes a privileged relationship between the two authors. Herbert, in effect, is hallowed as an interpreter of new experience; Vaughan is canonized as one of his followers.[5]

[5] In connection with Vaughan's usage of "convert," it should be noted that the word was beginning to assume a specifically secular connotation in his day. *OED*, s.v. convert, *sb*., 1b, cites W. Hakewill, *Liberty of Subject* (1641) as the first instance: "I did forsake my former opinion as erroneous, and do now embrace the contrary . . . and so am now become a convert."

Since the 1654 Preface also forms Vaughan's most complete statement about his poetic career and personal life, it has often been mined for evidence to support his actual "conversion," with the consequence that it is frequently read as if it were an early draft of *Grace Abounding by the Chief of Sinners*. Concentration is almost solely on the author's apology for having contributed to the burgeoning growth of "idle verse" in mid-century England. But if there are traces of Bunyan in the Preface, there are also shades of a politicized Sidney, who declares in the *Defence of Poesie* that nothing is so "vatic" as composing divine hymns in honor of God;[6] when Vaughan bemoans the contemporary fashions of verse—his own included—he does so as part of a larger argument in which the emphasis of a poet's new motives for eloquence falls harder than ever on the glories of rhetorical persuasion and verbal power. For a nation languishing in sickness, Vaughan concludes, the only possible remedy is for its "gifted persons [to make] a wise exchange of *vain* and *vitious subjects,* for *divine Themes* and *Celestial praise*" (p. 391, ll. 12-14). If this call for a "wise exchange" seems, moreover, a little fortuitous and self-congratulatory, the new relationship between poet and audience is also considerably heightened: "The *performance* is easie, and were it the most difficult in the world," Vaughan writes, "the *reward* is so glorious, that it infinitely transcends it: for *they that turn many to righteousness, shall shine like the stars for ever and ever.*" But for those who fail to hear the poet's voice, "I know nothing reserved for them, but *the blackness of darkness for ever.*" Poetry is not simply in the service of furthering God's Word; the service to God also furthers the poet. Conversion—turning "*many to righteousness*"—is both the ultimate challenge to poetry as well as a description of the ultimate response to its attributes.

If Vaughan seems slightly less than humble in this portrait, his subsequent attack in the Preface on Herbert's other followers, who have "more of *fashion,* then *force*" (ll. 27-28),

[6] *The Prose Works of Sir Philip Sidney,* ed. Albert Feuillerat, 4 vols. (Cambridge: Cambridge Univ. Press, 1962), 3: 9-10.

altogether destroys the image of him as a strictly "pious" poet. In a few quick strokes, he turns his rivals into hypocrites by questioning their poetry, their purpose, their output, and finally their religious spirit. Devotion to poetry, not just to the devotional way, is paramount to Vaughan's way of thinking, while his continued criticisms of "those wide, those weak, and lean *conceptions*" (ll. 32-33) of others leave us with a view of a person not rapt to the third heaven but of a poet reading the tradition with a measured eye, comparable to the one exercised in the verses to Cartwright and Fletcher. The "least pious" of Herbert's converts, Vaughan interprets the occasion of writing in the company of another as both an opportunity to adjudicate the individual demands of poetry and politics and a chance, once again, to bask in the reflected light of greatness, and the light is one he does not readily share with others.

His closing description of the poet's task is, accordingly, a careful balancing act between a reverent commitment to God's Word and an irreverent, or at least an ambitious, devotion to poetic fame:

> but he that desires to excel in this kinde of *Hagiography*, or holy writing, must strive (by all means) for *perfection* and true *holyness*, that a *door may be opened to him in heaven*, Rev. 4.1. and then he will be able to write (with *Hierotheus* and holy *Herbert*) A *true Hymn*. (p. 392, ll. 5-9)

Despite the allusion to Revelation, the toils of imitation have a reward that are not limited strictly to the afterlife: "*perfection*" and "true *holyness*" are still important virtues, but their value is defined largely by their place in a hierarchy that leads to the art of writing "A *true Hymn*" and ends with the election of a select group of poets. The enshrinement here is, above all, a verbal one. The Elysian Fields, populated by so many poets in the 1640s including the younger Vaughan, have now been fenced in to allow room for only a few: the mythical, first-century writer of hymns, Hierotheus, the Anglican poet, George Herbert, and the author of *Silex Scintillans*.

Whether Vaughan's "conversion" was a biographical event cannot be determined in any absolute sense from the poet's writings, least of all from the 1654 Preface. It, too, has elements of a pleasing fiction: the previously "idle" poet suddenly showing himself to be a "passionate lover of that unspeakable and everlasting bewtie to be seene by the eyes of the mind, onely cleared by fayth."[7] Vaughan would not have been the first person in the Renaissance to call on his life to authenticate his art; and insofar as the Preface fills this bill, it argues, perhaps more persuasively than some of his critics, that the poet's transition to religious verse is "continuous" and does not represent a sharp break with the secular poetry. Literary ambition still lies at the heart of the matter. The stakes are now higher, but the link to the other works remains visible, especially the link to *Olor*, for the step beyond the "transmigration of wit" attempted in the poems to Cartwright and Fletcher is a sustained effort at copying the work of another poet.

Nevertheless, what seems continuous from one perspective can appear radically disjunctive from another. Vaughan's decision to write devotional verse might not reflect a newly illumined spirit, but his commitment to following so ardently and assiduously one man alone certainly reveals a remarkable about-face in poetic strategy. In effect, Vaughan placed all his eggs in one basket since "without the inspiration and model of *The Temple*," as Pettet notes, "there would certainly have been no *Silex Scintillans*."[8] Furthermore, in turning to Herbert, Vaughan, ironically enough, had no better authority than the mentor of his earlier, secular efforts, "Great *B E N*" himself. Discussing methods of imitation, Renaissance theoreticians disagreed sharply over the issue of whether poets could profit most from copying the best works of several notable authors or by studying in detail the most distinguished examples of a single author of reknown. "Here riseth, emonges proude and envious wittes," writes Roger Ascham in *The*

---
[7] Ibid., p. 7.
[8] Pettet, *Of Paradise and Light*, p. 51.

Scholemaster (1570), "a great controversie, whether one or many are to be folowed: and, if one, who is that one; *Seneca* or *Cicero*; *Salust* or *Caesar*; and so forth in Greeke and Latin."[9] Jonson threw his prestigious weight in the direction of the one rather than the many. In his *Timber*, or *Discoveries*, published in 1640, he listed the requirement of imitation after both the gift of genius ("poetical rapture") and the need for patient industry to "forge and file" one's verse to perfection; but the ordering here is not of great importance since most early commentators agreed that the mind must have something to work on other than its own fancies. That something could be achieved, said Jonson, by making a "choise of one excellent man above the rest, and so to follow him, till he grow very *Hee*: or, so like him, as the Copie may be mistaken for the Principall."[10] Indeed, Jonson's fourth and final requirement of the poet, *Lectio* (study), follows naturally from this premise, since without "an exactnesse of Studie, and multiplicity of reading, which maketh a full man," it is only too easy for a quick aspirer to be deluded into thinking that "hee can leape forth suddainely a *Poet*, by dreaming hee hath been in *Parnassus*, or, having washt his lipps (as they say) in *Helicon*" (p. 639).

Vaughan, who washed his lips in Helicon in *Poems* and in *Olor* kept dreaming he had been in Parnassus, radically revised his approach toward poetry in *Silex*. He followed Jonson by following Herbert; he retained a theoretical allegiance to the father of coterie poetry but left his club for the practical example of another teacher, and nowhere is the blend of two influences into a single hierarchy clearer than in the 1654

[9] Ascham, *Elizabethan Critical Essays*, ed. G. Gregory Smith, 2 vols. (Oxford: Clarendon Press, 1904), 1: 7. For the origin of this controversy in the Renaissance, see the exchange of letters between Pietro Bembo and Gianfrancesco Pico collected in and trans. by Izora Scott, *Controversies Over the Imitation of Cicero* (New York: Teachers College of Columbia Univ., 1910), 2, 1-18, as well as the recent discussion of them given by Loren Partridge and Randolph Starn, *A Renaissance Likeness: Art and Culture in Raphael's Julius II* (Berkeley: Univ. of California Press, 1980), pp. 18-28.

[10] *Ben Jonson*, ed. C. H. Herford and Percy and Evelyn Simpson, 11 vols. (Oxford: Clarendon Press, 1925-1952), 8 (1947): 638.

Preface. It records how Herbert is, beyond doubt, the "one excellent man above the rest"; it underscores the process of growth and improvement within a theological context of "striving" that befits the subject matter; and it suggests how, in learning to write "A *true Hymn*," the copy may be mistaken for the principal. Vaughan's decision to make "a wise exchange of *vain* and *vitious* subjects, for *divine Themes* and *Celestial praise*" and learn to imitate the ways of Christ was predicated, first of all, on his willingness to learn to imitate the imitator of Christ, George Herbert.

One of Vaughan's first duties was to erase from his verse the memory of his past masters. Under Herbert's schooling, nearly all books of poetry other than *The Temple* become, at best, "broken letters scarce remembred" ("Vanity of Spirit," p. 419, l. 24). Traces of Jonson sometimes reappear in the octosyllabics of *Silex*, but the subject matter is usually so private and so un-Jonsonian as to mark the distance Vaughan has traveled since his early days as a tavern reveler. On the whole, what Louis Martz has termed "the action of the self"[11]— a practice Vaughan learned from Herbert—takes over and eradicates the "Son of Ben" from *Silex*. There are, for example, certain formal similarities between the wandering persona of "To my Ingenuous Friend, *R. W.*" and Vaughan's desire to "travell back" in "The Retreate," but the action in the latter poem has become internalized and pressurized to the point where even the verse registers the difference in a new tightening of rhythm, meter, and syntax. The one clear reminder of Vaughan's earlier mentor occurs with his little-known epigrammatic verse "The Burial of an Infant," which recollects specifically Jonson's brief elegy "On My first Daughter." Both poets lament the untimely death of an infant and seek consolation in the safety of innocence, and both poems, written in tetrameter verse, are exactly twelve lines long, although Vaughan's is in alernating rhyme and divided into

---

[11] Martz, "The Action of the Self: Devotional Poetry in the Seventeenth Century," in *Metaphysical Poetry*, ed. Malcolm Bradbury and David Palmer (London: Edward Arnold, 1970), pp. 101-21.

quatrains. But the resemblances are obvious—almost too obvious—as if the younger author is now casually poaching a poem from Ben without worrying about being a member of his tribe. In contrast to the many verse epistles in *Olor*, "The Burial of an Infant" seems a lonely tribute to their earlier relationship: imitative of the tiniest of Jonson's forms, the poem shrinks "Great B E N" to a manageable size.

The departure of Donne follows a similar route. Vaughan's greatest shows of "masculine, persuasive force" happen not from any recollection of his predecessor's battered heart, but through the poet's own vigorous refashioning of a line or two, or sometimes more, from *The Temple*. The most notable instance involves the interpolation of the "Author's Emblem" from *Silex* 1650 into the last stanza of "The Tempest":

> Lord! thou didst put a soul here; If I must
>   Be broke again, for flints will give no fire
>   Without a steel, O let thy power cleer
> Thy gift once more, and grind this flint to dust!
>   (p. 462, ll. 57-60)

Despite the surface similarities here to Donne in the marvelous closing apostrophe to God's grinding power, the achievement belongs to the younger poet and his desire to outdo his master, Herbert. Vaughan's stanza, a redaction of Jeremiah 23:29 ("Is not my word like as a fire? saith the Lord; and like a hammer that breaketh the rock in pieces?") remakes Herbert's more modest desire in "The Temper" to have God "stretch or contract"[12] him into a full-scale demolition attack on the stubborn heart. At the same time, the stanza also reverses Herbert's coyly presumptuous declaration that he will "gladly engrave [God's] love in steel" by returning the authority (the hammer itself) absolutely to God. Upgrading "The Temper" to "The Tempest," Vaughan transforms Herbert's neat engraving into God's ultimate grinding, while the vigorous "brunts" and

---

[12] All quotations from and references to Herbert's poetry are from *The Works of George Herbert*, ed. F. E. Hutchinson, 2nd ed. (Oxford: Clarendon Press, 1945). Vaughan is also specifically echoing here Herbert's "Dulnesse," ll. 23-25.

"starts"—as Lancelot Andrewes describes the experience of the first Christian's receiving the Holy Ghost[13]—have less to do with a few vestigial remains of Donne in *Silex* than with Vaughan's desire to return to the original scene of contact between man and God, one no longer mediated by Herbert.

If Vaughan was not quite a tabula rasa on which Herbert could write, he nonetheless did a good job keeping the slate well-scrubbed. Besides banishing Donne and Jonson, he also excluded from *Silex* some of the more mediocre poets who had left their print on his earlier work, like Habington and Browne. The rare appearance of a line from a writer other than Herbert, such as the famous echo in "The Retreate" from Owen Felltham,[14] seems an exceptional moment that only helps to prove the depth of Vaughan's commitment to follow one man above the rest "till he grow very Hee." Vaughan was, moreover, equally careful to remove other marks from the outside secular world that might seem to intrude into the design of *Silex* and disturb the colloquy between the poet, Herbert, and God. In contrast to *Poems* and *Olor*, there is in the religious verse no mention of individual names in either the titles or the texts of the poems, nor is there ever a hint of a specific occasion except as it refers to a Biblical event or a general celebration of the Christian year. The elegies all stubbornly withhold the names of the dead and the circumstances surrounding the loss. The epithalamion "To the best, and most accomplish'd Couple——" becomes simply "*Isaacs* Mar-

---

[13] Andrewes, *Ninety-Six Sermons by . . . Lancelot Andrewes*, ed. J. P. Parkinson, 5 vols. (Oxford: John Henry Parker, 1843-1860), 3 (1850): 126; preached on June 8, 1606, Whitsunday. The passage reads: "So in vigour, as His vigour is not brunts only or starts, *impetus*, but *habitus*, that it holdeth out habit-wise. Not only like the sparks before which will make a man stir for the present, but leaving an impression, such an one as iron red-hot leaving in vessels of wood: a fire-mark never to be got out more. Such doth the Holy Ghost leave in the memories: *In aeternum non obliviscar*, 'I shall never forget it.'"

[14] Compare "Bright *shootes* of everlastingnesse" (l. 20) with Felltham's "The conscience, the character of a God stamped in it, and the apprehension of eternity, do all prove it a shoot of everlastingness." *Resolves: Divine Political and Moral* (1631; rpt. London: Pickering, 1840), p. 142 [1. 64, "Of the Soul"].

riage" or the marriage of Christ, the bridegroom, to the Church. "An Invitation to *Brecknock*" is refashioned into an annual celebration of Christ's nativity or his crucifixion. And most important, the many commendatory poems, with their various salutes to friendship, are absorbed into Vaughan's single celebration in "The Match" of his "Dear friend," George Herbert.

In modeling his poetry after Herbert's, Vaughan transformed both the look and the feel, the outer edge and the inner life, of the earlier verse to create the substance of *Silex*. Not only did he considerably expand his total output of original verse in *Silex* 1650 to over five times that of *Poems* and almost four times the number in *Olor*, but Herbert's illuminating presence is also felt in the sudden burgeoning of stanzaic forms. For the seventy-three poems (not counting the "Dedication") in the first part of *Silex*, Vaughan generated fifty-eight different verse forms, and, of these, forty-five were used only once; the secular poems, on the other hand, were written almost entirely in standard pentameter or tetrameter couplets. Unlike some of Herbert's other followers, Vaughan usually avoided his master's most "conceited" forms: he wrote no neat anagrams or "Easter-wings," no "Altars" or "Aarons." He did learn, as Mary Ellen Rickey has shown,[15] such tricks as mending his rhyme in "Disorder *and* frailty" to indicate a repaired harmony between the speaker and God, something Herbert had done in "Deniall." He also copied in several poems ("Love-sick" and "The Wreath") Herbert's "wreathing" effects with language—the repetition of the rhyme word in the subsequent line to achieve what Renaissance rhetoricians called a sense of "*gradatio.*" More often, however, the formal resemblances do not constitute exact parallelisms but are of a more general kind: the adoption by Vaughan of a verse pattern in which the varied line lengths suggest a state of spiritual chaos; a decision to write a poem in which two

---

[15] Rickey, "Vaughan, *The Temple*, and Poetic Form," *SP* 59 (1962): 162-70.

different stanzaic patterns are employed; a habit of linking poems on the grounds of a common idea or in order to demonstrate the ebb and flow of the spiritual life; and a willingness to attempt more sophisticated practices with rhymes.

But even though the changes are often simple to chart, the process of transformation wrought by Vaughan's "conversion" and the advantages that it brought to his verse are not always so easy to assess. The difficulties stem from an excess, rather than a scarcity, of possibilities for criticism. In a remark that could serve as both a warning and a stimulus to interpretation, Hutchinson rightly observes that "a reader who knows well both *The Temple* and *Silex Scintillans* never comes to the end of the verbal parallels."[16] The consequence of such a plenitude is that critical attempts to determine the borrowings and survey the boundaries of each author's domain must necessarily settle for limited results: however accurate the conclusion usually reached—that one poet is weak where the other is strong[17]—the discovery is not a surprising one, nor is it altogether satisfying, since it rarely allows us to understand how Vaughan himself became strong where once he was weak. Usually left untouched are the techniques he learned from Herbert that make a comparison between the two of interest in the first place.

The single most important formal lesson that Herbert taught Vaughan was to "unpack" the pentameter line and, in doing so, to learn to work in a smaller, tighter, and more volatile verbal space. The change not only allowed Vaughan to inten-

---

[16] *The Works of George Herbert*, p. 42 (introduction).

[17] The observation is made by Joan Bennett, *Four Metaphysical Poets* (Cambridge: Cambridge Univ. Press, 1934), p. 89, echoed by Pettet, *Of Paradise and Light*, p. 70, repeated by Durr, *Mystical Poetry*, p. 10, and again by Lewalski, *Protestant Poetics and the Seventeenth-Century Religious Lyric* (Princeton: Princeton Univ. Press, 1979), p. 317. It should be pointed out, however, that Bennett's desire to separate the two authors was partly a response to the feud waged in the nineteenth century, described as comparable to "that between the Montagues and Capulets" (H. C. Beeching, intro. to *The Poems of Henry Vaughan, Silurist*, ed. E. K. Chambers [London: Lawrence & Bullen, Ltd., 1896], p. xxxiv), over which of the two was the better poet.

sify his (and our) focus on the specific value of a word or phrase—an important lesson for an Anglican apologist to acquire; it also led him to improve the structure of individual sections of a lyric and sometimes the movement of the verse as a whole. Although Vaughan's earlier mentors certainly appreciated order, Herbert's demanding precision with verse is a matter of legend, practically equal to that of his pious life. His "*measure* was eminent," the Welsh poet declared in the 1654 Preface, and his remark has been echoed and elaborated on all the way down to modern critical evaluations of *The Temple*. Joseph Summers speaks for many in his admiration of the poet's block-by-block method of constructing his verse: "Herbert characteristically considered his stanzas as inviolable architectural units. Each usually contained a complete thought, representing one unit in the logic of the 'argument,' and the great majority of his stanzas end with full stops."[18] Herbert's attention to precision and neatness was, of course, as poetically desirable as it was devotionally meaningful since "the ultimate method of reflecting God's glory was the creation of a work of decency and order, a work of beauty, whether a church, an ordered poem, or an ordered life."[19]

Of all of Herbert's admirers, it was Vaughan who best put into service Herbert's example. The opening stanza of the opening poem in *Silex*, "Regeneration," seems almost a textbook example of "inviolable" form already in full operation:

> A Ward, and still in bonds, one day
>   I stole abroad,
> It was high-spring, and all the way
>   *Primros'd*, and hung with shade;
>   Yet, was it frost within,
>   And surly winds

---

[18] Summers, *George Herbert: His Religion and Art* (Cambridge, Mass.: Harvard Univ. Press, 1954), pp. 132-33. For other representative remarks praising Herbert's form, see Mary Ellen Rickey, *Utmost Art: Complexity in the Verse of George Herbert* (Lexington: Univ. of Kentucky Press, 1966), p. 102; Arnold Stein, *George Herbert's Lyrics* (Baltimore: Johns Hopkins Univ. Press, 1968), pp. 138-39; and Martz, "The Action of the Self," p. 109.

[19] Summers, *George Herbert*, p. 84.

> Blasted my infant buds, and sinne
>   Like Clouds ecclips'd my mind.   (p. 397, ll. 1-8)

The intricacy of course impresses (8*a*, 4*b*, 8*a*, 6*b*, 6*c*, 4*d*, 8*c*, 6*d*), even though the stanzaic pattern is only slightly more complex than some employed in *Poems*; but what is appreciably new here is the way Vaughan uses the stanza to help create a poetry shot through with sustained energy. Precisely because the verse pattern imposes limits of its own on the thought (in contrast to the more "open" pentameter couplet of his epistolary style), Vaughan is able to regulate with greater efficiency the boisterous voice that he developed in *Olor Iscanus*. Achieved largely by joining alternating enjambed and endstopped lines with changes in rhyme, the verse keeps in tight balance the opposite attitudes of desire and restraint that form the ground rhythms of the regenerative experience. The first line, for example, manages to suspend the subject ("I") across a gap in space only to conclude the motion with an action (stealing abroad), while the next pair of lines repeat, with slightly less intensity, this process by enjambing "way" (and therefore leaving the way open), which it then partially closes off in the reference to "shade." These hesitations are themselves only brought to a definite point of conclusion in the subsequent four lines. Initiating with a "Yet" a new series of rhymes, and leaving, appropriately enough, the middle two open ("wind" and "sin"), they build to a final description of the mind being eclipsed by sin before the whole stanza is sealed off and the primary action of stealing abroad temporarily arrested. For a poem about continued false starts mediated only by prevenient grace, the first stanza is a beautifully constructed account of instability and hesitation amid strong desire. The jovial brashness of "Upon a Cloke"—a pilgrimage poem of another sort—is refined for its nuances and shifts, for the psychic uncertainties that hyperbole attempts to override.

If "Regeneration" forms a splendid alpha to *Silex*, the closing lyric of the first part, "I walkt the other day" (pp. 478-79) serves as its studious omega. Together, they indicate the sweep, if not all the details, of Herbert's influence in the 1650 volume and the younger poet's successful response to the challenge of learning much of his master's skill with form. In the case of the last poem, Vaughan leaves no doubt as to which Herbert poem supplied the blueprint for his. The allusion to "A gallant flowre" in the third line recollects "The Crown Imperial" ("A gallant flower") in the parson-poet's "Peace," while the formal design of the seven-line stanza (10a, 4b, 10b, 4a, 10a, 4c, 8c) is a variation of Herbert's in that poem (10a, 4b, 8a, 6c, 10b, 4c). Less compact than the stanza of "Regeneration," it is, nonetheless, equally well-organized. Instead of describing the quest as a hurried struggle up a mountainside, the pilgrimage is now played out on a flat terrain; the opening stanza expands immediately to admit the poet's leisurely search for peace in the face of personal loss:

> I walkt the other day (to spend my hour)
>   Into a field
> Where I sometimes had seen the soil to yield
>   A gallant flowre,
> But Winter now had ruffled all the bowre
>   And curious store
>   I knew there heretofore.   (p. 478, ll. 1-7)

In the careful articulation of the stanzaic pattern, Herbert's hand is evident here and throughout. The ebb and flow of thought, realized unobtrusively in the expansion and contraction of line lengths, comes to a full stop only once the idea has run its course. Moreover, the final line, in trimeter rather than pentameter, gives the effect of choking off the search with its quickened rhyme.

But there are also important differences between the first stanza in this poem and the beginning of "Peace," and they are signaled largely by the form of each poem. The taut, dialectical quality of Herbert's argument, precisely managed with each endstopped line, is revised by the younger poet, who loosens the structure of the verse and "reopens" the quest by enjambing all but one of the lines. The result is that Vaughan increases our sense of a mind brooding intently on the search for quiet; he interiorizes Herbert's poem and makes peace seem an even greater reward. Preoccupied, slightly careless, this pilgrim meanders and meditates as the rhymes bend with his thoughts and play a reduced role in directing the movement of the "argument." Furthermore, if digging deeper defines the way Vaughan differs from Herbert in his method of constructing the opening stanza, it is also the idea of Herbert that Vaughan singles out to develop: the activity of digging, of excavating the Crown Imperial, forms the structural and spiritual center of his poem and not just another step in the pilgrimage, as it does in "Peace." Vaughan's subjectivity, the "secretive self-communings"[20] so prized by critics yet missing from his secular verse, would be less impressive here if the poet did not first have the form of Herbert's poem to alter and remodel on his way to expressing a deeper penetration into the quest for peace.

Two of Vaughan's finest poems, "Regeneration" and "I walkt the other day" are only slightly exceptional among the verse of *Silex* for their new attention to the details of form. Although the second part of *Silex* is usually thought to be less "Hebertian," it is clear from "Ascension-Hymn" that Vaughan did not abandon his sense of the stanza as an "inviolable architectural unit." Again, like "Regeneration," no single verse from *The Temple* serves as an exact source, but it is evident that the poet who can chisel out the stanzas in this hymn is not far from the master carver of, say, "The Altar," "Easterwings," or "Vertue." The last two verses ought to demonstrate sufficiently the continued precision Vaughan sought under Herbert as well as the original way he could develop his own

[20] Robert Ellrodt, "George Herbert and the Religious Lyric," in *History of Literature in the English Language: Vol. 2, English Poetry and Prose, 1540-1674*, ed. Christopher Ricks (London: Barrie & Jenkins Ltd., 1970), p. 193.

"hieroglyphic" of ascension in the expanding dimensions of the line:

> Then comes he!
> Whose mighty light
> Made his cloathes be
> Like Heav'n, all bright;
> The Fuller, whose pure blood did flow
> To make stain'd man more white then snow.
>
> Hee alone
> And none else can
> Bring bone to bone
> And rebuild man,
> And by his all subduing might
> Make clay ascend more quick then light. (p. 483, ll. 31-42)

Both stanzas are remarkably tight rhythmically. Each gathers increasing energy in the shift from the initial three-syllable line to dimeter verse with alternating rhymes; each then achieves even greater expansion in the way Vaughan doubles the dimeter, drops the internal rhyme, and creates an octosyllabic couplet that gives a concluding sweep to the thought. Both stanzas also synchronize the increase in syllables (3, 4, 8) with Christ's expanding glory through comparisons that do not so much limit the initial terms of the metaphor as "recycle" them into a description of something more rich and strange. However astonishing Christ's "mighty light" might be, for example, Vaughan's account of it only prepares the way for the "fuller" and more stunning part He plays in purging man by purifying his blood. In turn, this role is extended in the final stanza with the complete reconstruction of man. Furthering Christ's magnificence, Vaughan develops Him as the only rebuilder of man and reserves His "all subduing might"—Christ's greatest feat—for the "fullest" lines in the last couplet: these describe the body's ascent to heaven with a speed that now surpasses the "mighty light" of the previous stanza. In this vision of the ascent, nothing is lost or left behind. Vaughan might not be able to build "bone to bone," but as a poet studying under Herbert, he has certainly learned to imitate Christ's action in the tightly evolving construction of his verse.

One of Vaughan's neatest efforts of verbal compression—one in which politics and poetry are strongly fused—occurs with "The Brittish Church." A haunting revision of Herbert's poem of the same title, Vaughan's describes religion as being on the tip of its tiptoes, ready, as Herbert points out in "The Church Militant," "to passe to the American strand" (l. 236). The first stanza, for instance, delivers a charge that adopts the persona of Herbert's British Church, his "dear mother," and melds it into a voice that has now grown as ragged and helpless as the coat it describes:

> Ah! he is fled!
> And while these here their *mists*, and *shadows* hatch,
> My glorious head
> Doth on those hills of Mirrhe, and Incense watch.
> Haste, hast my dear,
> The Souldiers here
> Cast in their lots again,
> That seamlesse coat
> The Jews touch'd not,
> These dare divide, and stain. (p. 410, ll. 1-10)

The urgency is again achieved in the way Vaughan uses the stanzaic form to heighten the stress of thought. After the initial, disyllabic exclamation, "Ah! he is fled!" the poet mutes the cry slightly by following it with a longer, reflective pentameter line of another (*b*) rhyme and then repeats this process of gathering and restraining energy as he brings the thought to a pause, not a complete stop, while the "glorious head" sits poised on top of "those hills of Mirrhe." The tension is held only for a moment, though, before it is broken with the double use of the spondee "haste." With this shift, the voice plunges abruptly forward, its progress "hastened" by the cut line and quick rhyme as the poet closes in on the pathos of religion's being decapitated. In one quick breath, the six lines are over; the full weight of the speaker's distress (and indignation) consolidates in a teeth-gritting final line: "These dare divide, and stain."

Vaughan's quintessential act of poetic closure occurs in *Silex* 1650 with the gnomic elegy, "Come, come, what doe I here?" Identical in stanzic length to "The Brittish Church" and similar in its varied pattern of rhymes, the lament further narrows the lines (trimeter is now the longest unit) and reduces the verbal scope by repeating "Come, come!" at the center of each stanza. The constrictions befit a poem in which fate or history has now completely played its hand, while the formal tightness is again central to the poem's meaning and the successful execution of its "mood of bereavement."[21] The opening stanza, for instance, bears the sting of death in its scant attention to grammatic propriety and syntactic links:

> Come, come, what doe I here?
>   Since he is gone
> Each day is grown a dozen year,
>   And each houre, one;
>   Come, come!
>   Cut off the sum,
>   By these soil'd teares!
>   (Which only thou
>   Know'st to be true,)
>   Dayes are my feares.   (p. 420, ll. 1-10)

The verse staggers to its conclusion. Not only is the diction starkly and unrelentingly monosyllabic, but even a line of eight syllables, like the third, could be compressed into six with only a slight slurring of "is" and "dozen." Vaughan's decision, moreover, to give the colloquial rather than the proper plural form of "year" seems a purposefully "careless" moment brought about not so much by the necessities of rhyme as by the sense

---

[21] Marilla, "The Secular and Religious Poetry of Henry Vaughan," p. 396. I certainly agree with Marilla about the poem's structural unity but resist his suggestion that Vaughan's earlier drab poem "To His Friend Being in Love" is only "a little less skillful" (p. 395) than "Come, come." It does not seem to me to follow that because two poems possess "progressive thematic development" (p. 397), they are necessarily of equal merit.

of paralysis that the speaker is experiencing. The whole idea of "cutting off the sum"—something done already to the person being mourned and which the poet is asking to be done to him—is presented in miniature through the missing *s*, a notion that might seem strictly fanciful if it did not keep recurring in varied ways throughout the stanza. What happens to the reader here orthographically happens again with the sudden appearance of "one" in line 4 when the parallel syntax (zeugma) has, on the contrary, led us to expect a word denoting "many." The "cutting off" happens once more with the repetition of "Come, come!" which intrudes again into the poem, and it happens for one last time in the abrupt closing confession, "Dayes are my feares," for which we have been only obliquely prepared in the course of the poem and certainly not at all in the lines that immediately precede it. For a poem that describes a tightening tourniquet of emotions in the speaker's conflicting response to death—extreme depression coupled with the desire to suppress extreme despair—the emphasis on formal compression is central to furthering the poet's sense of being cut off from himself, from the dead person, and possibly from God. Although Herbert's hand is barely apparent in the poem, it is still at work around the edges where Vaughan's attention to stanzaic detail is most visible.

The increased desire for stanzaic compression also allowed Vaughan to exploit the cumulative ordering value that formal repetition could lend to verse. Compared to his epithalamion "To the best, and most accomplish'd Couple———," the only poem in *Olor* written in stanzas, all the lyrics in *Silex* mentioned so far show an increased concern with verbal terseness and sequential movement of thought. If the middle sections of the marriage poem only barely further the cyclical design of the epithalamion, the center portions of poems so radically different in scope as "Regeneration" and "Come, come, what doe I here?" are dramatically developed moments in the full arc of the poet's plan. In the first instance, Vaughan constructs one of his finest stanzas ever in his vision of how "The unthrift

Sunne shot vitall gold," a vision whose marvels are meant to whet the appetites of pilgrim and reader for the land of spices at the poem's end. Considerably more reserved, the other poem uses the repetition of "Come, come!" in each stanza, including the middle one, like a drumbeat that marks the progress of the mourner's thought, or his failure to progress, even while it urges him forward to discover a new resolution for his despair.

Still more poems depend on stanzaic repetition to give shape to an otherwise loose series of meditations. "Rules *and* Lessons" (pp. 436-39), for example, a poem compassing the individual's daily responsibility to God, is set in twenty-four stanzas, with each one being, as Anthony Low has noticed,[22] made up of sixty syllables. Although "High-noon" does not appear until stanza eighteen (when it is "thus past"), the overall sequence of events is still more tightly integrated because of the approximate time of day to which the devotional action described in the individual verses should correspond. Not so dogmatic, Vaughan's translation of Psalm 104 in *Silex*, Part II (pp. 494-96) also organizes its celebration of God's boundless munificence into discrete units of praise. Adhering less rigidly to a time schedule, Vaughan's poem compresses the thirty-five verses of the King James version into twenty-four stanzas and suggests again the hourly ritual of honoring God through his Creation. The poet's decision to avoid the pentameter couplet, employed by Bacon, Carew, and Sandys in their translations, seems also to have been inspired by a desire to avoid a methodical line-by-line treatment of the Psalm.[23]

---

[22] Low, *Love's Architecture: Devotional Modes in Seventeenth-Century English Poetry* (New York: New York Univ. Press, 1978), p. 191.

[23] In the popular vein of the time, Vaughan's translations of three Psalms (65, 104, and 121) hardly represent a significant achievement by themselves, but they are superior to most attempts in the Renaissance and certainly deserve more attention than the few glances so far given them by modern critics. Translations of the Psalms tend to exaggerate, sometimes to the point of caricature, an author's stylistic traits, and for Vaughan this worked to his profit. Psalm 104, for instance—sometimes called the Creation Hymn—was an advantageous choice for a poet with Vaughan's belief in God's immanence. Whereas Bacon might make a medical prescription out of the King James's

Distinguishing among God's works was meant to be a pleasurable duty for the reader: the individual pleasures are discovered more readily when separated into stanzas and the poet's ingenuity given greater freedom to shape the thought.

The most important effect of Vaughan's rekindled interest in the stanza involved his developing the spectacular conclusions for which his devotional verse has always been famous. These occur almost without exception in the poems that make use of stanzaic divisions. The closing moments of "Regeneration," "Christs Nativity," "The Proffer," "Cock-crowing," and "The Night," regardless of their "otherwordly" attitudes, are certainly fashioned by an immediate concern for verbal effects. In each of these, Vaughan enacts a shift in direction, a change of pace, that tightens the rhythms of thought and desire by suddenly "overloading" the verse pattern with something new and unexpected. Sometimes it can be a simple process of readjusting meter and rhyme, such as at the end of "Christs Nativity" when the doubling of the internal rhymes in "Cure him, Ease him / O release him!" coincides with a quick shift to trochaic meter, which together produce a climactic finish to the hymn:

> Sweet *Jesu*! will then; Let no more
> This Leper haunt, and soyl thy door,
>   Cure him, Ease him
>   O release him!
> And let once more by mystick birth
> The Lord of life be borne in Earth.   (p. 442, ll. 25-30)

"And Wine that maketh glad the heart of man, and oil to make his face to shine: and bread which strengtheneth man's heart," and Carew an argument for courtly decadence, Vaughan could capture a sense of God's abundant generosity through the triple repetition of his gifts, summarized in "all," then driven into the reader (and man) through his use of "infuse" in the final, accented position in the line: "these (blest by thee) the earth / Brings forth, with wine, oyl, bread: All which infuse / To mans heart strength and mirth" (ll. 42-44). See, *The Works of Francis Bacon*, ed. James Spedding et al., 14 vols. (London: Longman, Green, and Co., 1857-1874), 7(1859): 282; and *The Poems of Thomas Carew*, ed. Rhodes Dunlap (Oxford: Clarendon Press, 1949), p. 140.

At other times the overloading is more complicated. At the end of "Cock-crowing" Vaughan prepares for the concluding apostrophe, "O take it off!" in the preceding stanza when, for the first time in the poem, he retards the movement of the verse in the triple repetition of "veyle" and the doubling of "broken," both of which are given a further note of suspense by the interjection of "I say." The sense drawn out, the rhythms slowed, the verse is ready to be reinfused with the charge "O take it off!" which Vaughan places in the first position in the last stanza and in a direct line with the repetition of the three "veyles":

> Onely this Veyle which thou hast broke,
> And must be broken yet in me,
> This veyle, I say, is all the cloke
> And cloud which shadows thee from me.
>   This veyle thy full-ey'd love denies,
>   And onely gleams and fractions spies.
>
> O take it off! make no delay,
> But brush me with thy light, that I
> May shine unto a perfect day,
> And warme me at thy glorious Eye!
>   O take it off! or till it flee,
>   Though with no Lilie, stay with me!
>
> (p. 489, ll. 37-48)

The finest endings—those of "Regeneration," "The Proffer," and "The Night"—are not just a matter of a sudden doubling of rhythm and language but involve, rather, a more extensive redirection of the poem's verbal pulse in order to indicate sweeping transitions in the argument. Since the latter two poems are discussed in detail below,[24] I will remark here only on the ending of "Regeneration," a prototype for the others in the way Vaughan, following his master, introduces a new voice into the fabric of the poem, one whose sudden intrusion has the effect of displacing all previous modes of speech. Usually assigned to the outpourings of a mystical fer-

---

[24] These poems are discussed respectively in chapters 6 and 7.

vor, these conclusions should also please precisely because the poet has remained levelheaded in his task.

"Regeneration" describes both a spiritual and a poetic rebirth, and in doing so it performs what Helen Vendler has generously called "an unexpected restitutive kindness of literary history": Vaughan delivers "the 'successful' pilgrimage poem that the more saddened Herbert could not write" in "The Pilgrimage," the immediate source for "Regeneration."[25] The heir apparent hears the voice his master has missed:

> I turn'd me round, and to each shade
>   Dispatch'd an Eye,
> To see, if any leafe had made
>   Least motion, or Reply,
>   But while I listning sought
>   My mind to ease
> By knowing, where 'twas, or where not,
>   It whisper'd; *Where I please*.   (p. 399, ll. 73-80)

Amid the speaker's turnings and hesitations, uncertainties intensified as they were in the first stanza of the poem by counterpointing line enjambment with an overall intricate, tight stanzaic structure, the poem builds to an even greater compression of energy in the sharply presented oppositions of "where 'twas, or where not" before it achieves the definitive response of "*Where I please*." The extraordinary entrance of God's voice is both surprising and yet also, in the rhythmic structure of the stanza, predictable. Completing a triad of "wheres," the rhyme clinches the presence of the divine with unmistakable conviction, but the message itself registers the endless evasiveness of God and his ways to the human mind. Like the idea of election that preoccupies the poet throughout,[26] the conclusion seems both whimsical and absolute, a mysterious ending which, in its powerful close, seems nonetheless preordained. Furthermore, without limiting its power or meaning,

[25] Vendler, *The Poetry of George Herbert* (Cambridge, Mass.: Harvard Univ. Press, 1975), p. 97.
[26] Joseph H. Summers, *The Heirs of Donne and Jonson* (New York: Oxford Univ. Press, 1970), p. 124.

the heir of Herbert inherits the divine afflatus which on this occasion has evaded his master; having been lying with others on "a banke of flowers" (l. 65) in the previous stanza—a scene that explicitly recollects the Elysian Fields in "To my Ingenuous Friend, R. W."—Vaughan is suddenly catapulted forward, separated now from the fellow poets of his earlier days because of his calling: "Lord, then said I, *On me one breath, / And let me dye before my death!*" (ll. 81-82).

One final example will suffice to show how Vaughan's renewed interest in the stanza as an architectural unit could lead him to build a poem, if not quite block by block, still with enough care to produce a fully satisfying work of art. His poem "Man" neither reaches after the ecstatic heights of devotional communion nor delves into the bittersweet depths of private mourning. It does achieve, though, a note of philosophic reserve and control appropriate to its subject, and the success is largely due to Vaughan's modulating the rhythms of the stanza to cut across the movement of the thought until the two finally resolve into a quietly definitive, almost neoclassical, statement about the human condition. The result is a poem that, as it unfolds, forms the perfect expression of its idea.

Again, a Herbert poem, this time identically titled, serves as the beginning point for Vaughan's. The idea central in Herbert's—that man is the stately center of the world and waited on by all things but God—is inverted by the younger author, who finds man "ever restless and Irregular"; he chases after every whim even though God is everywhere about him. To emphasize that difference and the greater historical "truth" of his mid-century vision, Vaughan opens on a Baconian note of skepticism that seems designed to rebut the initial premise of Herbert's verse, which begins as if spreading a casual rumor: "My God, I heard this day, / That none doth build a stately habitation, / But he that means to dwell therein." Vaughan's response is nothing if not studious, reflective to the point of being "weighty." The first stanza glosses the natural philosopher's axiom that "the best demonstration by far is experience,"[27] and the best source for proof, nature itself:

>   Weighing the stedfastness and state
> Of some mean things which here below reside,
> Where birds like watchful Clocks the noiseless date
>   And Intercourse of times divide,
> Where Bees at night get home and hive, and flowrs
>   Early, aswel as late,
> Rise with the Sun, and set in the same bowrs. (p. 477, ll. 1-7)

Filling out the verse with evidence taken from flora and fauna, the poet works methodically, in the best sense of that word. He uses the normal break in the stanza (8*a*, 10*b*, 10*a*, 8*b*, 10*c*, 6*a*, 10*c*) after the fourth line not to further the "argument" but to add more data, and, like a good inductive thinker, he does not undermine his evidence by quick generalizations: delaying the main clause of the sentence until the second stanza defers the possibility of anyone (poet or reader) jumping to easy conclusions. Moreover, Vaughan no sooner unfolds the purpose of his observations than he returns to the Book of Nature to add further ballast to his argument—that the creatures are more at home in the world than even the wisest of men, Solomon himself:

>   I would (said I) my God would give
> The staidness of these things to man! for these
> To his divine appointments ever cleave,
>   And no new business breaks their peace;
> The birds nor sow, nor reap, yet sup and dine,
>   The flowres without clothes live,
> Yet *Solomon* was never drest so fine. (ll. 8-14)

The final two stanzas reverse the emphasis and turn the minor premise into the major argument. In the third, Vaughan unveils the full effects of man's lack of "stedfastness" while the last extends and deepens the image of his restlessness before it concludes with a statement about final causes. All

---

[27] *The Works of Francis Bacon*, 4 (1858): 70 [*Novum Organum*, 1. 70].

of the counterexamples taken from nature now serve to buttress the poet's melancholy description which, with their added weight, corrects Herbert's cheerful account of man's relationship to his maker:

> Man hath stil either toyes, or Care,
> He hath no root, nor to one place is ty'd,
> But ever restless and Irregular
>   About this Earth doth run and ride,
> He knows he hath a home, but scarce knows where,
>   He sayes it is so far
> That he hath quite forgot how to go there.
>
> He knocks at all doors, strays and roams,
> Nay hath not so much wit as some stones have
> Which in the darkest nights point to their homes,
>   By some hid sense their Maker gave;
> Man is the shuttle, to whose winding quest
>   And passage through these looms
> God order'd motion, but ordain'd no rest. (ll. 15-28)

The overall argument of "Man" is not complicated. The truth of its position is formulated with an eye toward unfolding the inevitable rather than developing the new or the unusual: man has "not so much wit as some stones have." But the verse does have a kind of secret wit in its use of stanzas that corresponds perfectly to the philosophic tone of the poem, for the "weighing" that defines the natural philosopher's search for evidence also defines the poet's quest for the exact form, which materializes in the final stanza. There, Vaughan uses the natural advantages of the stanza to their fullest poetic value. The break after the fourth line, for instance, with the introduction of a new rhyme pattern, has been either overridden, ignored, or only partially obeyed in the previous three verses; though one senses its potential contribution to sharpening the thought, the poet's interest in accumulating more "evidence" has left the form of the verse slightly undone in places. But in the closing stanza, Vaughan uses the quatrain to give the clearest image of man's restlessness so far (knocking at all doors), then obeys the full stop completely, just at the moment when he also gives a summarizing analogy about the difference between human and natural responses to God, and concludes by formulating a definition of why this is so: "Man is the shuttle, to whose winding quest / And passage through these looms / God order'd motion, but ordain'd no rest." The tercet answers, in a precise image, to all that has gone before: it is the devotional man's explanation of what the natural philosopher has discovered, and the lines are uttered with a new authority that blends the "scientific" with the proverbial. At the same time, and for the only time, Vaughan closes off the stanza with a chiasmic twist that takes full advantage of the caesura: words with equivalent semantic sense ("order" and "ordain'd") are juxtaposed to develop antithetical attitudes toward motion. The cool, analytic note of this epigrammatic ending quietly detaches man from the witty and polite colloquy with God that Herbert has established in his poem, while the form of the last stanza, seen in relation to the preceding ones, answers to Bacon's account of how true induction should work: "Then indeed after the rejection and exclusion has been duly made, there will remain at the bottom, all light opinions vanishing into smoke, a Form affirmative, solid and true and well defined."[28] Although Vaughan might deny the meaning of Herbert's man, his discovery of "a Form affirmative" nonetheless affirms the teaching of his master's methods of making verse.

Stanzaic compression was the most important lesson Vaughan learned on his way to achieving a new intensity of lyric utterance in *Silex*, but there were also significant thematic rewards that a close reading of Herbert brought to the younger man's verse. Some are immediately apparent in the legacy of Christian topics that Herbert left to his "pious *Convert*." The two books of God—Nature and Scripture—are duly celebrated by both poets, with Vaughan ringing some witty changes

[28] Ibid., p. 146 [*Novum Organum*, 2. 16].

in the act of thievery: "The Morning-watch" (pp. 424-25), for instance, certainly his finest description of the "*Hymning Circulations*" of nature, begins ("O Joyes! Infinite sweetnes!") by echoing Herbert's poem on God's other book, "H. Scriptures" ("Oh Book! Infinite sweetnesse") so that the younger man's verse resonates with double praise for the Creator. In his own manner, Vaughan also replicates Herbert's poems of public worship. The holy days of Christmas, Easter, Trinity Sunday, and Whitsunday receive treatment by both poets; for good measure, and with the likely intention of keeping alive the liturgical echoes of *The Book of Common Prayer* (banned since 1645) in Puritan England, Vaughan adds to this list his "Ascension-day" and "Ascension-Hymn." Each poet also celebrates the Anglican rituals of morning and evening prayers, Holy Communion, and church music. Though Vaughan is certainly less involved in the visible Church than Herbert— a fact due as much to the political moment as to their different occupations—the younger author does carry on Herbert's ministerial purpose in the number of verses, appearing largely in *Silex*, Part II, that generate, in parsonlike fashion, specific interpretations of Scriptural passages and persons. Finally, both poets explore the inner configurations of the Christian life: "Affliction," "Unprofitableness," "Misery," and "Anguish"—to name only a few poems—all have their prototypes in *The Temple*. In these subjects and others, the master's stamp can be quickly reckoned, his poetry simultaneously absorbed and commemorated in the younger writer's echoing songs.

The most determining idea, however, involved not just a set of specific themes but a specific attitude toward a set of themes. The degenerative view of human history described in *The Temple*, usually neglected by modern criticism, is not unique to Herbert's Christian temperament, but Vaughan was sufficiently affected by the "reality" of the vision to refashion it into the profound note of "spiritual exile, estrangement, and severance from God"[29] that nearly every reader of *Silex*

[29] Pettet, *Of Paradise and Light*, p. 22.

has felt and most have admired. Over and over in the devotional verse Vaughan looks backward in an effort to glimpse a luminous past. Whether the subject is childhood or marriage, nature or religion, dawn or dusk, the poems are shaped by an abiding sense of time and its ruins, a vision of history more catastrophic than that glimpsed by Herbert in "The Church" section of *The Temple* and wider, deeper, and weightier than the one presented by Vaughan in either *Poems* or *Olor*.

There, in the secular verse, time seems to be little more than a series of individual moments. The poet woos Amoret, he lifts a glass, he praises another writer, with each occasion being presented as a separate instance of personal experience left generally unconnected to a larger view of human history. Even when the opportunity seems ripest for developing temporal resonances, such as his allusion to a Roman Wales in "An Invitation to *Brecknock*," Vaughan—cousin to one of the century's most famous antiquarians in John Aubrey—nonetheless resists exploiting the past in favor of representing the tensions of the immediate moment. Only through the allusions to Virgil in the funeral poems is there the suggestion of a frame wider than the one provided by the specific occasion; but here, too, the past lies generally undeveloped, the future unexplored: the poems remain elegies without ever being fully elegiac.

The religious works reverse this formula. The elegiac past often blends into a chiliastic future and shrinks the place of the present into an almost nonexistent moment between the two. Vaughan looks ahead and behind, to the occasion of God's fulfillment, to the time before man's expulsion; but either direction he casts his eyes, the result usually is an increased pressure on the temporal structure of the poem and a new awareness of the position of the self in its relation to beginnings and endings. In his fullest expression of human degeneration, "Corruption," Vaughan eulogizes the past by steeping the verse in Herbert's poem "Decay": both authors focus on the diminishing returns of faith; both celebrate the easy access that used to exist between man and God in a distant era but which now has gone awry. Herbert begins with a Nestor-like sigh for times gone by and signals all the pleasures of an imagined return in the first four words, "Sweet were the dayes," while the remaining lines of the first two stanzas lay out a past filled with the "heroics" of frequent religious encounters:

> Sweet were the dayes, when thou didst lodge with Lot,
> Struggle with Jacob, sit with Gideon,
> Advise with Abraham, when thy power could not
> Encounter Moses strong complaints and mone:
>   Thy words were then, *Let me alone.*
>
> One might have sought and found thee presently
> At some fair oak, or bush, or cave, or well:
> Is my God this way? No, they would reply:
> He is to Sinai gone, as we heard tell:
>   List, ye may heare great Aarons bell.

To Herbert's mind, the past can be immediately recovered and made present in the poem. The patriarchs of the Old Testament reappear without the need of a Biblical frame; the sound of "great Aarons bell" seems still to ring in the ear.

Vaughan's poem opens in response to Herbert's. The first four words, "Sure, It was so," replace the older man's initial exclamation and acknowledge the attraction provided by the backward glance of his master's account. But Vaughan quickly emphasizes that the snows of yesteryear, however comforting they are to the mind, are not always so vivid to the mind's eye, especially to the eye of a poet who, in looking about, has also learned the full lesson of "Decay." In the final two stanzas of Herbert, the heat of God's love turns cool, and Vaughan's recognition of this inevitable withdrawal colors his poem from the start. Man came "condemn'd hither." The perspective is decidedly gloomier and more self-consciously "fallen" than Herbert's, and it temporarily blocks Vaughan's vision of the Edenic past which was on the tip of his master's imagination.

> Sure, It was so. Man in those early days
>   Was not all stone, and Earth,
> He shin'd a little, and by those weak Rays

>   Had some glimpse of his birth.
> He saw Heaven o'r his head, and knew from whence
>   He came (condemned,) hither,
> And, as first Love draws strongest, so from hence
>   His mind sure progress'd thither.   (p. 440, ll. 1-8)

Compared to Herbert's account, everything here seems cut in half. Vaughan's focus is on man alone, not man and God, and instead of describing the many possible devotional encounters, the poet simply suggests that "man in those early days" might have been able to catch a glimpse of the past which the poet cannot; he, at least, "shin'd a little." But even this recognition is qualified by negatives ("was not all stone") and diminutives ("weak Rays" and "some glimpse"). Vaughan seems as far from imagining the beginning of Herbert's poem as he is from the past itself.

In order to achieve Herbert's vision and move from the end of "Decay" to its beginning, from a disenchanted and fully retrospective view of the past to apprehending it immediately, Vaughan delivers what is missing from his master's verse. He places himself right in the middle of "Decay," between stanzas two and three—a lacuna signaling the gap between present and past caused by the fall itself. As if to study the cause of all division that gave rise to the idea of nostalgia in the first place, the younger author focuses in on the moment with a splendid intensity missing earlier from the poem:

> He drew the Curse upon the world, and Crackt
>   The whole frame with his fall.
> This made him long for *home*, as loath to stay
>   With murmurers, and foes;
> He sigh'd for *Eden*, and would often say
>   Ah! what bright days were those?   (ll. 15-20)

The frame of the world cracks with a brittleness that matches the way the poet's own rigid encounter with the past collapses. With the mention of "*home*," Vaughan begins to reduplicate Herbert's initial "Sweet were the dayes" in the sigh for Eden that overflows into a Tennysonian lament for the bygone years and forms the exact center of the poem: "*Ah! what bright days were those?*" The times of old he was unable to glimpse before, he views now with measured enjoyment:

> Nor was Heav'n cold unto him; for each day
>   The vally, or the Mountain
> Afforded visits, and still *Paradise* lay
>   In some green shade, or fountain.
> Angels lay *Leiger* here; Each Bush, and Cel,
>   Each Oke, and high-way knew them,
> Walk but the fields, or sit down at some *wel*,
>   And he was sure to view them.   (ll. 21-28)

To signal his return, moreover, Vaughan "re-turns" Herbert's poem. He both recollects, sometimes through exact verbal repetition, the first two stanzas of "Decay," and he also structures the remaining section of his poem to follow the letter of his master's. Like "Decay," the second half of "Corruption" is exactly twenty lines long, and it, too, is divided into four units of thought whose ideas correspond precisely to those in the four stanzas of Herbert's poem: the vision of the past (ll. 21-24), the possible places for a divine meeting (ll. 25-28), the cooling of the Almighty's ardour (ll. 29-32), and a vision of the world growing old with a judgment to be pronounced shortly (ll. 33-40). The point of this delayed retrieval is to exaggerate further the length of time that separates poet and reader from a luminous past. For Vaughan the world is older and fouler than it is for Herbert; the vigorous heroics of frequent struggles described by the master are enacted by the pupil in a different spirit. It takes more effort to return to the moment before decay has begun—an elongated vision of history matched in the doubling of the narrative length in the later poet's verse. The few changes Vaughan makes in the original also help to underscore the greater sense of distance in his poem. Aaron's bell no longer tolls even to the imagination, human action has become decidedly wilder, and the judgment call is necessarily more militant: Herbert asks for justice; Vaughan demands that the Angel of Revelation "*Thrust in thy sickle*" (l. 40). The "strong complaints and mone" left to Moses and God now become the measure of all that has been lost as Vaughan extends Herbert's sighs into his own groans and advances a process of decay into a condition of corruption.

If "Decay" is not the sole source for the increased burden of history in *Silex*, the poem nevertheless contributed some important verbal cornerstones to the edifice of Vaughan's religious experience. The celebrated passage in "Rules *and* Lessons" in which the poet describes a sentient nature laden with divinity was made ripe to Vaughan's imagination by the account in "Decay" of man's search in ancient times to find God present in His works. For Vaughan the early days of faith can be recovered by being faithful early in the day:

> Walk with thy fellow-creatures: note the *hush*
> And *whispers* amongst them. There's not a *Spring*,
> Or *Leafe* but hath his *Morning-hymn*; Each *Bush*
> And *Oak* doth know *I AM*; canst thou not sing?
>   O leave thy Cares, and follies! go this way
>   And thou art sure to prosper all the day.
>
> (p. 436, ll. 13-18)

Herbert is not responsible for all that is going on here, but the echo of "Decay" in the middle of the stanza places him in the center of the experience. Moreover, the note of "mysticism" sounded here, and often praised, has its origin possibly in a less mysterious place than is sometimes supposed. The emphasis on spiritual quiet is Vaughan's being obedient to Herbert's command, "List ye may heare great Aarons bell," a request now revised to fit a situation when bells from the British Church no longer ring. It seems even possible that the phrase, "Each *Bush* / And *Oak* doth know *I AM*," is generated by Vaughan's wish to assign the voices of the angels at "some fair oak, or bush" in "Decay" to the geographical spots themselves, lest the younger man's description of a morning communion seem as potentially fanatical as some of those claimed by the sectarians the poet despised.

Indeed, the other poem from *Silex* in which "Decay" figures is given over to revealing one of the causes of continued corruption: church schism itself. "Religion" begins by showing how Vaughan can praise God for the opportunity to walk among His sacred leaves (the Bible) even while the poem itself has grown largely out of Vaughan's reading of Herbert:

> My God, when I walke in those groves,
> And leaves thy spirit doth still fan,
> I see in each shade that there growes
> An Angell talking with a man.
>
> Under a *Juniper*, some house,
> Or the coole *Mirtles* canopie,
> Others beneath an *Oakes* greene boughs,
> Or at some *fountaines* bubling Eye.   (p. 404, ll. 1-8)

As in "Decay," the vision of the past is anchored in the examples of Jacob wrestling with the Angel (l. 9) and Abraham hosting some "winged guests" (l. 13); and even though Vaughan adds several more instances from Scripture of divine messengers coming from heaven, his subsequent lengthy and embittered description of religion being polluted over the course of time points to the more profound, shaping influence of Herbert: in its allusion to contemporary events and the proliferation of sects, "Religion" gives an eyewitness account of "Decay" in operation.

Closely allied to this new sense of history in *Silex* is a deepened awareness of the brevity of human life. However commonplace such an idea might seem and whatever personal incidents lie behind the numerous elegies in *Silex*, it is clear that Vaughan's method of expression—his mode of counting the clock that tells the time—is radically different in the devotional verse from what it is in the secular poetry. Rather than resisting or recoiling from the event of death as happens for instance in the elegy to R. W., Vaughan now approaches the occasion with a much keener eye for uncovering the nuances of suffering and for responding with a purer lyric intensity to the fragility of life. Not the large actions but the small details absorb his attention and offer themselves as effective symbols for recounting loss.

Herbert, of course, wrote no elegies for *The Temple*, but his verse is sufficiently rich in elegiac expressions to allow Vaughan a foothold from which he could begin to develop the "distinctive group of elegies"[30] that has always been one of the recognized accomplishments of *Silex*. As Arnold Stein, among others, has shown, *The Temple* contains a number of poems that lament the passing of life;[31] the collection also possesses its share of death's-heads and *memento mori*—the stock in trade of religious verse and the *contemptus mundi* tradition.[32] "Church-monuments," "Mortification," "Time," "Vertue," and "Life" all have their obvious doctrinal messages and their moments of elegiac splendor, and each has an emblem, cadence, or idea that reappears in Vaughan. But the most important lyric in this group for influencing the tenor and construction of Vaughan's own laments was "Life," an ur-elegy that sufficiently moved the younger author to quote the verse entirely in one of his prose pamphlets, *Man in Darkness* (1652): it was the only time he was to so honor a poem by anyone. Vaughan described the poem as a "handful of *blossomes* gathered by [the author in which] he foresees his own *dissolution*" (p. 186). As a reflecting device for meditation, "Life" asks us to realize, with an evocative power only poetry can summon, that man "*hath his time appointed him upon earth, which he shall not passe*" (p. 186). A mirror within a mirror, Herbert focusing on his dissolution in the symbol of a "posie," the reader focusing on his own in Herbert's "poesy," the verse asks (and Vaughan asks us to ask) that all thoughts be directed to one end: the contemplation of death.

When Vaughan set about writing the elegies in *Silex*, he

---

[30] Pettet, *Of Paradise and Light*, p. 156.
[31] Stein, *George Herbert's Lyrics*, pp. 156-82.
[32] The foundations of the English lyric of death have been amply surveyed by Rosemary Woolf, *The English Religious Lyric in the Middle Ages* (Oxford: Clarendon Press, 1968), pp. 67-113.

remembered the lesson of "Life": not just the final cause to which all things move but how Herbert makes the activity of the speaker the center of the poem. He also remembered the rhetorical importance of "Times gentle admonition" to the genre. When the speaker in "Life" praises the fading "posie" for how it "did so sweetly deaths sad taste convey, / Making my minde to smell my fatall day," Herbert is glossing, in effect, the poetic virtues of his own symbol as well as describing the emblematic purpose of the flowers; immediate, sensuous, and resonant, they mediate the shock of death itself and stimulate the imagination of the speaker (and reader) to touch the threshold of another world ("my fatall day"). The experience of crossing over, so violently presented in *Olor*, is made smoother, even desirable, in this verse and in *Silex*, not necessarily because of a sudden effusion of Christian faith on the part of the speaker, but because the author recognizes that poetry, like the "posie" in "Life," is perhaps the best, if not the only, way to sweeten the time while waiting for decay.

The eleven elegies in the two parts of *Silex* stand as eloquent testimony to this fact. No other follower of Herbert mined this vein so thoroughly or with such skill. Christopher Harvey gives us only a single poem, on the church yard predictably enough, while some of Herbert's more distant heirs such as Herrick and Ralph Knevet simply accept human frailty without attempting to develop this recognition into a statement of personal loss. Vaughan, though, realized that to be a "pious *Convert*" to Herbert meant that one had to become a willing pupil of death, and he fastened onto this part of his role as religious poet with determined enthusiasm. In fact, he signals the importance of this task in his poem entitled "The Call," a revision of Herbert's lyric of the same title. Vaughan approaches the idea of a calling not, as his master does, by celebrating a communion with Christ, but by directing his attention to the vanities of life. It is the dust that captures the younger man's attention, the many forms of dissolution that the spirit must confront, and, significantly, he places the poem immediately before his first attempt at elegy in *Silex*, "Thou that know'st for whom I mourne," which in turn anticipates the group of elegies that follow shortly thereafter. Indeed, Vaughan's recognition of the initially somber course of his calling—a task certainly developing out of a sense of failing at it in *Olor*—receives its most resonant representation near the end of "Retirement," a verse that "might be mistaken for one of his master's minor poems,"[33] when the younger author declares his intention to enroll in

> A faithful school where thou maist see
>   In Heraldrie
> Of stones, and speechless Earth
>   Thy true descent;
> Where dead men preach, who can turn feasts, and mirth
>   To funerals, and *Lent*.   (p. 463, ll. 45-50)

One of the most haunted moments in all of *Silex*, the echoing here, mainly from "Church-monuments," seems so strong as to form a seal between the two poets. Herbert's disciple swears himself into a discipleship of death where he can hear dead men preach of "*Lent*" (the title of a Herbert poem) by using language from the dead man's verse. To learn one's "true descent" by studying the dust of mortification is a necessary prerequisite to joining "a faithful school" over which Herbert presides.

In giving himself to this task, Vaughan's genius was to apply theory to practice. He wrote not just of death but of the particular dead and turned what could otherwise be a conventional message from the *memento mori* tradition into an exquisitely personal preparation for the end. The true heirs of Herbert's "Life," these elegies simultaneously discover—or recover—value and meaning in this world even while they point to the more important "life" in the next. It is also clear that the "progress" of *Silex* shows a poet becoming more suited to his task. Death does not become "Dear, beauteous death" (p. 484, l. 17) until Part II when the defensive tone, dominant in Part I ("Sure, there's a tye of Bodyes!"), gives

---

[33] Summers, *George Herbert*, p. 12; see also n. 5 (p. 199).

way to an untroubled penetration into the occult properties of the grave:

> O calm and sacred bed where lies
>   In deaths dark mysteries
>   A beauty far more bright
>   Then the noons cloudless light
> For whose dry dust green branches bud
> And robes are bleach'd in the *Lambs* blood.
> (p. 512, "As time one day by me did pass," ll. 31-36)

In moments such as these, there is no seventeenth-century poet more at ease with death than Vaughan and few, if any, who have developed so rapidly their ability to be comfortable with the genre itself.

The intense activity of self-examination which Vaughan singled out in Herbert's "Life" distinguishes all of the elegies in *Silex* and separates them as a group from those in *Olor*. "Thou that know'st for whom I mourne," "Joy of my life! while left me here," "Silence, and stealth of dayes!," "I walkt the other day," "They are all gone into the world of light," and "Fair and yong light!" are the opening lines of poems whose central activity is to use the occasion, as Herbert puts it, to "smell my remnant out." Whether that "remnant" is the poet's recognition of his own frailty or that part of himself as reflected in the dead person(s) now lost, Vaughan's overwhelming desire is to internalize the experience and "track" down what is missing until he learns, like Herbert, to "follow straight without complaints or grief." His best-known elegy, for instance, sets out by balancing, or anchoring, the poet's vision of the departed with a description of his own melancholic state; in the oscillation between these two impulses, each line seems calculated to define the poet's sense of his separation from the dead:

> They are all gone into the world of light!
>   And I alone sit lingring here;
> Their very memory is fair and bright,
>   And my sad thoughts doth clear.   (p. 483, ll. 1-4)

But the division here becomes quickly absorbed in the poet's deeper recognition of what the experience of meditation has allowed. By the end of the quatrain Vaughan's "sad thoughts doth clear," and the way is paved for a continuing description of the visionary powers stimulated by the contemplation of death that also carries the poet into a further awareness of his frailty:

> It glows and glitters in my cloudy brest
>   Like stars upon some gloomy grove,
> Or those faint beams in which this hill is drest,
>   After the Sun's remove.
>
> I see them walking in an Air of glory,
>   Whose light doth trample on my days:
> My days, which are at best but dull and hoary,
>   Meer glimering and decays.   (ll. 5-12)

Besides the experience described here of the imagination beginning to open to the dead, one of the remarkable achievements in these lines is how the lament addresses the landscape and "revalues" it in light of the poet's particular angle of vision. Nature, fitted to a formula in the simile of the "well-built Elme" (R. W.), described distantly in the account of "some *Star* / Hurl'd in Diurnall motions from far" (R. Hall), and used conventionally in the figure of the ravished pastoral landscape (Elizabeth), now takes on a special and immediate significance. To describe the illuminating effects of memory, Vaughan singles out the afterglow on "this hill," not any hill, but the one on which he is now sitting, meditating, and presumably composing his poem:[34] the commonplace, like Herbert's "posie," is suddenly magnified. Furthermore, with his vision of the departed "walking in an Air of glory" following right after this local allusion, Vaughan suggests that the ascent

---

[34] Summers, *The Heirs of Donne and Jonson*, p. 128, writes of this stanza: "I do not know of an earlier passage in English poetry in which the reader is asked to respond to the details of a specific, privately-observed natural landscape . . . as if the afterglow on *this* hill were different from that on any other, and the reader must imagine and respond to an individual, natural peculiarity which only the speaker has seen."

of the elect is like an evening mountain climb, comparable perhaps to the one in, say, the *Purgatorio*, but occurring now on a nearby hill. In this elegy, as in "Life," the poet's thoughts of passing away sharpen his focus on what is directly before him.

Like Herbert, Vaughan looked studiously for fit symbols or emblems of death in mundane experience. The sixth stanza of "They are all gone," for example, reproduces Herbert's hominess by turning a death-walk into a little bird-watching, while the lamp in "Silence, and stealth of dayes" and the "gallant flowre" in "I walkt the other day" serve as both *unifying poetic images and the means by which the speaker* prepares to cross over into another world. The last-mentioned elegy perhaps shows better than any of the others a subliminal response to the grave comparable to Herbert's desire to "smell [his] remnant out." Drawn instinctively to the "gallant flowre," the speaker digs up the "warm Recluse" and confronts it as an image of his own reclusive self; but the mirroring stops here. Vaughan is faced instead with the crucial difference between the two in the cyclical regeneration of the plant versus the linear path of his own bodily dissolution: the recognition of "death's sad taste" delivers a sting of fear to the poet. But the sting is also educative. It jars him into uttering, almost subconsciously, a deeper truth about the dead, one that simultaneously orders the narrative for us (we learn the object of Vaughan's mourning) and turns the speaker in the direction "Where Light, Joy, Leisure, and true Comforts move" (l. 59):

> This past, I threw the Clothes quite o'r his head,
>   And stung with fear
> Of my own frailty dropt down many a tear
>   Upon his bed,
> Then sighing whisper'd, *Happy are the dead!*
>   *What peace doth now*
>   *Rock him asleep below?*   (p. 478, ll. 29-35)

Not so sweet as Herbert's "posie," the "warm Recluse" nonetheless still manages to point the way, and the younger poet "follows straight without complaints or grief."

In the elegies and other poems from *Silex*, Vaughan is most his master's pupil when he least attempts to canonize Herbert's piety in his own poetry. One of the "blessed Patterns of a holy life in the *Brittish Church*" (*Works*, p. 186), Herbert was a most dangerous model to his followers—Harvey and Vaughan alike—when they attempted to copy the "blessed pattern" at the expense of copying the poetry that created the image. Vaughan's beautiful and moving opening in his last elegy in *Silex*, "Fair and yong light! my guide to holy / Grief and soul-curing melancholy," is finally wasted because after ten remarkable lines describing the wayward spirit, he views "holy / Grief" from the side of too easy a salvation. "O holy, happy, healthy heaven" (*Works*, p. 513, l. 23) is a line Simmonds quite correctly points out as among the worst in Vaughan;[35] the only excuse for it (and this is less of an apology than an explanation) is that it results from the poet's attempt to take a short cut and canonize himself, as he did Herbert, as one of "the most obedient *Son*[s] that ever [the] *Mother* [church] had" (*Works*, p. 186). When Vaughan goes on to write in the same poem, "I did once read in an old book / Soil'd with many a weeping look, / *That the seeds of foul sorrows be / The finest things that are, to see*" (ll. 31-34) he seems literally to have traded Herbert's poems, with their splendid response to life, for an anchorite's ancient manual on the reasons for denying all pleasures. Barely in need of a hair shirt, the poet reduces the experience of "holy grief and soul curing melancholy" to a tract for the times—"*For he that's dead, is freed from sin*" (l. 46)—and so loses his poem along with it.

But when Vaughan concentrated not so much on patterns of piety but of poetry, no one read Herbert with greater benefit or imagination. His moving elegy, "Silence, and stealth of dayes," sums up the wisdom of his decision to follow one man "till he grow very Hee" and summarizes the eminent measure he discovered in *The Temple* and sought to reproduce in *Silex Scintillans*; in this poem, Herbert serves as the elixir that helped Vaughan turn to gold some of the tarnished metal

---

[35] Simmonds, *Masques of God*, p. 43.

found in his two earlier elegies to R. W. and R. Hall. The poem begins, as does the one to R. W., by measuring the time that has elapsed since the person was last alive:

> Silence, and stealth of dayes! 'tis now
>   Since thou art gone,
> Twelve hundred houres, and not a brow
>   But Clouds hang on.   (p. 425, ll. 1-4)

Written in alternate rhyming tetrameter and dimeter lines, the lyric reflects Vaughan's intensified search in *Silex* to discover the exact, individuated form for the particular expression: the pentameter line is cut and chiseled into smaller portions—a practice for which there is ample precedent in *The Temple*—as the younger author narrows his focus and discovers the verbal effects of loss. The "full years grief" of the earlier elegy has been pared down to "twelve hundred houres," and with this more exact computation, the burden of loss grows heavier: the days, like the syllables counting them, creep, as Vaughan readjusts the clock to calibrate each ounce of human suffering. Moreover, the histrionics that begin "R. W." have been tamed to realize a greater depth of sorrow. It is nearly impossible to question the sincerity of a speaker whose many words echo so unobtrusively the sound of "ow" ("now," "thou," "houres," "brow," and "clouds"), as if the expression of pain has become the root formation of language itself.

Like the poem to R. W., this elegy is also structured around a retreat back to a primal scene of loss, and in both cases the journey involves a confessed failure of vision. But in "Silence, and stealth of dayes," the quest is now the sole point of focus. Vaughan excises all material irrelevant to this purpose as he extends Herbert's metaphor of "smell[ing] out his remnant" into the heart of the poem:

> As he that in some Caves thick damp
>   Lockt from the light,
> Fixeth a solitary lamp,
>   To brave the night
> And walking from his Sun, when past

> That glim'ring Ray
> Cuts through the heavy mists in haste
> Back to his day,
> So o'r fled minutes I retreat
> Unto that hour
> Which shew'd thee last, but did defeat
> Thy light, and pow'r,
> I search, and rack my soul to see
> Those beams again,
> But nothing but the snuff to me
> Appeareth plain.   (ll. 5-20)

Along with its purpose of extending the darkness of the present ("Clouds") into an even darker past and thus tightening the image structure of the poem, the simile is also perhaps the most perfectly crafted in all of Vaughan. Syntactically lean but verbally sumptuous ("thick damp," "lockt from the light"), the full weight of the dependent clause falls cleanly on "Cuts" and emphasizes how quickly the mind can return to the past and redeem those "twelve hundred houres" in a few "fled minutes." Yet the ease of the backward glance ultimately betrays the difficulty the speaker has in glimpsing the actual moment of death. Memory recollects, circles around, but comes up empty-handed: "nothing but the snuff to me / Appeareth plain." "Snuff," like "remnant," is the well-chosen, colloquial synecdoche that shrinks the value of the body even while the search has initially increased its stature. But the word has also a further purpose. In Vaughan's day, "snuff," used figuratively, also meant to purge, in the sense of someone preparing his soul for God,[36] and through the play on its meaning the poet underscores how the exercise of looking backwards and inwards should end in darkness but not in despair. The discovery of nothing in the past is part of learning one's "true descent."

The structure of the poem pivots on the pun. Vaughan feels

[36] See *OED*, s.v. snuff, *v*.¹ 1b: "It shall not be overmuch . . . everie weeke . . . once or twice to purge and snuffe the soule"; and "The ministers of Christ must be . . . thoroughly snuffed from all affections of the flesh."

no guilt, as he does in "R. W.," for having "fail'd in the *glories* of so known a grave" (l. 70) because the glories no longer involve commemoration but reunion, and for this end the speaker has been throughout preparing. As he readies himself to "follow straight without complaints or grief," the poet is busy revising and tidying up the ending, not to "R. W.," but to "R. Hall":

> That dark, and dead sleeps in its known,
>   And common urn,
> But those fled to their Makers throne,
>   There shine, and burn;
> O could I track them! but souls must
>   Track one the other,
> And now the spirit, not the dust
>   Must be thy brother.
> Yet I have one *Pearle* by whose light
>   All things I see,
> And in the heart of Earth, and night
>   Find Heaven, and thee.

At the center of the final paragraph in "R. Hall" (ll. 59-74), Vaughan also describes the separation of the flesh and soul and expresses the same belief that "bodies cannot trace the *Spirits* flight" (l. 66); but even though he recognizes that "we can only reach thee with the mind" (l. 70), the union is presented as a consolation prize, and it increases the burden of memorializing on a poet already uncertain about his muse.

In "Silence, and stealth of dayes," Vaughan tightens the reins, not just to ascend, but to describe the ascension with a clarity and compressed simplicity absent from the other elegy. He banishes all echoes from other poets that cause the simile in "R. Hall" (ll. 59-64) to swell without a clear referent,[37] reduces its sixteen lines of pentameter into twelve, half of which are already in a meter less than half the length of a pentameter line, and refines the fuzzy geographical description

---

[37] See both Marilla, *SPHV*, pp. 230-31, and Rudrum, *CPHV*, p. 496 for the many possible echoes in ll. 59-74, and the parallels each editor finds to gloss this densely packed and allusive conclusion.

in that poem into a series of oppositions presented in sharp relief: dark/light, dead/elect, body/soul, dust/spirit, and earth/heaven. The syntactic pressures increased, the energy of the self concentrates and intensifies, while the narrower verbal scope allows the poet to underscore the role of the "one *Pearle*" and the paradox of finding heaven in the heart of earth.

Vaughan attends to his muse here instead of calling attention to his muse, but the role of inspiration has not been forgotten. He buries it in his allusion to the "one *Pearle*." Certainly a reference to Christ as the pearl of great price (Matt. 13: 45-46), it is also a quiet reminder of Herbert's poem entitled "The Pearl," which glosses these lines by turning the many labyrinths made by man into the single "silk twist" of our salvation. Imitating the imitator of Christ, Vaughan gives us in the cave simile only one labyrinth, but it is one that "miraculously" turns into a silk twist when the speaker "in the heart of Earth, and night / Find[s] Heaven and thee." The pleasure we discover in this poem and in *Silex Scintillans* at large is not just the comfort of a speaker wending his way successfully to God; it is the satisfaction of a poet warming his muse in the fire of another and discovering how sparks can come from flint.

CHAPTER FIVE

Making the Purchase Spread

> A shame were it therefore for us to imitate so painefulie as manie do in eloquence Cicero; in philosophie Aristotle; in lawe Justinian; in Physick Galen for worldlie wisedome; yea to imitate as, most do, the French in vanitie, the Dutch in luxurie, in braverie the Spanish, the Papists in idolatrie, in impietie and al impuritie of life the Atheists, and not to folowe our Savior Christ in heavenlie Wisedome, and in al godlines of manners.
>
> —Thomas Rogers, *Of The Imitation of Christ*

"THE BEST MEN are but Problematicall, Onely the Holy Ghost is Dogmaticall," wrote Donne in his first Prebend sermon preached on May 8, 1625.[1] The Dean of St. Paul's distinction between the best of men and the Best Man, between human and divine authority, was, of course, a commonplace in the Renaissance, and in *The Country Parson* (1652) Herbert gives his version when he observes how a person should "not so study others, as to neglect the grace of God in himself."[2] Vaughan's study of Herbert might easily have led him "to neglect the grace of God in himself" and to imitate only the word of the poet instead of the Word of God—a charge he, in fact, levels against others in the 1654 Preface—but he was unwilling to read his master in the literal and narrow way of a Christopher Harvey. Vaughan was attempting to "reconstruct" his own temple of worship; he was not simply making an addition to an already completed edifice, as Harvey admitted doing when he subtitled his *Synagogue, The Shadow of The Temple*. A bold, sometimes careless, but rarely meek imitator of Herbert, Vaughan realized that if he was to succeed

---

[1] *The Sermons of John Donne*, ed. George R. Potter and Evelyn M. Simpson, 10 vols. (Berkeley: Univ. of California Press, 1953-1962), 6 (1953): 301.
[2] *The Works of George Herbert*, ed. F. E. Hutchinson, 2nd ed. (Oxford: Clarendon Press, 1945), p. 229 ("The Parsons Knowledge").

in turning "*many to righteousness*" (Preface to *Silex*, p. 391), he had to convince his audience that he was a member of the elect, that he, too, was spoken to by Christ; and his way of doing so was to organize his own works—the original prose, the various translations of Jesuit works, and, most of all, the two parts of *Silex Scintillans*—around his desire to "match" his master and move beyond copying the letter of *The Temple* to capturing its spirit: the steady illumination of faith that came with Herbert's vaunted "independencie upon all others" except Christ.[3]

Despite his insistence on being the least of Herbert's followers, Vaughan clearly viewed his privileged poetic relationship to his master as granting certain religious prerogatives. Not only does the 1654 Preface challenge the spiritual authority of his rival poets and insinuate Vaughan's own "true, practick piety" (p. 391), deemed essential for the successful creation of any religious verse; but the younger poet also stands alone among Herbert's disciples in being the only one who answers specifically to his master's call in "Obedience" for another to join him in following the holy way. In characteristic fashion, Vaughan draws attention to this distinction by placing his response at the exact structural center of *Silex* 1650. The thirty-seventh of the seventy-three poems (not counting the "Dedication"), "The Match" appears midway between the author's baptism in "Regeneration" and his transfiguration in "Ascension-day" and helps to locate the poet within a specific order of the Church Militant: in private fashion, the lyric recreates a surrogate for the Anglican rite of Confirmation, the means by which a novice in the church affirms his vows to Christ in the presence of a bishop.

Included in *The Book of Common Prayer*, the ritual had been dutifully excised from *The Westminister Directory for Public Worship* (1645) on the grounds that the ceremony was

---

[3] The phrase appears in "The Printers to the Readers" which prefaces all printed editions of *The Temple* from 1633 to 1695 and in all probability was written by Nicholas Ferrar. See *Works*, ed. Hutchinson, pp. 3-4 and p. 476n.

"Popish" and also unnecessary since the sacrament of Baptism was reputedly sufficient for an individual's salvation. But for Anglicans, Confirmation was a needed addition to regeneration. The ritual was—to paraphrase Humphrey Lord, Bishop of Sarum—a way of transforming the *"begetting word"* into the *"strengthening word"*: *"in Baptisme he regenerates us to life, after Baptisme he confirms us for the battell,* ad militiam fidei, *for the warfare of Faith."*[4] Nearly as important, the ceremony also reaffirmed the ties between the Anglican and the ancient Church. The "laying on of hands" which the bishop performed during the service was in imitation of the early apostles who "laid their hands" on the multitude to increase the number of the faithful (Acts 6:6), itself an action that recollected the manner in which Jacob declared the sons of Joseph to be his successors (Gen. 48:14-15). To ban Confirmation was tantamount to cutting the Anglican church loose from one of the sacred traditions that had nurtured it. Writing in 1663, John Riland, Archdeacon of Coventry, saw the outlawed service as inseparable from, and its absence perhaps contributing to, the chaos of the recent past: "No wonder it is to have such *turnings,* and *Over-turnings,* amongst us, when *Confirmation* itself could not *stand.*"[5] In "Obedience," Herbert only symbolically extends his hand to another, but when Vaughan frames his response in "The Match" with a preceding resolution to follow "an ancient way" and "There turn, and turn no more" ("The Resolve") and then immediately afterwards delivers "Rules *and* Lessons"—his most parsonlike poem and clearest imitation of Herbert ("The Church-porch") in all of *Silex*—it is impossible to escape the suggestion that in the interim the younger poet has been confirming his vows to Christ along a specifically Anglican and subtly militant line of succession.[6]

[4] Lord, *Confirmation Confirmed,* ed. John Priaulx (London, 1662), pp. 7 and 23. See also Richard Baxter, *Confirmation and Restauration* (London, 1658), esp. pp. 1-4, 10-40, and 91-93.

[5] Riland, *Confirmation Revived* (London, 1663), p. 20.

[6] Although it is not possible here to do more than suggest how the sacramental order in *Silex* parallels that established by *The Book of Common*

"The Match" itself defines the necessary ingredients for a successful transfer of power. With the triple pun in its title on that which is ignited, a contest between two forces, and a marriage of true minds—all meanings current in Vaughan's day[7]—the younger author traces the extent of his debts to Herbert and the terms of the overall "match" struck between himself and Christ. The poem opens by duly honoring Herbert's verse for its power to "inflame" holy thoughts in its readers:

> Dear friend! whose holy, ever-living lines
>   Have done much good
>   To many, and have checkt my blood,
> My fierce, wild blood that still heaves, and inclines,
>   But is still tam'd
>   By those bright fires which thee inflam'd.
>   (p. 434, ll. 1-6)

Isaac Walton had credited *The Temple* with a similar consoling or taming ability when he remarked how the volume has "raised many a dejected and discomposed soul, and charmed them into sweet and quiet thoughts,"[8] and the beginning of "The Match" certainly admits this view. But it goes beyond Walton in its realization that the comforts offered by Herbert are not to be confused with those offered by the Comforter: just at the moment when Vaughan might seem to succumb to the siren in his master's verse and thus number himself among the many whose "blood" has been "checkt," he snaps back at the end of the third line—as if to check Herbert's check— by repeating "blood," now with a further distinguishing stress on the possessive ("My"), and adds two new adjectives of turbulence ("fierce" and "wild") that together disrupt the ap-

---

Prayer, it is worth noting that, in accordance with the Prayer Book, Vaughan also does not approach the subject of Holy Communion until he has undergone his figurative confirmation in "The Match."

[7] *OED*, s.v. match, *sb.*², *v.*¹, 1 and 3.

[8] Walton, *Life of Donne* (1658, rev. ed. only); I quote from the 2 vols. Temple Classics edition, ed. Israel Gollancz (London: J. M. Dent, 1898), 1: 75.

parently completed verbal pattern into a new mode of periodic flux. The lines in their looseness demand a more authoritative ending than Herbert's "ever-living lines / Have" been able to provide, and that happens with Vaughan's mention of "those bright fires which thee inflamed." Terminating the stanza yet neatly ambiguous, the "bright fires" refer either to the heat of divine love or to Vaughan's poetry that celebrates the divine way, but in neither instance does Herbert's verse play anything more than an initial, mediating role: by the end of the stanza it has been transumed by God's Word, the original source and end for all inspiration.

As if to consecrate the grounds on which this understanding has passed, Vaughan chooses precisely this moment to extend his hand to Herbert:

> Here I joyn hands, and thrust my stubborn heart
>   Into thy *Deed*,
>   There from no *Duties* to be freed,
> And if hereafter *youth*, or *folly* thwart
>   And claim their share,
>   Here I renounce the pois'nous ware.   (ll. 7-12)

The pact acknowledged, Vaughan performs a few final alterations that insure his distance from Herbert and his recognition that their friendship is in, or through, not independent from, Christ. The "heart" mentioned in "Obedience" acquires the appropriate modifier of "stubborn" in "The Match," and the "thrust" the younger poet performs is not "into these lines," as Herbert had requested, but into "thy *Deed*" which dates explicitly back to Christ ("Obedience," l. 10). The only codicil in Herbert's poem indicating the difficulty of the challenge—"if he to it will *stand*" (italics added)—has already been partially met: separate from his master, Vaughan stands free to give himself entirely to God.

The division of the poem into two parts underscores the twofold, hierarchic nature of Vaughan's loyalty. The second half of the lyric, addressed solely to Christ, forms the younger man's prayer of servitude. In it, he confirms his choice of calling—to extend his imitation of Herbert into an imitation of Christ—and he fashions a union between his "dread Lord" (l. 13) and himself that is completed on a figural level within the poem. Head bent in humility, Christ looks down from the cross while his servant asks that his eyes be lifted toward heaven and pinned "to thy skies" (l. 27). Their intersecting glance is a final gesture of *obedience* that serves to number Vaughan with Herbert as an apostle who will help make the purchase of Christ spread, and the image of Jesus crucified acts as a constant reminder to the poet of both the means of his redemption and of the personal sacrifices he has yet to make.

Self-confirmed successor to Herbert of a Church that had been driven underground, Vaughan would undoubtedly have agreed with Lancelot Andrewes's acid remark that "it were better that a wiseman should be in a calling without the Church, than a foole within it."[9] From Vaughan's point of view, the Puritan ministry—the new "established" church of the interregnum—contained few wise men. Presumptuous, often poorly educated, and indifferent or hostile to Anglican traditions, they infiltrated the poet's homeland in increasing numbers with the passage of the Act for the Better Propagation of the Gospel in Wales on February 22, 1649/50. The act went into effect just three days before *Silex*, Part I was registered with the Stationer on March 28, 1650, and it called for the immediate sequestering of all clergy who could be proven derelict in their duties. As a result, almost three hundred rectors, vicars, or curates were expelled from their benefices in Wales, with the south being deprived of nearly twice as many as the north. Brecknockshire alone lost twenty-five.[10] Among the dispossessed were Henry's twin brother, Thomas, rector of the parish church of Llansantffraed, who was evicted under the dubious charges of being a "common drunkard, a common swearer, no preacher, a whoremaster, & in armes personally

[9] Andrewes, *The Pattern of Catechistical Doctrine* (London, 1650), p. 358.
[10] Thomas Richards, *A History of the Puritan Movement in Wales* (London: National Eisteddfod Assn., 1920), pp. 120-22.

against the Parliament,"[11] and their tutor, Matthew Herbert. Two of the poet's closest friends, Thomas Powell and Thomas Lewes—both dispossessed of their holdings—were still engaged in minor skirmishes of a sort with the authorities. Several letters have survived in which they (along with a third person, Griffith Hatley) challenge unsuccessfully Parliament's right to punish ministers who reopen the doors of their church in an effort to avert a famine of the Word.[12] With the nearby parish of Llansantffraed remaining vacant for the next eight years and with Thomas Vaughan departing from Wales, an action later repeated by Thomas Powell who went "beyond the Seas,"[13] Herbert's "Church-rents and schismes" certainly deserves the prophetic status Henry Vaughan assigns to it: "Only shreds of thee, / And those all bitten, in thy chair I see" (ll. 9-10) accurately describes the crippled posture of the visible Church in the immediate vicinity of the Vaughans and in southern Wales in general.

In its place was substituted an itinerant ministry under the general leadership of Walter Cradock, Morgan Llwyd, and Vavasor Powell.[14] "*The glorious stile of Saints*," as Vaughan drily referred to their preaching methods in the Preface to *The Mount of Olives* (p. 140) was basically evangelical, ranging

[11] F. E. Hutchinson, *Henry Vaughan: A Life and Interpretation* (Oxford: Clarendon Press, 1947), p. 93; see also, John Walker, *Sufferings of the Clergy*, 2 vols. (London, 1714), 1: 152 and 2: 389.

[12] Hutchinson, *Life*, pp. 118-20; see also, Theophilus Jones, *History of Brecknockshire*, 2 vols. (Brecknock: Blisett, Davies & Co., 1909), 1: 191.

[13] Walker, *Sufferings of the Clergy*, 2: 337.

[14] Modern research into the Puritan movement in Wales begins with Thomas Richard's work cited above as well as the same author's *Religious Developments in Wales, 1654-1662* (London: National Eisteddfod Assn., 1923). Geoffrey Nuttall's brief study, *The Welsh Saints, 1640-1660* (Cardiff: Univ. of Wales Press, 1957), is still the most valuable single account of these three men; but B. S. Capp's *The Fifth Monarchy Men: A Study in Seventeenth-Century English Millenarianism* (London: Faber and Faber, 1972) has done much to clarify the central position of Powell and Llwyd in the Fifth Monarchy movement. The works of Christopher Hill, especially *The World Turned Upside Down* (New York: The Viking Press, 1972) and *Milton and the English Revolution* (New York: The Viking Press, 1977), have also helped to make the Welsh saint, William Erbery, seem a respectable thinker and influential spokesman for radical ideas during the Revolution.

from an enthusiastic teaching of the Gospels to a militant focus on the Second Coming. Modeled, or presumed to be modeled, on the habits of the original apostles, their purpose was to convert others by delivering "the *simple Gospel* [once] preached by *fishermen*."[15] Cradock, especially, wanted to cut through the "high *conceits*, and *ideas*, and *notions*" that "*Sublimate* the *Gospel* almost into *air* . . . and leave *poor Christ crucified*."[16] His fundamentalism was aimed at his listener's heart, his approach antirationalistic without being irrational: "to take books, and say, Jerome thinks this, and Austin that, and fill our heads with notions, they blind us that we cannot see the will of God."[17] Along with Vavasor Powell and Morgan Llwyd, Cradock preached mainly of the saint's fullness of joy—the glories of being united with Christ—where his nearly exclusive focus on the "good news" earned him, along with the other two and their occasional comrade, William Erbery, the reproach of Richard Baxter, who branded them all as antinomians.[18] Worried mainly that "the meere preaching of two Sermons a week . . . doth not reach the practice of the Apostles,"[19] these men turned the Gospel into something of a moveable feast: Powell was said to have preached "in two or three places a day" and sometimes to have ridden "a hundred miles in a week"; Erbery needed at the most only five days to travel between Brecknock and Cardiff, preaching in each place his millenarian message.[20]

Vaughan's stubborn resistance to this incursion of the Puritan Word is signaled by the new role he determines for himself with the publication of *Silex 1650*. Changing from "Gent." to "Silurist" (*Olor* was yet to be published), Vaughan

[15] Walter Cradock, *Divine Drops Distilled From the Fountain of Holy Scripture* (London, 1650), p. 227.
[16] Ibid.
[17] Cradock, *Mount Sion* (London, 1649), p. 311; quoted by Nuttall, *The Welsh Saints*, p. 25.
[18] Nuttall, *The Welsh Saints*, p. 20.
[19] Cradock, *The Saints Fulnesse of Joy* (London, 1646), p. 11.
[20] See, respectively, *The Life and Death of Mr. Vavasor Powell* (London, 1671), pp. 107-8, and *The Testimony of William Erbery* (London, 1658), pp. 242-51.

adopts the title of his ancient British countrymen who were famous, William Camden tells us, for their "hearty, stout [and] warlike" character. "Averse to servitude, of great boldness and resolution, [they were] not to be wrought upon either by threats or kindness: and their posterity have not degenerated in any of these particulars."[21] They were also part of the legendary ancient British Church so important to Protestant apologists of the sixteenth century in defending the Church of England. Initiated by the conversion of King Lucius in the second century, the early Church had grown quickly in size and flourished, in the words of John Foxe, for "the space of 216 yeeres, till the coming of the Saxons, who then were Pagans." An age of faith, "the Gospell [was] received generally almost in all the Lland"[22] and the government was a model of charity: "when the Britains ruled," Foxe tells us, "they were governed by christians."[23] But with the coming of the Saxons, the fabled Church was destroyed and the remaining Britons driven into Wales.

Inheriting his ancestors' vigor, Vaughan also inherited their sense of righteousness. To his enemies, he was prickly and recalcitrant, to his friends a source of continuity amid turmoil, a connecting link between the "true" Church of early England and what was to him its closest approximation, the reformed Church of the Elizabethan Settlement. Vaughan's devotional writings are consequently double-edged, offering at once, as he says of his translation from Anselme, a portrait "to vex the age" (*Man in Glory*, p. 193), and also a vision of assurance to fellow Anglicans in the description of a poet's regeneration, growth, and triumph during the days of "our sad captivity," appropriately enough the last words of the last poem in *Silex*, Part II. Defender of the faith, Vaughan offers a wide range of Anglican attitudes including celebrations that recollect the

[21] *Camden's Britannia Newly Translated into English: with Large Additions and Improvements*, published by Edmund Gibson (London, 1695), p. 574.
[22] Foxe, *Acts and Monuments*, 3 vols. (London, 1641), 1: 139. Foxe's enormously popular work first appeared in English in 1563.
[23] Ibid., p. 140.

primitive worship associated with the first churches, but he does not attempt to repeat his master's "transcendent Dexterity"[24] in threading his way between Geneva and Rome. To the younger poet, the dangers to the Church all came from one direction—within: that is, from Puritan enthusiasts like Cradock, Erbery, and Powell, whose "*painted* and *illuding appearance[s]*" (p. 181) threatened to destroy the remaining truths of a Church that had already been seen by Herbert, for whatever reasons in 1633, as "Readie to passe to the *American* strand" ("The Church Militant," l. 236).

Connected to the original Church by ancestry, the Welsh poet was also, because of his location, potentially one of its last descendants before the British Church emigrated from England altogether. Embracing both the apparent beginning and potential end of his native devotional tradition, Vaughan nonetheless sought to reestablish the middle ground of institutional worship; he was not simply "locked into nostalgia for the past," as Leah Marcus invites us to believe.[25] The past could at any moment be translated into the present and made available to the reader's imagination. In *The Mount of Olives* (1652), for instance, following God's saints in the primitive Church, Vaughan reinstates a version of *The Book of Common Prayer* reported to be "the Sole Comfort of the people

[24] Barnabas Oley, [Life of Herbert], collected in *The Works of George Herbert*, 2 vols. (London: William Pickering, 1853), 1: 107; Oley's account was originally prefixed to *Herbert's Remains* (London, 1652).

[25] Marcus, *Childhood and Cultural Despair: A Theme and Variations in Seventeenth-Century Literature* (Pittsburgh: Univ. of Pittsburgh Press, 1978), p. 175. Despite disagreeing here with Marcus, who tends to view Vaughan's entire poetic career, especially his reponse to the political turbulence, through this one trope, her study is nonetheless one of the most stimulating accounts of the poet to appear in recent years. The more I think of Vaughan's "Anglicanism," the less I am sure that it can be separated from his own role as an "underground" minister, of which the desire to "escape" into childhood formed only one of many responses to Puritan domination; and I certainly resist Marcus's suggestion that the childhood for which he longs is his own (pp. 169-72). Even though Vaughan unquestionably thought of himself as a loyal and devout Anglican, his most intense religious experiences seem to have appreciably little to do with the Laudian church. See also below, pp. 196-98.

of South Wales"[26] but banned by Parliament in 1645. Like the Prayer Book whose sacramental center, John Booty reminds us, "falls upon the communion,"[27] *The Mount of Olives* is structured to lead up to this central event. Morning and evening prayers frame the opening service, whose focus is on the proper preparation of the individual for church, those "reverend and sacred buildings (however now vilified and shut up)" (p. 147). Indeed, the subversive nature of Vaughan's manual clearly surfaces when he reminds those unable to attend service of the actions of "the holy men of God detain'd either by Captivity, or other necessary occasions" (p. 147); in solitude, Daniel and Judith continued their ritual worship, while David is exalted for his stubborn attachment to his religion: "*I had rather be a doore-keeper in the House of my God, than to dwell in the tents of wickednesse*" (p. 148), a particularly appropriate sentiment for a time when gathered churches were becoming the norm.

The middle portion of *The Mount of Olives* is given over to recreating the structure and the experience of Holy Communion, as Vaughan plays both minister and communicant. In line with the Prayer Book, he defines the spiritual prerequisites needed before approaching the table, and he supplies a model "confession of sins"; but in place of the responsive, public parts of the ceremony—the Creed, the Collect, and the Lord's Prayer—Vaughan delivers a model "life of Christ," the archetypal sufferer, on whom the partaker is to meditate before, during, and after the ceremony. As the political conditions dictate, his service is decidedly more private, and as his personal desires are emphatically to "match" or imitate Christ, so are his commands to others. But the full range of the manual is decidedly Anglican and anti-Puritan, from the opening quotation from Chrysostom to the closing prayers "*in time of persecution and Heresie*" and "*in adversity, and troubles occasioned by our Enemies*" (p. 166), both of which are personal

---

[26] Richards, *The Puritan Movement in Wales*, p. 53.
[27] Booty, ed., *The Book of Common Prayer: The Elizabethan Prayer Book* (Charlottesville: The Univ. Press of Virginia, 1976), p. 370.

expansions, tailored to the immediate circumstances, of the prayer "In the Time of War" found in *The Book of Common Prayer*.

As both Marilla and Simmonds have repeatedly emphasized, it is precisely Vaughan's position as a surrogate minister of Christ opposing Puritan attitudes that informs his writings with so much sense of purpose and bite. In the Preface to the same work, for example, the Silurist takes aim against the current mode of latter-day saints like the high-minded Vavasor Powell who, blustering against the Prayer Book, charged that "no man, or men in these days, can pretend to have such an infallibility of spirit, as either to *compose* or *enjoyn* a perfect Rule for others; and if it bee not perfect, they cannot tye any *Saint*, much less the Churches of Christ thereto."[28] Defending his right to "compose" these "*faithful and necessary Precepts*," Vaughan pricks at their sense of inflated independence: "*Nor should they . . . be uncharitably moved, if we that are yet in the body, and carry our treasure in earthen vessels, have need of these helps*" (p. 140). The lower station he defends is, of course, the true Christian posture, but Vaughan does not leave his readers or himself altogether prostrate. His closing salute of encouragement—from "Thy Christian friend" to the "Peaceful, humble, and pious Reader"—returns both to a triumphant height: "*Think not that thou art alone upon this Hill*," he writes, "*there is an innumerable company both before and behinde thee*" (p. 141). Two occupants of "*this Hill*," Christ on the Mount of Olives and the poet among the hills of Wales, "J E S U S the Authour and finisher of thy faith" and the author and finisher of these "*necessary Precepts*" that sustain the faith, are together symbols of endurance, figures who incur persecution but who will ultimately transcend their earthly circumstances. Neither is explicitly stoic—both suffer—and neither is "*rapt into some other place*" like those currently affecting saintly postures: their "reality"

---

[28] Powell, *Common-Prayer-Book: No Divine Service* (London, 1660), p. 4.

is to be human, to recognize weakness, and to minister to these needs.

Vaughan's Christ—the Christ he chooses to imitate—is decidedly unprophetic. He is not a visionary who has come to prepare the way for the New Jerusalem, "a *renovator mundi* who by overthrowing the reigning orthodoxies will establish new, enduring values."[29] He moves but not necessarily forward; His "wearisome journeys" (p. 157) take Him always to Golgotha where His crucifixion and ascension cut through any sense of linear progression associated with the prophetic stance, described recently by Joseph Wittreich as "the art of the forward gaze."[30] Viewed principally as a physician, Christ is a healer not a concealer, a repairer not a maker of wounds. Vaughan interprets His life as "nothing else but a pilgrimage and laborious search after sinners, that [He] mightst finde them out and make them whole" (*Mount of Olives*, p. 161). As a result, Vaughan's writings possess visionary interludes without ever attaining visionary status. Instead of gazing ahead, the poet is more interested in holding a glass up to his audience, to arrest movement, rather than to further it, so he can play physician and heal those whom he meets. *Man in Darkness, or, a Discourse of Death*, the prose work that follows *Mount of Olives*, reveals only an intermittent relationship to history which helps to make apposite the quotations and echoes from Old Testament seers (Amos, Isaiah, and Ezekiel), but the piece as a whole is so saturated with sayings from the Church Fathers and classical and contemporary authors alike that sustained personal exhortation—the lofty ascent—is continually impeded. Rather than inviting us to see through a glass darkly, the Silurist, like the satirist making ready to perform his surgery, demands at the outset of *Man in Darkness* that his readers see in this discourse only a reflection of themselves:

> Draw neer, fond man, and dresse thee by this glasse,
> Mark how thy bravery and big looks must passe

[29] Joseph Anthony Wittreich, Jr., *Visionary Poetics: Milton's Tradition and His Legacy* (San Marino, Calif.: Huntington Library, 1979), p. 75.
[30] Ibid., p. 130.

Into corruption, rottennesse and dust;
The fraile Supporters which betray'd thy trust.
O weigh in time thy last and loathsome state,
To purchase heav'n for tears is no hard rate. (p. 168, ll. 1-6)

Satire is not necessarily inimical to the visionary perspective, but in Vaughan it certainly chastens the imaginative leap into sublimity. Surrounding his most "inspired" poem, "The World," is the notorious controversy about the relationship between the first seven lines of heavenly "majestic utterance" and the remaining body of the poem most favorably described as a "vividly dramatic account of prominent followers of the world."[31] But regardless of whether we choose to lament or applaud the poet's changing angle of vision—to interpret it as a lapse in the lyric imagination or an intentional shift in dramatic focus—the change nonetheless exists, and it certainly tempers the grand sweep of the initial expression while it prepares for the more radical criticism given at the end of the poem. There, a voice intervenes to halt the verse: "*This Ring the Bride-groome did for none provide / But for his bride*" (p. 467, ll. 60-61); and the speaking persona, who has been discussing the "madness" of others, stops suddenly short. Though often noted but rarely emphasized, the point of the intrusion, which is to separate the speaker from the ring, also furthers the distance between the now obviously fallen visionary and that other ring glimpsed at the beginning—the circle of eternity—which now seems altogether removed from conscious human reach. Vaughan was openly critical of those who pretended to be "*rapt into some other place*" and in "The World" he filters these suspicions into a criticism of his speaker and of the visionary mode itself. The impulse to in-

---

[31] See, respectively, Hutchinson, *Life*, p. 99, and Simmonds, "Vaughan's Masterpiece and Its Critics: 'The World' Revaluated," *SEL* 2 (1962): 88. Further notable discussions of this much-examined poem are by Leland B. Chambers, "Vaughan's 'The World': The Limits of Extrinsic Criticism," *SEL* 8 (1968): 137-50; Earl Miner, *The Metaphysical Mode from Donne to Cowley* (Princeton: Princeton Univ. Press, 1969), pp. 193-94; Joseph H. Summers, *The Heirs of Donne and Jonson* (New York: Oxford University Press, 1970), p. 123; and A. J. Smith, "Appraising the World," in *Poetry Wales* 11 (1975): 55-72.

dulge the human imagination is clearly tempting and in many respects satisfying as two centuries of Vaughan readers have testified, but the voice at the end of the poem pointedly reminds us that these raptures are necessarily momentary and fictitious, perhaps enlightened or inspired by truth yet not truth itself. Only the Word of God has this undisputed claim to authority, and its dogmatic appearance at the end in the form of an inscription from John 2:16-17 completes the process of effacement begun in line eight and advanced by the whispering intruder. Instead of being a prophetic mediator of divine experience, separate from but with special access to God's ways, Vaughan's visionary enthusiast is finally absorbed into the will of God, his voice overridden by that of the Bible, the supreme vehicle of understanding.

If Vaughan was suspicious of the visionary imagination, he was altogether opposed to some of the more radical statements that developed out of it. For obvious reasons, prophecy was heavily dependent on Revelation and during the 1640s and '50s when millennialism was highly infectious, the Book was constantly reinterpreted for evidence of the Second Coming and portions of it frequently cited as a justification for military actions by the saints—those who viewed themselves as God's chosen instruments. Both Erbery and Powell, for instance, emphasized at various points in their careers how the saints may "lawfully fight" their oppressors since "the army of the lamb" has been given by Scripture both a two-edged sword and the sanction of revenge:[32] "He that leadeth into captivity

---

[32] See, Erbery, *The Lord of Hosts*, (London, 1648), p. 31 and Powell, *Christ Exalted* (London, 1651), p. 58. Both men were voicing common, albeit extreme, millenarian attitudes of the day. See, *Puritanism and Liberty*, ed. A.S.P. Woodhouse (Chicago: Univ. of Chicago Press, 1951), pp. 229-39, 323-35, 474-78; and William M. Lamont, *Godly Rule: Politics and Religion, 1603-1660* (London: St. Martin's Press, 1969), chaps. 4-6. Although Vaughan was obviously removed from the center of action, it would seem almost certain that his awareness of continued militant activities by the saints after the Civil War involved more than just a general recognition of the threats they posed to peace. As Capp has shown, the head of the Commission for the Propagation of the Gospel in Wales was Major General Thomas Harrison, a leading Fifth Monarchist. Furthermore, Jenkin Jones, the person with whom Vaughan's

shall go into captivity" (Rev. 13:10). Indeed, it was precisely attitudes such as these that caused one contemporary to remark that "a great inlet to our late civil wars hath been the misinterpretation of the Revelation."[33]

As a member of the Church Militant but no longer of the military itself, the Silurist clearly directed his attacks against such "misinterpretations," even if he did not have either of these Welsh Saints specifically in mind. In *Silex*, Part II, when the confirmed poet is noticeably more public in his stance, he demonstrates his ability to possess "a clearer knowledg of Christ, and the Mysteries of the Gospel"[34] by writing on Biblical topics. Two of these on Jesus weeping (Luke 19:41 and John 11:35) prepare the way for a third, "The Men of War" (Luke 23:11) by underscoring Christ's patient suffering and humanity. The first (p. 502), with its focus on Jesus' peaceful entry into Jerusalem, casts a glance at the immediate chaos, perhaps even toward Brecon or London, both of which were occupied by Puritans, while in the second Vaughan pledges to imitate "A grief so bright / 'Twill make the Land of darkness light" (p. 505, ll. 50-51). In both poems, however, the tears of Christ's suffering are contrasted with the strife at large, with Vaughan conceding in the first that "This land . . . Will nothing yield but thorns to wound thy head."

"The Men of War" moves beyond an imitation of a tearful Christ (and thus avoids the histrionics to which "Jesus Weeping [II]" falls prey) and focuses on Christ's patience as interpreted by His *true* saints. The title is a cryptic reference to Herod's soldiers who mocked Jesus "and arrayed him in a gorgeous robe, and sent him again to Pilate" (Luke 23:11) in

---

friend, Thomas Powell, exchanged letters (see above), was closely associated with Vavasor Powell, and together they helped to rally a millenarian task force against an invading Scottish army in 1651 sympathetic to Charles II. Vavasor Powell was engaged in leading other uprisings as well. See, Capp, *The Fifth Monarchy Men*, pp. 54-55, 65, 101, and 109-10.

[33] R. Hayter, *A Meaning to the Revelation* (London, 1676), dedicatory epistle. Quoted by Lamont, *Godly Rule*, p. 21 and Christopher Hill, *Antichrist in Seventeenth-Century England* (London: Oxford Univ. Press, 1971), p. 78.

[34] Richard Baxter, *Confirmation and Restauration*, p. 107.

the final hours before his crucifixion. Within the poet's private scheme of criticism the suggestion is made that the soldiers in "The Brittish Church" responsible for shredding Christ's coat are now preparing Him for the final slaughter. The versified lines from Revelation that begin the poem extend these personal fears into a public admonition:

> *If any have an ear*
> *Saith holy John, then let him hear.*
> *He that into Captivity*
> *Leads others, shall a Captive be.*
> *Who with the sword doth others kill,*
> *A sword shall have his blood likewise spill.*
> *Here is the patience of the Saints,*
> *And the true faith, which never faints.* (p. 516, ll. 1-8)

Included within the poet's warning is also a lesson in reading. "*If any have an ear*," Vaughan abruptly begins—implying of course that many do not—then listen; and he proceeds to quote the complete sense of the verse, not, like Erbery and Powell, just the portions from it that support their particular arguments. In this case, the difference between a partial and a full reading is the difference between violence and peace, the imposter and the true saint. Those who take out of context only the lines on captivity invariably conceal the one possible solution to the endless bloodshed: patience. The misreading of Revelation on this point banishes Christ, not Antichrist (the reason almost always given for drawing swords in the first place) and creates the possibility for another "inlet to our late civil wars." Vaughan, who apprehends the full text here, also apprehends "thy word," and he ratifies the correctness of his reading by citing as evidence the simple fact that he is not running "to endless night"—an image that suggests the dark, repetitious action of revenge itself:

> Were not thy word (dear Lord!) my light,
> How would I run to endless night,
> And persecuting thee and thine,
> Enact for *Saints* my self and mine.
> But now enlighten'd thus by thee,

> I dare not think such villany;
> Nor for a temporal self-end
> Successful wickedness commend.
> For in this bright, instructing verse
> Thy Saints are not the Conquerers;
> But patient, meek, and overcome
> Like thee, when set at naught and dumb. (ll. 9-20)

Without the fanfare of rapturous claims, Vaughan offers himself as someone who, in Richard Baxter's terms, reads with "that illumination of the Holy Ghost which is so often mentioned in Scripture as given to all true believers."[35] Restrained, reasonable, and absolutely limpid, the poem attempts a reflection of the "bright, instructing verse" it commends, in which the greatest act of poetic license involves a modest but "instructive" pun on "enact": meaning both to legislate and to impersonate,[36] the verb aptly summarizes the methods of pseudo-sanctification Vaughan saw currently being adopted by Puritans. Otherwise, not only are Biblical and poetic texts perfectly integrated—the one developing out of, intertwining with, complementing and interpreting the other—but Vaughan is careful not to darken his verse by deliberately confusing heavenly with earthly matters, actions that might, paradoxically, only add to the distance between the poet and his "Crown":

> Armies thou hast in Heaven, which fight,
> And follow thee all cloath'd in white,
> But here on earth (though thou hast need)
> Thou wouldst no legions, but wouldst bleed.
> The sword wherewith thou dost command
> Is in thy mouth, not in thy hand,
> And all thy Saints do overcome
> By thy blood, and their Martyrdom. (ll. 21-28)

Working with obvious care, Vaughan defuses and eliminates the Christian radicalism embedded in Revelation as the poet frames and, in effect, restrains the prophetic ecstasy of John

---

[35] Baxter, *The Divine Life* (London, 1664), p. 261.
[36] *OED*, s.v. enact, v., 2 and 5.

of Patmos with a gloss from the literary physician, Luke, one of the indisputably true propagators of the Gospel. There are no heavenly armies on earth; down here there are only men of war.

The final section of the poem is devoted to Vaughan's prayer for patience, and the turn inward tests whether the interpreter can copy his own interpretation. The energy usually released by Vaughan in celebrating God, following Herbert, or satirizing others is rechanneled into the effort of simply holding on—toward being patient—as if the poet can halt the confusion, or at least his share in it, by the sheer power of his centripetal vision and the stasis imposed by the triple repetition of "give me." But it is also clear that the ritual repetition of prayers serves as a forceful restraint on passions not easily tamed: "A sweet, revengeless, quiet minde" exists in the implied future. Not until the end of the poem when Vaughan imagines all the earthly struggles being over and himself "Amongst that chosen company" created *after* the Last Judgment does the verse finally relax into the passive indefinite ("I may be found") signaling the rest (in both senses of that word) of eternity:

> Give me, my God! a heart as milde
> And plain, as when I was a childe;
> That when *thy Throne is set*, and all
> These *Conquerors* before it fall,
> I may be found (preserv'd by thee)
> Amongst that chosen company,
> Who by no blood (here) overcame
> But the blood of the *blessed Lamb*.   (ll. 45-52)

Vaughan's increasing concern over the true meaning of sanctification led him to translate those "Certain Rare and Elegant Pieces" collected in his *Flores Solitudinis* and published in 1654 with the inscription from *Georgics*, "*tantus amor florum & generandi gloria mellis*" (so deep is their love of flowers and their glory in begging honey). The quotation from Virgil recollects the poet's pledge in "The Match" to help Herbert make the purchase of Christ spread while the immediate literary context reminds us of the personal sacrifices Jesus demands of his disciples: "often, too, as they wander among rugged rocks they bruise their wings, and freely yield their lives under the load."[37] Despite their "Rare and Elegant" nature, though, these works are not strictly the products of a precious isolation. Reported to be "Collected in [the poet's] Sicknesse and Retirement" (*Flores Solitudinis*, p. 211), they survive as documentary proof of the charges made against the commonwealth by Thomas Powell and others that because of the repressive measures taken against Anglican ministers, many persons "do daily relapse to Popery."[38] All the pieces are "Romish" in outlook. The first two, written by the Spanish Jesuit, Juan Eusebius Nieremberg, are laced with mementos of Catholic "superstition"—rosaries, beads, candles and the ever-present Virgin—to say nothing about passages devoted to the individual triumphs of Jesuit missionaries working in "dark corners of the land."[39] The next, a letter by Eucherius, the fifth-century Bishop of Lyons, to his kinsman Valerianus "*breaths that* togatam elegantiam *which in most of the Roman Senatours was not more acquired, then natural*" (p. 312) and defines an attitude of the early Church clearly repugnant to Puritan reformers and mechanic preachers. The final work in the collection, the summary *Life of Paulinus*, describes an exemplary servant of Christ laboring faithfully to spread the Gospel in the primitive Church under Constantine, a time

---

[37] Virgil, *Georgics*, 4. 203-5 (Loeb translation).

[38] Hutchinson, *Life*, p. 119 (letter to Jenkin Jones on the punishment of ministers).

[39] The phrase, adopted by Christopher Hill from E[dward] B[ush], *A Sermon preached at Pauls Crosse, 1571* (London, 1576), is used to describe the heathenish, outlying regions in the north and west of England associated with papacy. See Hill, "Puritans and 'The Dark Corners of the Land,'" collected in his *Change and Continuity in Seventeenth-Century England* (London: Weidenfeld and Nicolson, 1974), pp. 3-47. For a further account of "Roman survivals" in Wales, see David Walker, "The Reformation in Wales" in *A History of the Church in Wales*, ed. David Walker (Glamorgan, Wales: D. Brown and Sons Ltd., 1976), pp. 54-77.

when, for many Puritans, "*Antichrist* began first to put forth his horne."[40]

The works in themselves do not necessarily argue Vaughan's own recusancy even though, as Hutchinson notes, the poet was descended from one of Wales' more infamous Catholics in Thomas Somerset and connected to other recusants by kinship or friendship.[41] They do, however, play on continuing Puritan fears about Wales being a stronghold of adherents to the old faith. The *contemptus mundi* attitude flavoring all the works is of course an invitation for others to dig in and resist "Gospel reform" while the prefatory "To the Reader" goes even further by placing "*those wise* Hermits, *who have withdrawne from the present generation*" in a line with "*the rough and severe* habit *of the* Franciscans" (p. 216). Such monkish behavior has its own militant strategies designed to challenge and cut through, perhaps even to disorient further, Puritans and the lunatic fringe, "*those Melancholy* Schismaticks, *who having burnt off their owne hands in setting the world on fire, are now fallen out with it,* because they cannot rule it" (p. 216). But Vaughan also salts each piece with plenty of anti-Puritan propaganda. *Of Temperance and Patience,* for instance, pivots around the Silurist's insertion that "Having now taught you how to master *Adventitious, Personal Evils,* and to prevent the *Evils* of *Conscience*; It orderly followes, that I should teach you how to subdue and triumph over *Publick Evils,* or *National Calamities*" (p. 267). *Of Life and Death* includes a timely addition to the original criticizing those who "plot to forfeit a Crown of Eternall glory, by usurping a transitory one: They murther their owne soules by shedding the blood of some innocent persons" (p. 288). And Paulinus's model life is repeatedly set against the "*Schismaticks* and *seditious raylers*" in this later age who cover "their *abominable villanies* with a pretence of *transcendent holinesse,* and a certain *Sanctimonious excellencie* above the Sons of men" (p. 371).

---

[40] *Complete Prose Works of John Milton,* ed. Don M. Wolfe et al., 8 vols. (New Haven: Yale Univ. Press, 1953-), 1 (1953): 557 (*Of Reformation*).

[41] Hutchinson, *Life,* p. 7.

Beginning with *Of Temperance and Patience*, whose title recollects Herbert's translation of Luigi Cornaro's *A Treatise of Temperance and Sobriety*, *Flores Solitudinis* works gradually toward incarnating a model of primitive holiness in the figure of St. Paulinus, Bishop of Nola. Pointed and homiletic, the two works of Nieremberg are rather severe examples of what Douglas Bush has broadly defined as "literature of conduct."[42] Less sumptuously written than Jeremy Taylor's *Holy Living* and narrower in focus, *Of Temperance and Patience* divides between maxim and example, believing that "*Theorie* is nothing so beneficial as *Practice*" (p. 264). The rhetorical as well as spiritual center of the treatise is, of course, Christ, "that great *Arch-Type* of Patience in life and death" (p. 241) around whom the rest of the work revolves: the many illustrations, taken from Old and New Testaments alike, serve to define a doctrine of good works in which "discretion"—a fusion of patience with temperance—"orders the Action so excellently, that oftentimes there is more goodnesse in the *manner*, then in the *Action*" (p. 259). The companion piece, *Of Life and Death*, is, in fact, less about living than dying: an *ars moriendi* paralleling Taylor's *Holy Dying*, it presents virtue as "nothing else but an imitation of death" (p. 292) where, once again, Christ serves as the cutting edge of truth. By making "his entrance through the veile" (Vaughan's addition), He radically altered the ancient belief held by the Patriarchs that "the reward of righteousnesse and sanctity was long life" (p. 288).

Structurally, neither work is much more than a series of aphorisms, bits of stoic wisdom tempered by Christian humility and regathered in the subsequent epistle by Eucherius under the single title of *The World Contemned*. Here, they receive more flesh in the rambling fatherly advice the Bishop of Lyons gives to his young convert as the narrative begins to move toward biography. The "reverend witnesses" (p. 324) that Eucherius produces as testimonies of the value of conversion are designed to confirm Valerian in his decision while,

---

[42] Bush, *English Literature in the Earlier Seventeenth Century*, 2nd ed. (Oxford: Clarendon Press, 1962), p. 331.

within the larger frame of *Flores*, they serve to whet the reader's appetite for the saint's life to come. Bound along with the epistle in the Latin original, the *Vita Paulina* is—to quote Vaughan's marginal note to Eucherius—"*a precedent after these precepts*" (p. 324). The biography at once encapsulates and provides a living model of the lessons taught so far. Patient and temperate, performing his works in a spirit of charity until his final hours, Paulinus everywhere reveals a proper contempt for the world as he discloses the richness in serving Christ, symbolized above all by his friendship with Augustine: their souls "(like *Jonathan* and *David*, or *Jacob* and *Joseph*) were *knit together*, and *the life of the one was bound up in the life of the other*" (pp. 357-58). His death, moreover, is as artful as any prescribed by Taylor or Nieremberg: the final vision of Paulinus's being rewarded "a kind of Heavenly foode in form like a honey-combe" (p. 381) neatly returns us to the inscription on the title page of *Flores* itself.

Paulinus's exemplary life certainly anchors us in the heart of Anglicanism with its frequent praise of primitive holiness, but Vaughan's portrait of old-style worship is not strictly an exercise in piety. For one thing, the appearance of this "real" saint's life literally mocks the appearance of those "who saint themselves" and their attempts to banish all liturgical traditions in favor of the Word of God. Paulinus preaches, but much of his episcopal dignity comes from his "*Works of Piety*" (p. 374), the most notable of which are the lavish churches he either repaired or built and which Vaughan recovers to the Anglican memory through the lengthy descriptive passages he quotes from the Bishop's own poetry. Beyond such pugnacious recollections, Vaughan prefaces the *Life* with a quotation from 2 *Kings:* "*My Father, my Father, the Chariot of* Israel, *and the Horsmen thereof*" (2:13). Spoken by Elisha at the moment of Elijah's ascension, the appellation, as Richard Bernard notes,[43] was a common euphemism for the ministry, while the line itself was thought to signal Elisha's despair over the loss of his country's guiding light. "That we have foregone a father,

[43] Bernard, *The Faithfull Shepheard* (London, 1607), p. 2.

should not so much trouble us, as that Israel hath lost his guard," writes Joseph Hall, who continues: "The prayers of an Elijah are more powerful, than all the armies of flesh. The first thing that this seer discerns, after the separation of his master, is, the nakedness of Israel in his loss. If we muster souldiers, and lose zealous prophets, it is but a woeful exchange."[44]

In this transitional moment of history, Vaughan suggests—when England has lost her guard—there are horsemen and there are opportunists who ride horses. Some, like Paulinus, are authentic descendants of Elijah who guide the chariot of the state and minister to its needs; others masquerade on horses in the style of saints, like Powell and Erbery:

> [Resolved,] that Three or Four *Itinerary Teachers* should be imployed in most of the Counties, to supply the same; and because it shall not seem too hard a work, for so few to supply a whole County, which some of them consist of 120 Parishes, and the least of 50 or 60. *Resolved* also, that in their *expedition*, they should be supplyed with fresh horses at every stage, which commonly are 10 or 20 miles, and sometimes more, to ride post from place to place, to spread their *Doctrine*.[45]

Vaughan's use of the Biblical inscription is necessarily more muted than the sardonic account given here by Alexander Griffith, the evicted clergyman from Glasbury (Radnorshire) who spent much of his time in Brecknockshire, but it nonetheless allows the Welsh poet to take a similar swipe at these peripatetic preachers who desecrate the holy office. "Every man can speak, but every man cannot preach," says Vaughan, elaborating in the *Life* on the criticisms implied in the quotation from Kings:

> Tongues and the gift of tongues are not the same things.... Wee have amongst us many builders with *hay and stubble,* but let them, and those that hired them, take heed how they build; The tryal

---

[44] *The Works of Joseph Hall*, 12 vols. (Oxford: D. A. Talboys, 1837-1839), 2: 86.

[45] Alexander Griffith, *Mercurius Cambro-Britannicus* (London, 1652), pp. 5-6.

will be by fire, and by a consuming fire. The *hidden things of dishonesty, the walking in Craftinesse*, and *the handling deceitfully of the word of God* they are well versed in; but true sanctitie, and the Spirit of God (which Saint *Paul* thought he had) I am very sure they have not. (p. 348)

Stylistically and psychologically, politically and emotionally, Vaughan was deeply implicated in his account of the life of Paulinus to the point of seeing himself through his subject's eyes. Not only is the "translation" the freest the author ever produced, one in which he frequently cuts, interpolates, and shapes the original to his own liking, but the saint's life and the poet's are in many remarkable ways mirror reflections of each other and meant to be viewed as such. Hutchinson partially glimpsed this doubling process when he noted how both men were poets and both were influenced by Ausonius,[46] to which we might add that both subsequently came to represent this author as the epitome of wordly temptation. But the mirroring is more complete and complicated than this one example allows.

Both men, for instance, claimed noble ancestry; each was born into a place of retirement, the one in a country estate outside of Bordeaux, the other in Wales. Each man also experienced a conversion to religious writings, with Paulinus achieving acclaim for doing precisely what Vaughan was seeking to do—inspire others to devotion: "O that I were able (saith [Jerome]) to extoll and publish your ingenuity and holy learning, not upon the *Aonian* hills, or the tops of *Helicon* (as the Poets sing) but upon the Mountaines of *Sion* and *Sinai*; that I might preach there what I have learnt from you, and deliver the sacred mysteries of Scripture through your hands" (p. 342). Both men, moreover, received a late Baptism that brought upon them the enmity of their "friends" and caused each to seek a deeper retirement into "those *Western* parts" where few received "the *Christian* Faith" (p. 345). There Paulinus, like Vaughan, "preferred the indignation and hatred of

[46] Hutchinson, *Life*, pp. 134-35.

the multitude to their love, he would not buy their friendship with the losse of Heaven, nor call those Saints and propagators, who were Devills and destroyers" (p. 346). Paulinus, of course, was officially ordained whereas the "Silurist" was not, but the later author's free rendering of the original on the subject of ecclesiastical corruption and the admission of "Lay-men, and unseason'd persons into the Ministry" (p. 354) certainly reflects his understanding of the immediate circumstances and questions the validity of external sanctification in the first place. Finally, in their dedication to Christ, both men also suffered captivity, Paulinus to the Goths and Vandals, Vaughan to the Puritans, and in each instance relief is provided both by Christ and the true companions one discovers in Christ: Saints Augustine, Ambrose, Jerome, and Martin form the nucleus of Paulinus's community, while the single figure of George Herbert makes a solitary but conspicuous appearance near the end of the *Life* to remind us of Vaughan's (p. 379).

The point of these parallels, reinforced by interpolation, is not that they reveal the *Vita Paulini* to be a work of its age, one in which the seventeenth-century biographer (in this instance, the pseudo-biographer) was unable to resist "the impulse to identify all of himself with one aspect of his subject."[47] They create, in fact, just the opposite effect. The many alterations indicate a Vaughan intent not so much in making Paulinus in his own image as in remaking himself in the image of a saint; a saint, moreover, who had already received official sanction from the Church as one of Christ's chosen few and not like the many around who were simply usurping that title for themselves. Vaughan might be subtly guilty of sainting himself, but he would undoubtedly argue that at least in his case the original from which the copy was made was authentic. Indeed, with the inscription of Elisha's cry affixed to the title page, a cry designated in Kings as a sign that Elisha was to

[47] David Novarr, *The Making of Walton's "Lives"* (Ithaca: Cornell Univ. Press, 1958), p. 486.

be the rightful successor to Elijah, the Silurist firmly incorporated himself into a distinguished line of true bearers of faith, a line which Marjorie Reeves has shown to connect with English monasticism.[48] Monkish without being a monk, interested in the Franciscans without actually putting on their habit, Vaughan translates through Paulinus's life many of their ideals of primitive holiness as he blends with his portrait to become a representative of those values himself. In doing so, the Silurist at once incarnates and realizes the role posterity had defined for Herbert: "A companion to the primitive Saints, and a pattern or more for the age he lived in."[49]

In the shadow of Paulinus, Vaughan sketches a portion of a saint's life for himself, but the final configuration wrought in this mold was left to the completion of *Silex Scintillans*. "It is one thing to be an *Idol*, or *Counterfeit*," said the Welsh author in translating Nieremberg, "and another to be a *lively Figure* and *likenesse*":

> To the *Politure* and *sweetning* of the Divine *Image*, there are some *lines* expected from thine owne hand. If some expert Statuary, suppose *Phidias* himselfe, should leave unfinished some excellent peece, like that Statue of *Minerva* at *Athens*, and out of an incurious wearinesse, give himself to some obscure and Artlesse imployment, or to meere Idlenesse, wouldst not thou much blame and rebuke him for it? (p. 260)

Written alongside the major prose and reflecting many of its attitudes, the second part of *Silex* supplies the significant finishing touches to the Silurist's devotional works. Some have resisted its concluding role, arguing that the collection represents a falling off of poetic inspiration;[50] but it seems clear that Vaughan felt compelled to polish and sweeten the divine

---

[48] Reeves, *The Influence of Prophecy in the Later Middle Ages: A Study of Joachimism* (Oxford: Clarendon Press, 1969), pp. 158-59.

[49] Hutchinson, *Works*, p. 3 ("The Printers to the Reader").

[50] See, for instance, Louis L. Martz, *The Paradise Within: Studies in Vaughan, Traherne, and Milton* (New Haven: Yale Univ. Press, 1964), pp. 4-5, and James D. Simmonds, *Masques of God: Form and Theme in the Poetry of Henry Vaughan* (Pittsburgh: Univ. of Pittsburgh Press, 1972), p. 203.

image uncovered in *Silex* 1650 and developed in the prose works into some final *"lively Figure* and *likenesse."*

That *"lively Figure,"* of course, is a canonized version of the regenerated self. Created in the image of Christ, or, more accurately, in the image of the Christ Vaughan imagines, this figure functions rhetorically and dramatically both to convince the reader of the authenticity of the poet's religious experience and to invite him to be a sharer—a communicant—in it. "When thou hast considered [Christ] in his acts of love and humility," Vaughan writes in leading his reader to Holy Communion in *The Mount of Olives*, "consider him again in his glory, take thine Eyes off from *Bethlehem* and *Golgotha*, and look up to the mount of *Olives*, yea, to heaven where he sits now upon the right hand of his Father" (p. 158). For the most part, *Silex* 1650 is grounded in "*Bethlehem* and *Golgotha*," birth and suffering, the two principal events in the early phases of the individual Christian life. Indeed, the holy days celebrated in *Silex*, Part I—Christmas and Easter, Christ's Nativity and His Passion—show just how closely Vaughan identified his speaker's experiences with those of Christ: the pledge at the beginning of *Silex* to take up the cross in "Day of Judgement," and reconfirmed in "The Match," finds its liturgical fulfillment in the sequence on the Passion beginning with "Dressing" and progressing through "Easter-day," "Easter Hymn," and "The Holy Communion." In this cluster of poems Christ's sufferings—his crucifixion—is finally confronted directly by the speaker who, because of the knowledge gained by the encounter, discovers almost immediately afterwards in the poem entitled "Affliction" that his own sufferings are minimal and part of a larger divine plan.

But Bethlehem and Golgotha represent only phases in Jesus' life, the speaker's development, and the reader's experience. The seal to the communicant's "worthiness," Vaughan tells us, is to imagine Christ in his glory, a transition initiated by our looking up to the Mount of Olives. *Silex* 1650 concludes with just such a glance. Three poems from the end, Vaughan writes his second "Mount of Olives" poem, and the difference between the two is the difference, in several senses, between promise and fulfillment. Retrospective, elegantly poised, and assured, the lyric stands apart from those surrounding it, indeed from all the poems in Part I, in the distance in vision it achieves of the regenerated self. Like Christ, the author inhabits the Mount of Olives and inherits its perspective. He surveys his "progress," and the view he presents is of an illuminated disciple-poet who has climbed the mountain and received inspiration, the extent of which he attempts to flesh out in the richly sensuous, pentameter couplets:

> When first I saw true beauty, and thy Joys
> Active as light, and calm without all noise
> Shin'd on my soul, I felt through all my powr's
> Such a rich air of sweets, as Evening showrs
> Fand by a gentle gale Convey and breath
> On some parch'd bank, crown'd with a flowrie wreath;
> Odors, and Myrrh, and balm in one rich floud
> O'r-ran my heart, and spirited my bloud,
> My thoughts did swim in Comforts, and mine eie
> Confest, *The world did only paint and lie.* (p. 476, ll. 1-10)

Witholding the main clause, Vaughan holds out for the benefit of his reader the experience of being infused with divine radiance. "Through all my powers" begins a series of quiet rhythmic flexes that luxuriously conveys the fullness of God's "glance" (l. 15), a look that even subsumes "the glance" which fell on Vaughan's master in the poem of that title and which serves as the immediate source for the younger author's lyric. In that poem, Herbert, too, had recounted the similar experience of being eyed by God, but compared to Vaughan's description the language in it seems cropped of its fullness, as if God's glance has not penetrated so deeply. The giddy raptures Vaughan reports, besides exceeding in their sensuous detail those in "The Glance," also recollect the misguided zeal of Herbert's "Affliction I" but now disarmed of its potential treachery: "My thoughts did swim in Comforts" is not a prelude to a series of severe renunciations but an unmistakable sign of the poet's election. Vaughan carries that recognition right through to the poem's end where the conclusion, with its resounding echo of Herbert's dedicatory challenge prefacing *The Temple* to see *"who shall best sing thy name"* (l. 4), argues that the younger poet is presenting himself to be in every way his master's "match":

> Thus fed by thee [God], who dost all beings nourish,
> My wither'd leafs again look green and flourish,
> I shine and shelter underneath thy wing
> Where sick with love I strive thy name to sing,
> Thy glorious name! which grant I may so do
> That these may be thy *Praise*, and my *Joy* too.   (ll. 21-26)

"Mount of Olives" begins the process of canonizing the *"lively Figure"* of the regenerated self, but the poem is an intermediary, rather than a final, step between Bethlehem and heaven. Emblematically and spatially, it asks the reader, as Vaughan has asked the communicant, to direct his thoughts vertically; and insofar as the figure of the poet feels increasingly responsive to God's grace and reflects this attitude in the creation of his verse, he, too, participates in and even serves as a measuring point to chart this movement. The concluding sweep is reserved for Part II. "Ascension-day," the opening poem in that volume, inaugurates this action just as the final, imaginative preparation by the communicant on his way to receiving "those sacred and mystical Elements to that blessed end for which they were ordained" (p. 158) begins with a meditation on Christ's Ascension. "Call to mind," Vaughan tells us in *The Mount of Olives*,

> his Joyful resurrection, his most accomplished conquest, and triumph over the world, death and hell; his most gracious and familiar conversation with his Apostles before his Ascension, with his most loving and comfortable carriage towards them at his departure, *leading them out as farre as* Bethanie, *and lifting up his hands, and blessing them.* (p. 158)

In "Ascension-day," the poet walks among Christ's apostles. One of Vaughan's more astonishing performances, it begins, as Alan Rudrum notes,[51] by fusing lines from the Book of John and the Epistle of James which together help to unify the poet and Christ in their upward flight:

> Lord Jesus! with what sweetness and delights,
> Sure, holy hopes, high joys and quickning flights
> Dost thou feed thine! O thou! the hand that lifts
> To him, who gives all good and perfect gifts.   (p. 481, ll. 1-4)

The muted echo from John, partially occluded by the more familiar echo from James ("every good gift and every perfect gift is from above" [l. 17]), is Christ's remark to his disciples, "And I, if I be lifted up from the earth, will draw all *men* unto me" (John 12:32). But the way Vaughan blends his Biblical sources with the vocative address suggests that it is Christ's, not God's, hand that is doing the lifting, and the "him" being lifted is the poet, who, with heaven's touch, now "gives all good and perfect gifts": the eclipsed portion of Christ's words—"will draw all *men* unto me"—figure as the "gifts" that the poet extends to others in his efforts to lift them to heaven. With recourse to the Bible, the orthodox reading can, of course, be established (God is lifting Christ who gives all good and perfect gifts), but the point of the swift, twisting beginning is that the poet, who feels himself to be "a sharer in thy victory" (l. 8), quickly dramatizes his "independencie upon all others" except Christ, to whom he is now "sealed."

"Very little indebted to George Herbert," the poem is an "original achievement"[52]—at least in its use of poetic material. Once the Shelley-like somersault into the eternal present is performed (ll. 9-14), Vaughan gives us a re-vision of all of Mark 16, part of which is prescribed by *The Book of Common Prayer* to be read on that holy day. Besides conflating the first days of Genesis with the early days of the apostles, Vaughan performs one substantive change in Mark; he excises Christ's

---

[51] *CPHV*, p. 588, ll. 3-4n.
[52] Louis L. Martz, "The Action of the Self," in *Metaphysical Poetry*, ed. Malcolm Bradbury and David Palmer (London: Edward Arnold, 1970), p. 117.

harsh words to his disciples who "believed not them which had seen [Jesus] after he was risen" (l. 14). Faith is not at issue here. Indeed, a questioning note of any sort would only undermine the purpose of the poem, which is to celebrate the poet as one of Christ's original worshippers, arriving early at a scene still savoring of the savior:

> I greet thy Sepulchre, salute thy Grave,
> That blest inclosure, where the Angels gave
> The first glad tidings of thy early light,
> And resurrection from the earth and night.
> I see that morning in thy Converts tears,
> Fresh as the dew, which but this dawning wears[!]
> I smell her spices, and her ointment yields,
> As rich a scent as the now Primros'd-fields:
> The Day-star smiles, and light with the deceast,
> Now shines in all the Chambers of the East.   (ll. 15-24)

Within the festive structure of *Silex*, this poem, like the day it commemorates, is designed to open "the kingdom of heaven to all believers."[53] Unlike Part I, dominated by the sense of Christ's suffering and His Passion, Part II begins with an unmediated vision of the past, one in which the speaker and the early heroes of faith are no longer separated by a vast channel of time ("Corruption") and a religion that insinuates that all miracles have ceased ("Religion"):

> Thy forty days more secret commerce here,
> After thy death and Funeral, so clear
> And indisputable, shews to my sight
> As the Sun doth, which to those days gave light.
> I walk the fields of *Bethani* which shine
> All now as fresh as *Eden*, and as fine.   (ll. 33-37)

The opening sequence of poems in Part II all play on and expand the enthusiastic statements of "Ascension-day" to assure the reader that the poet's sense of election is more than a momentary rapture; it is also probably the finest sequence

---

[53] Anthony Sparrow, *A Rationale Upon the Book of Common Prayer* (London, 1655), p. 77.

of verse Vaughan ever wrote. With heaven opened, there assumes a regular "commerce," as Vaughan says in "The Star," between the Father of Lights and the poet. "Ascension-Hymn" describes how the "Walk to the skie / Even in this life" (ll. 10-11) is accomplished, while in "They are all gone into the world of light," the poet meditates on the recent ascension of his dead friends. "White-Sunday," celebrated only a week later in the Church calendar, places the poet again in the position of one of the early apostles now receiving the Pentecostal flames, and the sequel to that, "The Proffer," shows him battling to retain his "Crown." Finally, "Cock-crowing" and "The Star" expand the celebration of light into the Book of Nature: in the first, the echo from James—"every good gift . . . cometh down from the Father of lights"—is recollected in the opening apostrophe, "Father of lights! what Sunnie seed / What glance of day hast thou confined / Into this bird?"; and the second redefines the poet as an able lecturer in cosmic sympathy.

The devotional antecedents to the heightened sense of worship in this sequence can probably, with a few Hermetic modifications, be traced back to Ficino; but the celebrations of divine light and the poet's enlightenment also reveal Vaughan's "troping" "The Glance" of his master and thereby placing himself in the center of God's vision. Not only is the younger author everywhere surrounded by a radiance exceeding that described by Herbert, but he also plays deliberately with the "thousand suns" of heaven which in "The Glance" Herbert has reserved only for the elect after Judgment Day: "When thou shalt look us out of pain, / And one aspect of thine spend in delight / More than a thousand sunnes disburse in light, / In heav'n above" (ll. 21-24). Vaughan discovers this experience in the immediate present where the dazzling brightness—"A thousand Suns, / Though seen at once,"—easily outshines the account given by Herbert:

Wellcome white day! a thousand Suns,
Though seen at once, were black to thee;

> For after their light, darkness comes,
> But thine shines to eternity.   ("White Sunday," p. 485, ll. 1-4)

Equally remarkable is how in "Cock-crowing" Vaughan "matches" and excels his master in his praise of God by conflating the opening lines of "Love I" ("Immortall Love, author of this great frame") and "Love II" ("Immortall Heat, O let thy greater flame") to achieve an even greater sense of God's love penetrating and inflaming the frame of the universe:

> O thou immortall light and heat!
> Whose hand so shines through all this frame,
> That by the beauty of the seat,
> We plainly see, who made the same.
>   Seeing thy seed abides in me,
>   Dwell thou in it, and I in thee.   (p. 488, pp. 19-24)

Last of all, the reversal of roles—or the sense of Herbert and Vaughan being equally matched in Christ—is neatly effected in "The Palm-tree," a poem that serves as a coda to this opening sequence on the Ascension. Vaughan begins as he began "The Match," by calling to his "Dear friend," who in this case is asked to "sit down, and bear awhile this shade / As I have yours long since" (ll. 1-2). We need not restrict the appellation to Herbert, but it is also hard to escape the association. The only "friend" elsewhere referred to in *Silex*, Herbert is also the only one in whose "shade" Vaughan has rested for any length of time; and now after the devotional "heat" of the first seven lyrics during which time the younger author has fully established himself as a recipient of divine favor—favor essential to the poet who "desires to excel in this kinde of *Hagiography*, or holy writing" (Preface to *Silex*, p. 392)—it is appropriate, witty, and generous that the young author should turn to offer his "Dear friend" some of the fruits.

In this context, "The Palm-tree" resembles a giant pun more than the emblem poem for which it is usually taken to be. Serving as an umbrella for the poet's accomplishments, the lyric reveals Vaughan delivering a capsule version of his readings in Nieremberg, Eucherius, and the *Vita Paulini* in a voice that mimics his master's in "Love Unknown." None of the lore is extraordinary, but the doctrine is absolutely sound, with his definition of a saint's life based on a perfectly proper and peaceful imitation of Christ. The closing stanza, though, finishes with a bit of bravado that distinguishes Vaughan in dialogue with another and returns us, once more, to Herbert's "Obedience." The older poet had concluded his offer for another to join him in the holy way by remarking how it would be "to both our goods"—his as well as his companion's—and as a further enticement, he suggests that the sum of their combined achievements would be greater than their separate efforts; together their lines would be "by winged souls / Entered for both, farre above their desert" (ll. 44-45). In the last stanza of "The Palm-tree," Vaughan plays with the complementary dimensions of their salvation in the garland he promises to gather for his friend:

> Here is their faith too, which if you will keep
> When we two part, I will a journey make
> To pluck a Garland hence, while you do sleep
> And weave it for your head against you wake.
>
> (p. 491, ll. 25-28)

Symbolizing the twin accomplishments of piety and poetry, the victory wreath naturally calls to mind the triumphant values Vaughan discovers in Herbert and reincarnates in *Silex*, itself a garland testifying "to both our goods" and in a sense woven while his master is asleep: completed, it will provide further evidence of Herbert's worth and protect his "head against you wake"—that is, at Judgment Day. But Vaughan does not leave the compliment in such general terms. Two poems later in his journey, he presents "The Garland," a poem in which he gives a miniature account of his conversion, and the "story" he weaves includes, once again, the (now) suspiciously familiar figure of "a dead man" (l. 26) who addresses the poet "at the height of [a] Careire" (l. 25) of fruitless living and "posie" making to warn him of the vanities he is pursuing. Slyly recollective, "The Garland" enshrines the dead man by enshrining the fruitful encounter between the two, one that is further sealed and elevated by the fact that the advice the regenerated poet gives to others is a repetition of what he has received from Herbert.

In a popular nun's prayer of the seventeenth century, the penitent speaker asks to be kept "reasonably sweet": "I do not want to be a Saint—some of them are so hard to live with." One effect of Vaughan's "coronation" in the Ascension series is to make a handful of his later preacherly poems like "The Ass," "The Daughter of *Herodias*," and parts of "The Timber" and "Mary Magdalene" hard to live with in a way that few of his weak performances in *Silex* 1650 are. Rigorously sober, defensive, and plaintive to the point of irritability, they give the sour side of sanctification and picture a surrogate priest who has turned poetry into statement by trying too hard at his task. But the posture, and the failures stemming from it, are of one piece with the attitude that has helped to shape the best verses in Part II (almost certainly greater in number than the most accomplished performances in *Silex* 1650), and together they prepare the way for the final "politure and sweetning of the divine image" in the coronation sequence at the end:

> Lastly, close up these thoughts with a serious and awful meditation of that great and joyful, though dreadful day of his second coming to judgement, promised by himself, and affirmed at the time of his Ascension by the two men in white apparel.
> (*Mount of Olives*, p. 158)

Recollecting Christ's promise in its allusion to the "two men in white" (l. 59), "Ascension-day" links the beginning with the end, the opening of *Silex* II with the poems on the Last Things. Vaughan completes the two parts of *Silex* by having them conform to the overall plan in *The Mount of Olives* for preparing the communicant for the holy sacraments, the point at which an imitation of Christ gives way to an identity of the individual with Christ. But Vaughan does not leave his readers in a state of hypostatic ecstasy, nor, like Herbert, does he terminate his collection with a heavenly banquet: "You must sit down sayes Love, and taste my meat: / So I did sit and eat" ("Love III"). The communion prepared for on both a large and small scale, within the full arc of *Silex* and the narrower range of the poems immediately leading up to "The Feast"—"The day of Judgement," "Psalm 65" (used in the Introit to the Funeral Mass), "The Throne," and "Death"—remains an imagined possibility rather than an immediate experience. "O come away, / Make no delay, / Come while my heart is clean & steddy!" ("The Feast," ll. 1-3) testifies to the speaker's readiness, but the poem refrains from fulfilling these expectations. Indeed, the whole feast sequence is deprived of its concluding role by the fact that it terminates when we are still eight poems from the end.

In its place, however, we are given a vision hardly less rewarding. Led toward becoming a communicant in Christ, the reader is redirected toward being a sharer in the poet's victory in Christ as he prepares to take his place among "the triumphant saints."[54] Passing through the poems on the Last Things, we participate not in the speaker's death but in the form of his recovery—an experience that serves to intensify further the author's sense of his own elected status: "But *the God of the spirits of all flesh*," Vaughan writes in a gloss on these poems, "hath granted me a further use of *mine*, then I did look for in the *body*" (Preface to *Silex*, p. 392). The typological perspective in *Silex* in which "the speaker's present experience becomes a type of his perfected life at the Apocalypse"[55] comes close to finding its fulfillment in the final few poems when the poet is still "in the *body*." Although Vaughan continues to create "a twin'd wreath of *grief* and *praise*" ("The Wreath," p. 539, l. 9)—that is a poetry that sustains the values of humility—the finest lyric in the series serves as a type for all previous nature poems in its presentation of the speaker as both an exemplary reader of God's book and an emblem of the illuminated soul, while the pe-

---

[54] Barbara Lewalski, *Protestant Poetics and the Seventeenth-Century Religious Lyric* (Princeton: Princeton Univ. Press, 1979), p. 325.
[55] Ibid., pp. 324-25.

nultimate verse in the collection attempts to turn the poet's life into a sacred text for others to contemplate.

In "The Water-fall," Vaughan regards nature with a "pensive eye" (l. 14). Easily penetrating its shimmering, vital surface to "Lodge in thy mystical, deep streams!" (l. 28), the poet plays with the underlying freedom of the water in its hieroglyphic descent and quick ascension. Being called and in turn calling the reader, he traces in speech all the hesitant but divinely orchestrated movements of the stream—the sudden forward cascade of dimeters, the slow retention of liquid sounds carried gently over the enjambment—that describe "*a quickness, which my God hath kist*" ("Quickness," p. 538, l. 20) and a mind perfectly at ease with its subject, which in this instance reaches out to embrace poetry, nature, and death. If Vaughan seems at his most Wordsworthian here, it is because both poets, however much they might disagree over origins, were deeply committed to retrieving from nature intimations of immortality—"the deep murmurs through times silent stealth":

> With what deep murmurs through times silent stealth
> Doth thy transparent, cool and watry wealth
>   Here flowing fall,
>   And chide, and call,
> As if his liquid, loose Retinue staid
> Lingring, and were of this steep place afraid,
>   The common pass
>   Where, clear as glass,
>   All must descend
>   Not to an end:
> But quickened by this deep and rocky grave,
> Rise to a longer course more bright and brave.
>
>   (p. 537, ll. 1-12)

But the celebration of nature here becomes ultimately for Vaughan (as for Wordsworth) a celebration of the inspired mind, both in its immediate perceptions and in its growth. Vaughan refines the dazzling display of language into a meditation on creation; the spirit that moves in these waters reminds him both of the spirit "in the beginning" that "moved upon the face of the waters" (Gen. 1:1-2) and of the creative potential given only to those regenerated by that other fountain of life, Christ:

> What sublime truths, and wholesome themes,
> Lodge in thy mystical, deep streams!
> Such as dull man can never finde
> Unless that Spirit lead his minde,
> Which first upon thy face did move,
> And hatch'd all with his quickning love. (ll. 27-32)

The mind led by "that Spirit" is the mind in growth, and "The Water-fall" stands as Vaughan's measure of his own development. The ability of his speaker to be able to interpret the waterfall allegorically—as a fountain of life—exactly reverses the situation in "Regeneration" where the poet-pilgrim is only a figure in an allegory, pondering, without really understanding, the cistern he has been drawn to by the sound of "a little Fountain" (l. 49). The bonds of sin which shadow the figure in that poem are conclusively released in "The Water-fall":

> O my invisible estate,
> My glorious liberty, still late!
> Thou art the Channel my soul seeks,
> Not this with Cataracts and Creeks. (ll. 37-40)

The "last" poem in *Silex* (if we think of "L'Envoy" as an afterword) is ostensibly addressed to God's other book; but "To the Holy Bible" delivers instead a valedictory address in which the poet, who has written so many elegies for others, finally composes his own epitaph and thus inscribes as a permanent lesson to his readers the story of his regeneration:

> O book! lifes guide! how shall we part,
> And thou so long seiz'd of my heart!
> Take this last kiss, and let me weep
> True thanks to thee, before I sleep. (p. 540, ll. 1-4)

Immaculately ordered, the lines that follow provide a final, clarifying vision of the author of *Silex*. An index to the poet's life—at least of the life he incarnated through his art—the lyric retraces his fall from childhood innocence into a "rash" youth, a descent interrupted only by "A sudden and most searching ray / Into my soul" (ll. 20-21) from the Bible, which developed into a struggle with sin and then into an eventual triumph over temptation. The paradigm is certainly a familiar one in Vaughan, indeed in most Christian writings. What is striking here is how the recollective view tidies up the past, sharpens the outlines of the author's life, and in effect retrieves the idea of childhood by placing it in a context that looks forward rather than backward—a context that presents "those early days" not as the last stages of innocence but the first step in the poet's regeneration. Like Dante's pilgrim who has traveled the distance to God, the fully regenerated speaker in *Silex* now measures personal time from the prospect of eternity. Within the developmental scheme of *Silex*, moreover, this version of *felix culpa* also neutralizes and rescues a view of the past that has even been fading before the poet's eyes. Clearly glimpsed in "The Retreate" (*Silex* 1650), the vision of innocence and the tender recollection it inspires shrinks noticeably in "Childe-hood" (*Silex* 1655): "I cannot reach it, and my striving eye / Dazles at it, as at eternity" (ll. 1-2)—a perspective further clouded by the intruding practices of "worldlings." But in "To the Holy Bible" the intimacy reappears where it is now directed not to a passing memory of "Angel-infancy" but to the story of the poet's regeneration in which infancy is only a prelude to "Fruition, union, glory, [and] life" (l. 31).

Not completely forgotten, the Bible in this epitaph occupies a protective position similar to the "genii" who preside over the casket of Elizabeth in Vaughan's lament on the death of the "Second Daughter to his late Majestie": it consecrates the grounds around the place of his approaching death just as it helped to show him "the way" in life; and insofar as the Bible and the poem share a common purpose in serving as a "lifes guide"—the one to the poet during his life, the other to the reader interpreting the progress of the poet's life—they work together to transform the Silurist into a shrine (like Elizabeth) and *Silex* into something of a sacred feast. Hoping to *"turn many to righteousness* [and thus] *shine like the stars for ever and ever"* (Preface to *Silex*, p. 391), Vaughan prepares the reader for a communion with Christ by structuring his collection to parallel the approach to the sacraments. But the feast that he finally provides to lure others to God is the *"lively Figure"* of a converted poet, whose discovery of "Gladness, and peace, and hope, and love" (l. 27)—a line taken almost *verbatim* from Herbert's "Prayer I"—reminds us of the ultimate rewards of "the match" struck between two poets in Christ.

CHAPTER SIX

Spitting out the Phlegm: The Conflict of Voices in *Silex Scintillans*

> There must be some "sons," and some "servants," to prophesy to, to whom these Prophets may be sent, to whom this prophecy may come. "All flesh" may not be cut out into tongues; some left for ears, some auditors needs. Else a Cyclopian Church will grow upon us, where all were speakers, nobody heard another.
> —Lancelot Andrewes, "Sermon Preached on May 24, 1618"

HERBERT'S "Obedience" is central to understanding the personal, poetic, and political links that developed between Vaughan and his master. Indeed, it would only be a slight exaggeration to suggest that the poem contains in miniature the proper "code" of behavior for all Christian poets, but especially for the poet whom the Anglican Herbert viewed as his companion in Christ. Without actually sealing a tribe in the manner of Jonson, he nonetheless called for a tribe of his own and so returned Jonson's Biblical metaphor (Rev. 7:8) to its original spiritual source. There were, of course, many differences in being sealed to Herbert rather than to Jonson, to a devotional lyricist rather than to an ethically minded and worldly poet, and among these one of the most important surely centers on the kind of language an author chooses in attempting to establish the correct relationship to his audience, human and divine alike. In "Obedience," Herbert singles out for special criticism the "wrangler" (l. 15), a disputatious caviler still tied to the pleasures of the world however these might be defined. In the poem immediately following "Obedience," entitled "Conscience," Herbert further reveals his contempt for the noisy quarreler by explicitly favoring a devout silence—thoughts as harmonious as "A noiselesse sphere"

(l. 8)—to the unruly chatter of his prattling conscience; and in "The Familie," a poem of obvious importance to a younger author aware of his filial ties to his master, the older poet spells out in no uncertain terms what he assumes should be God's response toward the obstreperous and contentious: "Turn out these wranglers, which defile thy seat: / For where thou dwellest all is neat" (ll. 7-8). The impious generate only purposeless noise; they ignore altogether the purposeful message contained in quiet penance, a devotional posture whose meaning Herbert explores in the paradox: "What is so shrill as silent tears?" (l. 20). The paradox also forms the beginning of Vaughan's "Admission" ("How shrill are silent tears?"), a poem whose title puns on the notion that admission into Christ's family is determined by the ability of the person to be able to make the proper admission from the heart.

Herbert's attention to quiet is strictly doctrinaire given the commonplace Christian belief that the meek shall inherit the earth, but the doctrine itself could become a problem to an Anglican poet writing during a time when, to many in his Church at least, it seemed that every one except the meek was in the process of taking over the earth. Annabel Patterson has recently summed up the dilemma facing the devotional polemicist of the seventeenth century in two juxtaposed and contradictory verses from Proverbs 26:4, 5: "Answer not a fool according to his folly, lest thou be like unto him. Answer a fool according to his folly, lest he be wise in his own conceit."[1] Taking these alternative responses as defining, respectively, Anglican and Puritan rhetorical strategies during the 1640s, Patterson subsequently demonstrates how these distinctive attitudes were reversed by Samuel Parker in 1669 when "the moderation formerly associated with the Anglican position was no longer an adequate response to enthusiasm; he identified with the position defined and defended by Milton, the Juvenalian satirist and scourge who nevertheless believes

[1] Patterson, *Marvell and the Civic Crown* (Princeton: Princeton Univ. Press, 1978), pp. 181-82.

that his anger is not incompatible with 'Meekness and Charity' " (p. 187).

Parker's usurpation of a Miltonic method was perhaps inevitable given the treacherous terrain on which the polemicist walked, but for a poet like Vaughan, who began his career on a Juvenalian note and then subsequently "converted" to the school of Herbert with its distaste for "wranglers," it was not so easy to gloss over the potential "incompatibility" of these responses. The hawk threatened to displace the dove; the voice of the Church Militant might easily become the voice of a militant only. Always conscious of the conflict in his verse between "*Philomel*" and the "hoarse bird of Night," Vaughan further refines and attempts to reconcile these opposing attitudes in *Silex* as he incorporates the savagery of political attack within the meeker posture of the Herbertian devotional poet. As the defender of a Church "now trodden under foot" (p. 186), the Silurist speaks out but always at the risk of destroying the solitude, moderation, and quiet that were the traditional values of the Anglican Church. As one of the "sons" to whom a "seer" was sent, Vaughan needed also to be a good listener; otherwise he might only contribute further to the growth of a "Cyclopian Church . . . where all were speakers [and] nobody heard another."[2]

One consequence of this double impulse toward fusing the voice of Juvenal with Herbert's, the hawk with the dove, is the extraordinary role the auditory imagination plays in the religious verse. Along with his master, Vaughan was scrupulously attentive to the sound of language, or rather the language of sounds, and even though he is principally remembered for the stunning ocular effects in his verse,[3] he none-

[2] *Ninety-Six Sermons by . . . Lancelot Andrewes*, ed. J. P. Parkinson, 5 vols. (Oxford: John Henry Parker, 1843-1860), 3 (1850): 314.

[3] Discussions of Vaughan's visionary power date back to the nineteenth century when the poet was thought a precursor of Wordsworth and continue into the present to cover the full range of Vaughan criticism, regardless of whether the poet is viewed as a nature worshipper, religious mystic, Renaissance hermetist, or simply as an author of some fine lines. Representative examples of each include: *The Works in Prose and Verse of Henry Vaughan,*

theless falls within an established line of Christian thought, intensified by the Protestant Reformation, that regarded the ear and not the eye as the superior sensory organ.[4] The basic authority for elevating one over the other was, of course, the familiar cry of the Apostle Paul that "faith *cometh* by hearing" (Romans 10:17), a claim repeated by Christians as distant in time as Augustine and Bunyan and asserted with increasing frequency during Vaughan's day when the visible Church was forced underground. The poet's own translation from the fifth-century Bishop Eucherius's *The World Contemned* dilates on the central reason for valuing sound over sight:

> Why with so much dotage do we fixe our Eyes upon the deceitfull lookes of temporal things? Why do we rest our selves upon those thornes onely, which wee see beneath us? Is it the Eye alone that wee live by? Is there nothing usefull about us but that wanderer? We live also by the eare, and at that Inlet wee receive the

---

ed. Alexander B. Grosart, 4 vols. (Lancashire: The Fuller Worthies Library, 1871), 2:13-14 and 68-88 in the Intro.; Itrat-Husain, *The Mystical Element in the Metaphysical Poets of the Seventeenth Century* (London: Oliver and Boyd, 1948), pp. 210-36; Patrick Grant, *The Transformation of Sin: Studies in Donne, Herbert, Vaughan, and Traherne* (Amherst: Univ. of Massachusetts Press, 1974), pp. 155-60, and E. C. Pettet, *Of Paradise and Light* (Cambridge: Cambridge Univ. Press, 1960), pp. 3-11 *passim*.

[4] William G. Madsen, *From Shadowy Types to Truth: Studies in Milton's Symbolism* (New Haven: Yale Univ. Press, 1968), pp. 155-62, gives a brief but excellent account of classical and Christian attitudes toward the rival senses and cites the lines I quote below from Eucherius to place Vaughan in that tradition. Objecting to Madsen's placement of Vaughan with Humanists rather than with Neoplatonists, Florence Sandler, "The Ascents of the Spirit: Henry Vaughan on the Atonement," *JEGP* 73 (1974): 209-26 has argued that "no reader of Vaughan will be reassured by [this quotation], for it is doubtful that he took to heart Eucherius's maxim, let along attached to it the significance that the Protestant Reformers had placed upon the ministry of the Word" (pp. 209-10). Barbara Lewalski, *Protestant Poetics and the Seventeenth-Century Religious Lyric* (Princeton: Princeton Univ. Press, 1979), pp. 317-51, esp. pp. 332 and 493, demonstrates Vaughan's pervasive debt to Protestant Reformers; but even if there is still room for disputing theological influences on this most eclectic of authors, I hope to show in this chapter how Vaughan, as a poet, was certainly responsive in his verse to the auditory imagination, a sensitivity with inevitable theological overtones that places him in a line with Protestant Reformers, like Luther and Calvin, who valued the "inner voice" over visual ceremony.

glad tydings of Salvation, which fill us with earnest grones for our glorious liberty and the consummation of the promises. (p. 326)

Not every image leads to a vision of eternity. The Odyssean eye could easily be tricked in its wanderings while the humbler ear offered some of the securer comforts of home: always open to the "glad tydings of Salvation," it seemed a surer passage for Christian truth to enter. As the endings of both "Regeneration" and "The Collar" tell us, it is the presence of God's voice, not a vision of God in His works, that serves finally to calm the questing or rebellious spirit. Moreover, a person need only hear the sounds of his own "earnest grones" to realize that a "*Hymning Circulation*" ("The Morning-watch," p. 424, l. 10) had once more been restored between the chime of heaven and the tongue of man.

But if Vaughan followed Herbert in his belief in speech as the fundamental point of mediation between God and man, he exceeded his master in his deeper attention to both the moral attitudes reflected in a person's tone of voice and the corruptibility of language itself. Like his contemporary, Milton, he was keenly aware that the fall of man brought about also a fallen language in which words surrendered the pristine clarity of their original signifying powers to the corrupt habits of the flesh. In his well known poem "The Retreate," for instance, the author looks back to the past through a haze created partly by language, and he indicts the tongue for its Satanic powers to wound the conscience and soil the other senses: Adamic innocence exists in a time

> Before I taught my tongue to wound
> My Conscience with a sinfull sound,
> Or had the black art to dispence
> A sev'rall sinne to ev'ry sence,
> But felt through all this fleshly dresse
> Bright *shootes* of everlastingnesse. (p. 419, ll. 15-20)

Vaughan seems almost to Platonize language here when he divides it into two realms in which the "black art" of the fallen tongue stands in direct contrast with the flesh that feels "Bright *shootes* of everlastingnesse." The distinction is an absolutely traditional one, of course, with clear verbal ramifications. Dante and Milton assign the greatest linguistic confusion to the characters in hell and the purest modes of communion to those in heaven, and Vaughan follows suit. His one view into "that dark, dreadful pit" in *Silex* ("The Relapse," p. 433, l. 3) concentrates almost solely on the cries of the damned while his many visions of heavenly splendor are often inaugurated by song.[5] "Howling is the noyse of hell," Donne reminds us, "singing the voyce of heaven."[6]

Given these traditionally polar views of language, Vaughan's own affiliation with Juvenal and Herbert, and the immediate historical context in which the Welsh poet wrote, it is hardly surprising to discover the presence of two voices in *Silex*. There are perhaps others, but these two seem particularly conspicuous in the way the poet plays one off against the other, with each receiving clearer definition in the light of its opposite and both serving as a synecdoche of sorts for a broad spectrum of human behavior with precise moral equivalents. The first is the voice of fallen Adam, whose language, when unrestrained, could easily move toward chaos. Inevitably associated with the Tower of Babel, the confusion of tongues that radiates from the entire species also identifies the particular individual:

> For whereas our mindes are distracted with varietie of opinions, and our hearts carried headlong to divers inordinate lusts; so the tongue should likewise bee confounded with many base and barbarous languages, some of them very harsh in pronunciation, that

---

[5] See, for instance, "The Search" (p. 407), "Me thought I heard one singing thus" (l. 74), which transforms the "call" at the end of Herbert's "The Collar" to emphasize the shift to song (ll. 75-94), one that prepares the reader for "another world" (l. 95). "Ascension-day" (ll. 9-14) also depends on the sudden intrusion of "song" into the pentameter norm to signal the spirit's ascent.

[6] *The Sermons of John Donne*, ed. George R. Potter and Evelyn M. Simpson, 10 vols. (Berkeley: Univ. of California Press, 1953-1962), 7 (1954): 70.

a man must wrong his owne visiage, and disfigure himselfe to speake them.⁷

Vaughan only occasionally draws such caricatures through language, but the many changes he rings on "loud" in *Silex*—and their association with the fallen—show him equally sensitive to the disruptive and barbarous potential of human speech. Whether describing the impulsive murmurings of the heart or the more conspicuous clamorings of God's foes, the young poet, to be sure, knew the tones of disobedience.

The other voice of course is Christ's, whose sounds Vaughan identifies with all true followers of God. "How comes He?" asks Lancelot Andrewes, "He shall come down like the dew in a fleece of wool,' and that is scarce to be heard. 'He, He shall not roar nor cry, nor His voice be heard out into the street.' "⁸ In *Silex*, Christ, while potentially present to all who are obedient, is also "scarce to be heard": the ear needs to be finely tuned to catch the whisperings at the end of "Regeneration" or the "still, soft call" at the center of "The Night." Nowhere in the verse does He roar or cry. As the antitype to fallen man's "babble," moreover, Christ's voice speaks instead with clarity and precision, and his language has a palpable "softness" that contrasts with either the crudeness of man's sometimes clumsy cadences or the shrill tightening of accents that occurs with intemperance. During the mid-century strife, Vaughan thought of God's Word as his sole guide—"Were not thy word (dear Lord!) my light, / How would I run to endless night" ("The Men of War," p. 517, ll. 9-10)—and as a model for imitation, it had only one tone and one message: "Let *Mildness*, and *Religion* guide thee out, / If truth be thine, what needs a brutish force?" ("Rules *and* Lessons," p. 437,

---

⁷ Godfrey Goodman, *The Fall of Man* (London, 1616), p. 293. For a survey of Renaissance commentaries describing the effects of the fall on the human tongue, see Beverly Sherry's helpful essay "Speech in *Paradise Lost*," *Milton Studies*, VIII, ed. James D. Simmonds (Pittsburgh: Univ. of Pittsburgh Press, 1975), pp. 247-66.

⁸ *Ninety-Six Sermons by . . . Lancelot Andrewes*, 3 (1850): 267. Andrewes is quoting respectively from Psalms 72:6 and Isa. 42:2.

ll. 38-39). Indeed, to an author claiming a distant descent from Elijah, the very means by which that prophet, in fact, received the call of God would certainly have served as an ironic gloss on the "brutish force" of Puritan enthusiasm:

> And, behold, the Lord passed by, and a great and strong Wind rent the mountains, and brake in pieces the rocks before the Lord; *but* the Lord *was* not in the wind: and after the wind an earthquake; *but* the Lord *was* not in the earthquake:
> And after the earthquake a fire; *but* the Lord *was* not in the fire: and after the fire a still small voice. (1 Kings 19:11-12)

To see how Vaughan interpolates these different voices into his verse is to appreciate that his poetry is not always so haphazardly composed as is sometimes thought. The spiritual fullness of the Edenic past and the resurrected future, for instance, is repeatedly defined by the way language verges on silence and highlights a present riddled with the strains of verbal abuse and confusion. "Religion" (pp. 404-5) and "*Isaacs* Marriage" (pp. 408-10), Vaughan's most complete portrayals of an earthly paradise in the devotional verse, evoke many of the familiar, Christian-pastoral views of an harmonious ideal where man communes with both angel and animal; they also underscore the necessity of civilized discourse made possible only by "soft" voices. Both poems take considerable care to describe an ideal tone of speech; both counterpoint these descriptions with a disturbing cacophony of sounds. Whether it is the "mild, chast language" of Rebecca (l. 41) or the soothing, natural tones of God's "*soft voice* as He speaks in "*fire, / Whirle-winds*, and *Clouds*" (ll. 17-18), each of these ritual acts of communion have been destroyed by the intruding noise pollution: the "False *Ecchoes*, and Confused sounds" of religious disputes ("Religion," l. 38) and the "*Antick* crowd / Of young, gay swearers, with their needlesse, lowd / Retinue" ("*Isaacs* Marriage," ll. 21-23). The possibility of a quiet "Conf'rence in these daies" ("Religion," l. 20) is a dream as far removed as the golden age itself. In each poem, also, Vaughan gives his verbal thematics a summary twist. He sharpens his resentment in "Religion" by acidly concluding, "Nor must we for the Kernell crave / Because most voices like the *shell*"—the kernel at the heart of Puritanism is as hollow as the "False *Ecchoes*" it generates—while in the second poem he underscores the current perversion of language by drawing a picture of a modern Adam in the "odde dull sutor" who spends his time coining "twenty / New sev'ral oathes, and Complements" (ll. 15-16): the act of naming has degenerated into the art of defaming.

Vaughan also extended his ideal of "soft" voices in the past into the future where he could further refine it into an image of quietude. One of his most anthologized poems, "Peace" describes a remote outpost of the elect more picturesque than sublime. Ordered, aesthetic, and still, the poem envisions a new "model army" neatly detached from any real acts of military destruction:

> My Soul, there is a Countrie
>   Far beyond the stars,
> Where stands a winged Centrie
>   All skilfull in the wars,
> There above noise, and danger
>   Sweet peace sits crown'd with smiles,
> And one born in a Manger
>   Commands the Beauteous files.   (p. 430, ll. 1-8)

The "noise, and danger" of the world have been mediated and transcended, not conquered, by Christ, whose "commands" create "Beauteous files" of order. Furthermore, as one who does not actually speak in the poem, Christ's smile seems to be a beckoning gesture of the silent rewards that await the obedient but which the speaker's sleeping soul has yet to enjoy (l. 10). The waking for which Vaughan prays is to the tranquility of Christ: the soul that sleeps in this poem can only hear the noise of life below.

Living in a world, though, "where all [things] mix and tyre" ("The Night," p. 523, l. 44), Vaughan rarely sculpted such statuesque visions of peace. More often, he would frame momentary communions against a larger backdrop of chaos and noise and heighten the tension of a poem by fusing antithetical attitudes toward sound with larger image patterns of contrasting light and darkness. "The Night," for instance, develops the paradox of speaking with the "Sun" (Christ) at midnight—a time naturally suited to hearing His voice—and in the central stanzas, five and six, darkness of night becomes the tent in which the poet listens to the private and selective voice of Christ's "still, soft call":

> Dear night! this worlds defeat;
> The stop to busie fools; cares check and curb;
> The day of Spirits; my souls calm retreat
>   Which none disturb!
> *Christs* progress, and his prayer time;
> The hours to which high Heaven doth chime.
>
> Gods silent, searching flight:
> When my Lords head is fill'd with dew, and all
> His locks are wet with the clear drops of night;
>   His still, soft call;
> His knocking time; The souls dumb watch,
> When Spirits their fair kinred catch.   (ll. 25-36)

God's "silent, searching flight" is a version of what Vaughan describes in "The Constellation" as "motion without noise"; it is a delicate spiritual hovering easily shattered for both poet and reader by the intruding noise of the larger world:

> Were all my loud, evil days
> Calm and unhaunted as is thy dark Tent,
> Whose peace but by some *Angels* wing or voice
>   Is seldom rent;
> Then I in Heaven all the long year
> Would keep, and never wander here.   (ll. 37-42)

The real "hauntings" here belong not to the whispering sounds of the night but to the loud utterances of the day. Temptation lurks "where the Sun / Doth all things wake" (ll. 43-44); without the ritualized communion with the "Sun" that should be occurring during the day in the form of traditional Anglican services, the wanderings of man cannot be checked. It is not up to Christ to increase the volume of His voice in His offer of salvation to man: "He shall not roar, nor cry, nor His voice be heard out into the street."

Wider in geographic scope but even more precise in the verbal distinctions it makes, "The Constellation" like "The Night," combines both auditory and visual senses to discriminate between proper and improper modes of religious behavior. The poem pairs off the "Fair, order'd lights whose motions without noise / Resembles those true Joys" of heaven (ll. 1-2) against the sounds this time created not just by the world at large but by the "zeale" (l. 40) of Puritan enthusiasm. Identified throughout with "Silence, and light" (l. 13), the stars serve as distant patterns of obedience for all to observe; they also serve as a means for the reader to measure and imagine degrees of human depravity during these war-torn years. The speaker comes across as an individual attentive to the constellation, and his meditative address and quiet ruminations at least imitate, if not equal, the serene motion of the stars. Man in general, though, gropes in an intermediary range of darkness associated with "Musick and mirth (if there be musick here)." In this case, music is no symbol for heavenly harmony in the traditional Pythagorean scheme; Vaughan's crystalline spheres are silent, and the sounds heard characterize only the sensual pleasures on which man slavishly depends:

> Musick and mirth (if there be musick here)
>   Take up, and tune his year,
> These things are Kin to him, and must be had,
>   Who kneels, or sighs a life is mad.   (p. 469, ll. 21-24)

This description of a general indifference to God and partially apprehended noise prepares us in turn for a further descent into the demonic particulars of Puritan behavior. More than halfway through the poem, Vaughan takes us deep into the center of his version of the *Inferno*:

> But here Commission'd by a black self-wil
>   The sons the father kil,
> The Children Chase the mother, and would heal
>   The wounds they give, by crying, zeale.
>
> Then Cast her bloud, and tears upon thy book
>   Where they for fashion look,
> And like that Lamb which had the Dragons voice
>   Seem mild, but are known by their noise.   (ll. 37-44)

"Silence and light" have been extinguished by the cries of the damned. Here, the inversion of all moral codes, symbolized in Dante by Satan's inverted posture (as viewed from God's perspective), finds its equivalent in the deadly primitive rites of offspring killing their parents. Like the devil, the children repudiate their source of life, and again, like him, they dissemble and feign; but their failure to keep silent gives them away: they are "known by their noise" (l. 44). The dragon in their voice links them with the Beast of the Apocalypse (Rev. 13:11) who, for a while, is allowed to overpower God's saints before being driven to perdition. After such a journey, Vaughan returns to contemplate the heavens with increased urgency, but he does not forget the role of sound in the poem. The concluding line of "The Constellation" locates the restoration of social order at a time only when man can "say," not cry, "*Where God is, all agree*" (l. 60); the manner is as important as the matter. Speech cannot be separated from action. Without a return to simple, familiar (and Vaughan would say humane) discourse, it is both foolish and hypocritical to preach of Christ and religious toleration.

Vaughan's sharpest division of voices belongs to his finest "war poem"—"Abels blood." Indeed, one of the best of the many poems about mid-century strife, Vaughan's attempts to balance the cries of vengeance against a plea for patience, and the result testifies to the poet's ability to imagine, even to identify with, both impulses. Like Milton's sonnet "On the Late Massacre in Piemont," "Abels blood" taxes God to protect the righteous and punish the wicked. Abel, of course, was the archetype of all martyrs; despite being murdered he was not silenced: his "blood crie[d] unto [God] from the ground" (Gen. 4:10) and put a curse on Cain. Vaughan begins by establishing the lines of continuity between past and present symbolized in the sound of Abel's cry that still rings loudly around the land:

> Sad, purple well! whose bubling eye
> Did first against a Murth'rer cry;
> Whose streams still vocal, still complain
>   Of bloody *Cain*,
> And now at evening are as red
> As in the morning when first shed.   (p. 523, ll. 1-6)

But after drawing the initial parallel, etched precisely in the scarlet image of the setting sun, Vaughan lets his auditory imagination work on the basic difference between the first murder and the present slaughter. Abel's voice is but a whisper when compared to the sounding complaints of the accumulated dead:

>   If single thou
> (Though single voices are but low,)
> Could'st such a shrill and long cry rear
> As speaks still in thy makers ear,
> What thunders shall those men arraign
> Who cannot count those they have slain,
> Who bath not in a shallow flood,
> But in a deep, wide sea of blood?
> A sea, whose lowd waves cannot sleep,
> But *Deep* still calleth upon *deep*:
> Whose urgent *sound* like unto that
> *Of many waters*, beateth at
> The everlasting doors above,
> Where souls behind the altar move,
> And with one strong, incessant cry
> Inquire *How long?* of the most high.   (ll. 7-23)

There is much to admire here poetically, particularly the sustained imagery of spreading blood: the streams of the third line are more than "a shallow flood" by the thirteenth, when they expand quickly into a "deep, wide sea" (l. 14) before they broaden into *"many waters"* (l. 18) that collectively beat on heaven's doors above. But the poet's voice also demands attention. One "long cry" (the sentence covers sixteen lines), Vaughan's initially low-pitched description quickly increases in volume and power through a series of verbal repetitions and appositional phrases that sweep forward and backward on their way to gathering energy for the "one strong, incessant cry" of *"How long?"* (ll. 21-22). One phrase fades impatiently into another—the *"Deep* still calleth upon [the] *deep"* (l. 16)—as the murmur of confusion builds steadily into a challenge of God's authority.

With the mention of "most high," though, the poem turns back on itself. Exactly halfway through (line twenty-three of the forty-four-line poem), the speaker redirects his attention to face the "Almighty Judge," and he adopts a new tone, a new voice, and a new message. Vaughan remembers that the blood of Abel is canceled by the blood of Christ (Heb. 12:14), a cancellation that penetrates into the fabric of the verse and results in a new address identical in length to the first one. The revisions begin theologically with the poet's assertion that at God's "just laws no just men grudge" (l. 25); they continue in the images of blood that now should remain "Speechless and calm" (l. 35); and they are summed up in the restrained posture of prayer the poet adopts throughout. The only cry to reach heaven should *"speak better things"* (l. 40), and Vaughan's does:

> Almighty Judge!
> At whose just laws no just men grudge;
> Whose blessed, sweet commands do pour
> Comforts and joys, and hopes each hour
> On those that keep them; O accept
> Of his vow'd heart, whom thou has kept
> From bloody men! and grant, I may
> That sworn memorial duly pay
> To thy bright arm, which was my light

> And leader through thick death and night!
>   I [Aye], may that flood,
> That proudly spilt and despis'd blood,
> Speechless and calm, as Infants sleep!
> Or if it watch, forgive and weep
> For those that spilt it! May no cries
> From the low earth to high Heaven rise,
> But what (like his, whose blood peace brings)
> Shall (when they rise) *speak better things*,
> Then *Abels* doth! may *Abel* be
> Still single heard, while these agree
> With his milde blood in voice and will,
> *Who* pray'd for those that did him kill!   (ll. 24-44)

Moreover, the second half of the poem seems literally to transform or "reform" in the light of Christ's "mild blood" the turbulent wake of voices in the first half of the poem. Clearly marked, each thought begins with an apostrophe (ll. 23, 27, 33, 37, and 41); each proceeds in a similar tone of penitence, with the poet concluding that Abel should still be "single heard" (l. 42)—to remind us of the sufferings of the slain—but that it is Christ whom we should follow, "not for revenge, but for 'remission of sins.'"[9]

"Abels blood" is exemplary for showing the devotional Vaughan trespassing into the sounds of the world and making a successful return to the ways of Christ. But the gap in language represented here so clearly has broader implications for the writer of "heavenly poesy." As a descendent of Adam, Vaughan, like Sidney, understood that the corruption of language could be momentarily refined by Christ but not altogether restored to its original Adamic purity: the poet makes us, "*as it were*, see God coming in his majestie" (italics added); the need for similitude is still necessary since "our erected wit maketh us know what perfection is, and yet our infected wil

---

[9] *Ninety-Six Sermons by . . . Lancelot Andrewes*, 3 (1850): 321. The passage from which this quotation is taken describes at some length the different "keys" in which Abel and Christ speak. See also *The Sermons of John Donne*, 7 (1954): 69-70, and the discussion of Abel in Vaughan's 1654 translation of Nieremberg's *Of Temperance and Patience* (pp. 236-37).

keepeth us from reaching unto it."[10] For Vaughan, the gap is felt most deeply in the verbal alternatives before him. Not enough of a precursor of Romanticism to wish away altogether the need for language, he was sufficiently a child of the Reformation to realize that the "wilde / Murmurings" of his youth ("Dedication," p. 395, ll. 35-36) did not simply stop with his "conversion" to religious verse. Along with those whom he criticized, Vaughan knew that he also possessed the "black art" of the tongue; he, too, inherited the potential to "babble," to speak without Christ, where the noise from his own throat might reveal him as a disciple of the devil rather than an apostle of Christ.

He signals this concern in a place no less conspicuous than the epigram to the finished *Silex Scintillans* (1655). While a number of Herbert's other followers explicitly identified themselves with David—the traditional type of the devotional poet—Vaughan thought of himself as a latter-day Job, in some respects the prototype of David, whose eloquent plea for knowledge of God's favor the Welsh poet fixes on the title page to his collection: "*Where is God my Maker, who giveth Songs in the night? / Who teacheth us more then the beasts of the earth, and maketh us wiser then the fowls of heaven?*" (Job 35:10-11).[11] The inscription fuses the political with the per-

---

[10] *The Prose Works of Sir Philip Sidney*, ed. Albert Feuillerat, 4 vols. (Cambridge: Cambridge Univ. Press, 1962), 3: 7 and 9, respectively (spelling slightly modernized).

[11] Lewalski, *Protestant Poetics and the Seventeenth-Century Religious Lyric*, pp. 31-53 *passim*, gives the most recent discussion of the pervasive influence of the Psalms of David on sixteenth- and seventeenth-century poets. She is undoubtedly right in downplaying the generic influence of the Book of Psalms on Vaughan (p. 332) given the importance he attached to *The Temple* as a literary model; but David was also thought of as "The most glorious pattern, not only of the sacred music of the day, but of Songs also in the Night" (*The Works of Joseph Hall*, 12 vols. [Oxford: D. A. Talboys, 1837-1839], 7:524). The quotation comes from Hall's pamphlet, *Songs in the Night* (1660) and forms a valuable though histrionic gloss on these lines from Job, particularly in connection with the issue of election discussed below: "And if we, out of the strength of our moral powers, shall be setting Songs to ourselves in the Night of our utmost disconsolation [as opposed to the songs which God puts in our mouths], woe is me, how miserably out of tune they are! how harsh,

sonal. An obvious choice for a poet conscious of writing "*out of a land of darkenesse*" (p. 217), the quotation from Job asks whether suffering is a sign of God's grace or of His indifference; it also underlines the poet's deep-felt concern about whether he has been the recipient of divine inspiration for his "Sacred Poems and Private Ejaculations" or whether, like Job, he "open[s] his mouth in vain [and] multiplieth words without knowledge" (Job 35:16). Sensitive to the sounds of others, Vaughan was equally sensitive to the sounds generated by his own voice. They, too, were a measure of grace.

It is not surprising, therefore, to find that a number of Vaughan's most "afflicted" moments take the form of a verbal struggle between the language of the world and the language of Christ. "The Check" and "Distraction," for instance, are designed to represent the difficulties that beset a poet who is unable to transform the voices of temptation into the sounds of Christ: in both poems language has surrendered its control to the corrupt flesh and, consequently, both poems are in the process of disintegrating. "The Check" is written precisely at the moment when things are falling apart, when the center is not holding because the poet can barely hear Christ's voice. As a result, the poem is on its way to becoming the "speechlesse heap" (l. 3) which is its threatened end. But first it must suffer the fate of all fictions that are created without God at the center and lose its symmetry and order before crumbling to dust. Vaughan begins by attempting literally to hush the sound of his own flesh:

> Peace, peace! I blush to hear thee; when thou art
>   A dusty story
> A speechlesse heap, and in the midst my heart
>   In the same livery drest
>   Lyes tame as all the rest;
> When six years thence digg'd up, some youthfull Eie
>   Seeks there for Symmetry
> But finding none, shal leave thee to the wind,

how mis-accented, how discordous even to the sense of our own souls" (p. 522).

>   Or the next foot to Crush,
>   Scatt'ring thy kind
>   And humble dust, tell then dear flesh
>   Where is thy glory?   (p. 443, ll. 1-12)

E. L. Marilla has insisted that we read this poem in connection with "The Charnel-house"[12]—another dramatization of human vanity—but such a connection needs to be mediated by Herbert. As the allusion to "dear flesh" (l. 11) indicates, Vaughan had his master's "Church-monuments" in mind when he wrote the opening stanza. The speaker, with teacherly condescension, chides his body, but the task is not so coolly performed here as it is in Herbert. There is obvious embarrassment on the speaker's part for even having heard the call of the flesh, the effects of which Vaughan represents in the fragmented structure of the verse itself. The verbally mimetic pattern of dissolution that occurs phonetically, rhythmically, and syntactically in Herbert's poem[13] reappears here in the way flesh and fiction become curiously fused to share in a parallel rite of disintegration. "The Check," like the body, possesses a certain skeletal symmetry in the fairly elaborate rhyme scheme and the parallel adverbial clauses, but the joints of the poem keep being jolted by the abruptly halting speech rhythms and the variously drawn out and suddenly truncated lines. Even down to the details of a crushed poetic foot, the formal disorderliness of the verse anticipates the "dusty story" of the flesh which some youth will later find. Moreover, the visual structure does not and, in fact, cannot impose "a diagram which otherwise has no existence,"[14] a situation that Wimsatt finds frequently in the shaped poems of the classical

---

[12] Marilla, "The Secular and Religious Poetry of Henry Vaughan," *MLQ* 9 (1948): 408.

[13] Joseph H. Summers, *George Herbert: His Religion and Art* (Cambridge, Mass.: Harvard Univ. Press, 1954), p. 134, followed by Stanley E. Fish, *Self-Consuming Artifacts: The Experience of Seventeenth-Century Literature* (Berkeley: Univ. of California Press, 1972), pp. 164-69, have commented extensively on these aspects of "Church-monuments."

[14] "In Search of Verbal Mimesis" in William K. Wimsatt, *Day of the Leopards* (New Haven: Yale Univ. Press, 1976), p. 72.

tradition. On the contrary, Vaughan's refusal to allow the speaker's response to achieve a firm symmetrical pattern is exactly the point: so long as he attends to the flesh, we will always witness a partially corrupted form of address. The "dusty story" (l. 2) cannot be the neatly carved devotional poem.

The reflexive process continues into the center of the poem. "All things," the speaker tells the flesh in the second stanza, "teach us to die" (l. 20). "View thy fore-runners," he goes on to say: "All that have growth, or breath / Have one large language, *Death*" (ll. 28-29); and it is impossible to escape the suggestion that the poem is just one more such emblem. Death seems writ large in the speaker's own breath and in the shape his words assume on the page itself. The only way to reverse the decaying process, Vaughan hints, is through Christ, whose word can make "true glory dwell / In dust, and stones" (ll. 35-36). His voice, if heard, cannot only save "dear flesh," but the way in which it can transform a "dusty story" into a dwelling of "true glory" bears significantly on the speaker's own mode of address. The final stanza brings to a point the conflict between Christ's voice "Of Love, and sorrow" (l. 38), and the speaker's own intensifying warnings to the unregenerate self:

> Heark, how he doth Invite thee! with what voice
>   Of Love, and sorrow
> He begs, and Calls; *O that in these thy days*
>   Thou knew'st but thy own good!
>   Shall not the Crys of bloud,
> Of Gods own bloud awake thee? He bids beware
>   Of drunknes, surfeits, Care,
> But thou sleep'st on; wher's now thy protestation,
>   Thy Lines, thy Love? Away,
>   Redeem the day,
> The day that gives no observation,
>   Perhaps to morrow. (ll. 37-48)

Shuttling between Christ's invitation and the obstinate flesh, the speaker only partially grasps the voice "Of Love, and sorrow" (l. 38) in the italicized lament, before he turns abruptly to castigating his body. At this point his own intemperance takes over—"Thou knew'st but thy own good!" (l. 40)—and his own reinterpretation of Christ's invitation as "Crys of bloud" (l. 41) makes the flesh shrink further away, with the speaker chasing choppily after him: "Wher's now thy protestation, / Thy Lines, thy Love?" (ll. 44-45). The remark seems one last reflexive gesture by Vaughan that indicts the tongue of the speaker as well as the unregenerate flesh: neither possesses lines of love. The speaker's stumbling conclusion, "Away / Redeem the day, / The day that gives no observation, / Perhaps to morrow" (ll. 45-48), seems almost to fall in on itself in a "speechlesse heap" (l. 3).

"Distraction" is the spiritual sequel to "The Check." The most visually chaotic lyric in all of Vaughan, the poem is a picture of human babble: "a man must wrong his own visage, and disfigure himself to speak [it]." Not only does it record a "world / . . . full of voices" (ll. 11-12), but the verse reflects in its own verbal disjointedness how one "Man is call'd, and hurl'd / By each [voice]" (ll. 12-13). The opening few lines initiate an experience of sudden stops and starts that continue throughout the poem and indicate the spasms of living without God:

> O knit me, that am crumbled dust! the heape
>   Is all dispers'd, and cheape;
>   Give for a handfull, but a thought
>   And it is bought;
>   Hadst thou
> Made me a starre, a pearle, or a rain-bow,
>   The beames I then had shot
>   My light had lessend not,
>   But now
> I find my selfe the lesse, the more I grow.   (p. 413, ll. 1-10)

Few lines measure the meter adequately. A phrase either fails to span the full line or it bends loosely around the end where the rhyme keeps catching the voice by surprise to add another jolt to the poem. It is little wonder that the speaker complains that "I find my selfe the lesse, the more I grow" (l. 10): the flips and starts weary.

Like "The Check," "Distraction," also records its debts to Herbert—this time to some of his master's wilder poems such as "Deniall" and "The Collar." The resemblances to the latter are expecially instructive since, like "The Collar," Vaughan's lyric is one long, disorganized poem that looks as if it should be divided into stanzas but offers no convenient place to do so. Moreover, the two poems are also nearly identical in length with Vaughan's falling just two lines short of Herbert's; but the shortcoming is a crucial one, for it is here that Herbert's rebellious speaker hears the sound of God's voice—"Me thoughts I heard one calling, *Child*!" (l. 35)—and the poem closes on a note of communion that orders all that has gone before: "And I reply'd, *My Lord*" (l. 36).[15] In "Distraction," there is no intervening voice, no "glad tydings of Salvation," that might assure the speaker that his groans have been in "earnest." Instead, the poem concludes with the speaker's confession that still "Amidst the noise, and throng" (l. 32) he is "full of voices" (l. 12) but none of them Christ's.

> Come, and releive
> And tame, and keepe downe with thy light
> Dust that would rise, and dimme my sight,
> Lest left alone too long
> Amidst the noise, and throng,
> Oppressed I
> Striving to save the whole, by parcells dye.   (ll. 28-34)

The final lines do give a clue, however, to Vaughan's "formal" purposes in the poem. Like the speaker who, in striving for all, has begun to disintegrate, so the poem is in the process of crumbling from the standard pentameter couplet that lies beneath the lines: both "by parcells dye"; each needs to be

---

[15] For an excellent discussion of the formal aspects of "The Collar" that describes how the final lines "order" the poem both theologically and structurally, see Summers, *George Herbert*, p. 92.

"reformed," but neither is given the chance. Unlike "The Collar," "Distraction" measures only the fall, for which there is no single pattern, either human or verbal.

The noise without was within, and in both locations it was equally difficult for Vaughan to ignore. "When the sounds will not unite," writes Walter Ong in pointing to the victimizing powers of the aural sense, "when they are cacophonous, hearing is in agony, for it cannot eliminate selectively—there is no auditory equivalent of averting one's face or eyes."[16] To escape from the weight of his own tongue, Vaughan was led at times into a practice of verbal self-effacement that paralleled his own ascetic instincts. The quotations from Scripture— "God in the *Voice*" ("H. Scriptures," p. 441, l. 8)—placed at the end of his poems, for instance, serve to absorb the poet's own language into that of another order. "Regeneration," "Religion," "The Brittish Church," "The World," and "The Mutinie" all conclude with sizeable inscriptions from the Bible that sometimes verify and at other times correct the speaker's attitude; but in either case they deliver an intervening voice that seals off the poem on a gnomic note of authority. Among seventeenth-century poets, Vaughan was unusual in this respect, and among his own verse, the most interesting example is perhaps "The Mutinie."

"The Mutinie" presents the paradox inherent in a rebellious deliverance, for what the speaker learns, reluctantly, is that no true deliverance can be rebellious. Vaughan begins by presenting the self's captivity in typological terms that have both personal and political significance. As Martin notes (*Works*, p. 743), the images of clay and straw are from Exodus; the speaker, like Israel, is in bondage, and the God to whom he initially prays is more theirs than his, more Old Testament than New:

Weary of this same Clay, and straw, I laid
Me down to breath, and casting in my heart

[16] Ong, *The Presence of the Word: Some Prolegomena for Cultural and Religious History* (New Haven: Yale Univ. Press, 1967), p. 130.

> The after-burthens, and griefs yet to come,
>   The heavy sum
> So shook my breast, that (sick and sore dismai'd)
> My thoughts, like water which some stone doth start
> Did quit their troubled Channel, and retire
> Unto the banks, where, storming at those bounds,
> They murmur'd sore; But I, who felt them boyl
>   And knew their Coyl,
> Turning to him, who made poor sand to tire
> And tame proud waves, If yet these barren grounds
>   And thirstie brick must be (said I)
>   My taske, and Destinie,
>
> Let me so strive and struggle with thy foes
> (Not thine alone, but mine too,) that when all
> Their Arts and force are built unto the height
>   That Babel-weight
> May prove thy glory, and their shame.   (p. 468, ll. 1-19)

Vaughan asks that his murmurings be channeled into action, not quieted. His wish is to join God in the punishment of the wicked and, incidentally, to share in the glory of His victory. But the speaker also keeps bargaining with God for favors. The unregenerate thoughts "storming at those bounds" (l. 8) continue in the speaker's wish to be part of a victory in which he remains protected by God from all the "frothie noise which up and down doth flie" (l. 25). He wants it both ways. Even as he begins the third stanza—"Not but I know thou hast a shorter Cut / To bring me home" (ll. 29-30)—he still partially resists complete identification with the milder ways of Christ and the New Testament. Only gradually does he assent to a will greater than his own that is not an extension of his earlier anger: concession ("O be pleas'd / To fix my steps" [ll. 35-36]) becomes desire ("O give it ful obedience" [l. 39]) that finally relaxes into an attitude of patient acceptance ("soft and mild / Both live and die thy Child" [ll. 41-42]). But the finishing touches are left to Christ, "the finisher / And Author of my faith" (ll. 22-23). His voice closes off the poem through an inscription from Revelation that plays on the two ways of "overcoming" and presents the only bargain of any importance to remember:

> To him that overcometh wil I give to eate of the hidden Manna, and I wil give him a white stone, and in the stone a new name written, which no man knoweth, saving he that receiveth it. (Rev. 2:17)

The "frothie noise" (l. 25) of the speaker, gradually refined from the poem, is altogether excluded from the quotation. Permanently fixed on the page, set in place with italic solidity, the inscription, like Christ's promise, buttresses the verbal order and assures us of the difference between a momentary mutiny and complete distraction.

"Joy" extends the ascetic into the hermetic and goes so far as to equate all unholy mirth with "False, jugling sounds" and "forc'd accents." The poem pushes the genre of melancholy complaints mediated by song into a realm of pseudo-suffering whose "course measures" offend the poet's ears. Associated most often with the literary pastoral, these "grone[s] well drest" contrast with nature's music—"a lesson plaid . . . by a winde or wave"—and threaten to lure the listener away from the harmonies of God's creation. To spoil our sense of their melodies, Vaughan twists these lesser creations into a series of "jugling" oxymora, highly conventional in their description but harshly presented by the poet:

> Be dumb course measures, jar no more; to me
> There is no discord, but your harmony.
> False, jugling sounds; a grone well drest, where care
> Moves in disguise, and sighs afflict the air:
> Sorrows in white; griefs tun'd; a sugerd Dosis
> Of Wormwood, and a Deaths-head crown'd with Roses.
>
> (p. 491, ll. 1-6)

The speaker, responsive to "the lesson plaid . . . by a winde or wave," delivers a different sound altogether, signaled by a change in the poem's meter that eventually tightens into the whispering dimeters describing the sounds around "Hermit-wells" before they expand into an epigram written, once more, in a pentameter couplet:

> Therefore while the various showers
> Kill and cure the tender flowers,
> While the winds refresh the year
> Now with clouds, now making clear,
> Be sure under pains of death
> To ply both thine eyes and breath.
>   As leafs in Bowers
>   Whisper their hours,
>   And Hermit-wells
>   Drop in their Cells:
> So in sighs and unseen tears
> Pass thy solitary years,
> And going hence, leave written on some Tree,
> *Sighs make joy sure, and shaking fastens thee.*   (ll. 17-30)

Like "The Mutinie," "Joy" seems to undergo its own rite of verbal purification. The closing couplet, precisely chiseled, points to its own well-carved art in the inscription the hermit should leave on the tree, one whose message neatly reverses the message usually left by lovers who roam the pastoral woods. Yet lest it seem that the hermit is presumptuous—too satisfied with his note of wisdom—we should remember that what he writes has already been written. All he is doing is what Vaughan, the poet, has been doing: imitating the imitator of Christ, George Herbert, whose "Affliction V" describes man as "We are the trees, whom shaking fastens more" (l. 20).

Finally, "The Proffer" extends the ascetic into the transcendent by way of the world as the poem represents perhaps the quintessential example in *Silex* of a battle of voices both within and without Vaughan. The poem is a tour de force, a remarkable display of verbal power. Viewing it either biographically or allegorically or as a fusion of the two,[17] its critics all agree that the good fight has been fought and fought well. Simmonds sums up this position when he sums up the

---

[17] See, respectively, F. E. Hutchinson, *Henry Vaughan: A Life and Interpretation* (Oxford: Clarendon Press, 1947), p. 125; R. A. Durr, *On the Mystical Poetry of Henry Vaughan* (Cambridge, Mass.: Harvard Univ. Press, 1962), pp. 101-11; and James Simmonds, *Masques of God: Form and Theme in the Poetry of Henry Vaughan* (Pittsburgh: Univ. of Pittsburgh Press, 1972), pp. 105-7.

poem in a gloss from the prose. The poem expresses "Vaughan's acceptance of the advice which he gave the reader of *The Mount of Olives*: 'running thy race with patience, look to JESUS the author and finisher of thy faith, who when he was reviled, reviled not again. Presse thou towards the mark, *and let the people and their Seducers rage*; be faithful unto the death, and he will give thee a Crowne of Life' (Martin, p. 141)."[18] The poem might be a demonstration of personal fortitude on Vaughan's part, but to read it retrospectively is ultimately to drain away from it the dramatic process of language and fail to appreciate the moral risks inherent in a devotional poet's very choice of words. For while the poem does end with Vaughan looking to Jesus, the first seven stanzas hardly reveal a poet running his race patiently, or refusing to revile his enemies, or even distinguishing carefully between his calm self and the raging world of seducers. Indeed, just the opposite is true. Vaughan simmers with indignation as he reviles his enemies with some of the most bone-cracking rhetoric he ever wrote. "Some *Syllables* are *Swords*," the poet writes in "Rules *and* Lessons": "Unbitted tongues are in their penance double, / They shame their *owners*, and the *hearers* trouble" (ll. 70-72). During most of "The Proffer," Vaughan forgets about the possibility of shame and concentrates on giving his "*hearers* trouble."

The poem does not unfold in a linear pattern marking a pilgrim's progress. Instead, Vaughan keeps using language to create, extend, and widen a gulf between his tempters and himself, one in which the poet's violent denunciations stand in sharp contrast with the "Sorcery / And smooth seducements" of the "Commonwealth." He begins by pummeling his opponents immediately. The alliteration stings throughout the first stanza but especially in the final line, which turns nature's symbiotic process into a parasitic raid that borders on the obscene:

> Be still black Parasites,
>   Flutter no more;

[18] Simmonds, *Masques of God*, p. 107.

> Were it still winter, as it was before,
>   You'd make no flights;
> But now the dew and Sun have warm'd my bowres,
>   You flie and flock to suck the flowers.   (p. 486, ll. 1-6)

In stanza after stanza, Vaughan attempts to "still" the sounds of the "poys'nous, subtile fowls" through the force of his verbal barrage; he slides between irony and invective but never softens in his attitude toward them:

> O poys'nous, subtile fowls!
>   The flyes of hell
> That buz in every ear, and blow on souls
>   Until they smell
> And rot, descend not here, nor think to stay,
>   I've read, who 'twas, drove you away.   (ll. 13-18)

But the language used to create a distance between the two on one front also serves to connect them on another. So long as the speaker directs his diatribe against these fiends, he is to some extent bound to their claims; and inasmuch as he continues in his cankered assault, he reveals, in fact, that he is in danger of being infected by their rotten breath. Righteous indignation has its problems as well as its rewards. The example, for instance, of Christ casting the money-changers from the Temple—sometimes seen as an authority for Vaughan's fuming[19]—was a tricky model at best to imitate. "Every Christian is not Christ," preached Donne:

> And therefore as he that would fast forty dayes, as Christ did, might starve; and he that would whip Merchants out of the Temple, as Christ did, might be knockt downe in the Temple; So he [that] knowing his owne inclinations, or but the generall ill inclination of all mankind, as he is infected with Originall sin, should converse so much with publicans and sinners, might participate of their sins. The rule is, we must avoid inordinatenesse of affections; but when we come to examples of that rule, our selves well understood by our selves, must be our owne examples.[20]

---

[19] Durr, *On the Mystical Poetry*, p. 109.
[20] *The Sermons of John Donne*, 4 (1959): 329.

The conclusion Donne reaches forms the conclusion of Vaughan's poem: "our selves well understood by our selves, must be our owne examples." In the final stanza Vaughan takes stock of his associations with the enemy and "Spit[s] out their phlegm":

> Then keep the antient way!
>   Spit out their phlegm
> And fill thy brest with home; think on thy dream:
>   A calm, bright day!
> A Land of flowers and spices! the word given,
>   *If these be fair, O what is Heaven!*   (ll. 43-48)

The first three lines continue in the imperative, but then one of those remarkable shifts occurs in Vaughan where the force of language suddenly alters its course, leaving a ripple in the seam of the poem that declares at once the gap that distinguishes the life of human fury and restricted movement from the world of transcendent calm, the restless activity of the verb from the motionless and atemporal noun in apposition. The former is the fallen world—a world of poets as well as publicans—whose limitations are best signaled in the tight closure on which each of the first seven stanzas end. The latter is, as Vaughan says, "the word given," a sign of grace bestowed from above and available for all to imitate; its endless potentiality for creation and freedom is marked through the openness of apostrophe.

Moreover, when Vaughan exhorts himself to "Spit out their phlegm," he repeats almost exactly Herbert's command for England to "Spit out thy flegme" in "The Church-Porch"; but through the simple substitution of "their" for "thy" and of himself as the implied subject for England, the poet admits to his recognition that in the act of writing, he has already been in contact too long with the slothful commonwealth. He has, in fact, begun to decay spiritually. Without necessarily knowing, or believing in, contemporary arguments that "satyr" and satire were etymologically linked to the devil,[21] Vaughan

---

[21] "This word *Satyr*, many verbal Grammatists labour to derive from the Greek . . . but we must derive it from the first *maternall* tongue, the *Hebrew*

nonetheless seems to have understood the risky position of the satirist in general, summed up by Alvin Kernan in the old adage: "He who sups with the devil needs a long spoon."[22] By spitting out their phlegm, Vaughan clears his throat of whatever sickness may have lodged in his lungs during his attack. He also clears the way for a new verbal order: for "where the Holy Ghost is received," remarks Lancelot Andrewes, "there is ever a change in the dialect, a change from cursed, unclean, 'corrupt communication,' unto 'such as becometh Saints.' "[23] The good fight in "The Proffer" is finally as much within the poet as it is with others, and it centers on Vaughan's own all-too-human impulse to indulge too fervently in the language of overkill, so that while winning this battle, he should lose the larger war for his soul. The victory assures us, and is meant to assure us, that on this occasion at least the poet of *Silex* has heard "the glad tydings of Salvation" and at last "giveth Songs in the night."

---

word *Shagnar*, *Lev.* 17:1: *Ye shall not offer your children* Leshegnirim, *to the hairie ones*, That is, to the Devils, who appeared in the liknes of hairy Goats, & therefore were called *Satyres* by some small enterchange." *The Workes of Mr. John Weemse*, 3 vols. (London, 1636), 1:16.

[22] Alvin B. Kernan, *The Cankered Muse: Satire of the English Renaissance* (New Haven: Yale Univ. Press, 1959), p. 24. For variations on this proverb in the Renaissance see, *The Home Book of Proverbs, Maxims, and Familiar Phrases*, selected and arranged by Burton Stevenson (New York: The Macmillan Co., 1948), p. 559.

[23] *Ninety-Six Sermons*, 3 (1850): 193. The punishment Dante assigns the wrathful in hell throws a macabre light on Vaughan's own actions in the final stanza: in the fifth circle, the incontinent are immersed in black mire where, unable ever to clear their throats, they nonetheless keep attempting to sing but only gurgle inarticulate hymns to God. See, *The Divine Comedy of Dante Alighieri: Inferno*, trans. John D. Sinclair (1938; rpt. New York: Oxford Univ. Press, 1961), pp. 104-5.

CHAPTER SEVEN

"The Night" and Vaughan's "Late and Dusky" Age

> In the kingdome of blind men the one ey'd is king.
> —George Herbert, *Outlandish Proverbs*, no. 469

IN THE MARGIN opposite his discussion in *Man in Darkness* of Herbert as "a most glorious true *Saint* and a *Seer*," Vaughan singles out from his master's "incomparable prophetick Poems" three works for special consideration: "Church-musick," "Church-rents and schismes," and "The Church Militant" (p. 186). As the common word in the title of each indicates, these poems share an obvious interest in the Church—its ceremonies, the potential agents of its destruction, and the history of its struggle on earth. Taken as a group, few poems better illustrate the gap that frequently divides contemporary from modern responses to Herbert. Except for "The Church Militant" (which has earned a place in recent criticism of *The Temple* largely because of its problematic relationship to the lyrics in "The Church"),[1] none of these is among Herbert's more admired performances today. But for an Anglican poet writing both in the direct shadow of his master and in the aftermath of the Civil War, it was only logical that these verses should loom large in his imagination and assume a greater immediacy than they now possess: it was an immediacy that sprang not just from the devotional commitment present in each poem but also from the powers of divination preserved in the order of their appearance in *The Temple* and "discovered" by Vaughan in the margin to

---

[1] The most recent extended discussion of "The Church Militant" belongs to Stanley E. Fish, *The Living Temple: George Herbert and Catechizing* (Berkeley: Univ. of California Press, 1978), pp. 137-69.

Man in Darkness. The three poems together provide a telling gloss on political events in mid-century England. "Church-musick" contains the ominous line *"God help poore Kings"* amid its otherwise sweet sounds. "Church-rents and schismes" describes the proliferation of sectarian attitudes in the image of the worm gnawing on the root of the "Brave rose." And "The Church Militant" gives a final, apocalyptic vision of corruption in which religion, once apparently free from sin, has now become so contaminated by it that the two are linked in a global assault on Gospel innocence until a time when "such a darknesse do the world invade / At Christs last coming, as his first did finde" (ll. 230-31). Only with the Last Judgment is the degenerative process of human history to come to a halt.

For Herbert, the great day of reckoning was to occur once the Church had completed its circumnavigation of the earth and returned to its place of origin in the east. But to many in England, both Anglican and Nonconformist alike, it was not at all clear if Christ's Second Coming would wait that long. "With the end of civil war," writes Christopher Hill, "when men naturally were everywhere discussing England's future settlement, apocalyptic overtones sound more clearly."[2] God did not always save poor kings, and for the zealous, who had branded Charles as Antichrist, his destruction seemed a sure sign that the kingdom of God was at hand. Rome was warned to beware of Cromwell's army;[3] new societies were envisioned and some even sampled; and prophecies of the coming End were a commonplace in the early 1650s, especially among the more radical Puritans who, following Revelation 20:4-6, anticipated a messianic kingdom on earth ruled by Christ for a thousand years before the Last Judgment.[4] In August of 1652, William Erbery proclaimed in Brecknock that he was now

[2] Hill, *Antichrist in Seventeenth-Century England* (London: Oxford Univ. Press, 1971), p. 103.
[3] Christopher Hill, *The World Turned Upside Down* (1972; rpt. Harmondsworth: Penguin Books, Ltd., 1976), p. 96.
[4] B. S. Capp, *The Fifth Monarchy Men* (London: Faber and Faber, 1972), p. 190.

going to preach only about the New Jerusalem's "coming down from God out of heaven."[5]

In a very different spirit, Anglicans, too, discovered a portentous message in the beheading of a king. "We could not have lived in an age of more instruction, had we been left to our own choice," declares Vaughan in *Man in Darkness*:

> We have seen such vicissitudes and examples of humane frailty, as the former world (had they happened in those ages) would have judged prodigies. We have seen Princes brought to their graves by a new way, and the highest order of humane honours trampled upon by the lowest. (p. 170)

Personal as well as human history seemed well on its westering way (p. 169, ll. 24-28), and an individual's final hours could take on the cataclysmic coloration of the Last Days: "How will they lie on their last beds, *like wilde Buls in a net, full of the fury of the Lord? When their desolation shall come like a flood, and their destruction like a whirle-wind*" (p. 170). With the recognition that "the day that *shall burne like an Oven*" (p. 170) might well be the event that takes the sinner unaware, the need for the soul's preparation had become all the more pressing. Vaughan's headnote from Ecclesiastes 11:7-10 banishes any illusions he might elsewhere create that by "meer playing" one can "go to Heaven" ("Childhood"): "*Therefore remove sorrow from thy heart, and put away evil from thy flesh, for childhood and youth are vanity*" (p. 168). Two years later, in the preface to the *Life of Paulinus*, the Welsh poet would drop his guard completely and state flatly that the end of the world "*truely draws near, if it be not* at the door" (p. 338).

Had Vaughan been left to his own choice, he might very well have still written about the Second Coming and Judgment Day since these topics were familiar fare to religious poets of the seventeenth century; but it is doubtful whether he would have been so receptive to the idea of an imminent End had he lived and composed poetry at any time other than during

---

[5] *The Testimony of William Erbery* (London, 1658), p. 243.

the 1640s and '50s. The invading darkness which Herbert had prophesied in 1633 had become the younger poet's reality by mid-century—a burden that seemed only to increase with time: Civil War led the way to regicide which, in turn, helped to create further religious schism. Historical change in any form brought to Vaughan only the prospect of a new set of disasters; the bleak vision of "The Church Militant" seemed more and more unavoidable. "*All that may bee objected is, that I write unto thee out of a land of darkenesse,*" the Welsh poet, with studied equanimity, informs his readers in *Flores Solitudinis*, "*out of that unfortunate region, where the Inhabitants sit in the shadow of death: where destruction passeth for propagation, and a thick black night for the glorious day-spring*" (p. 217). This *is* a world turned upside down, one in which creation (propagation) turns demonically back on itself and the natural cycle of time has been suspended; and even though Vaughan's allusion to the Propagation Act is a local one, the overtones of suffering (Job 10:21-22), combined with the imagery of darkness, quickly suggest a broader and more imminent context. "This last and lewdest age"—a description Vaughan gives to his situation in "White Sunday" (p. 486, l. 39)—clearly shows him associating the present spiritual depravity with that of the final days when, in Paul's words, "evil men and seducers shall wax worse and worse" (2 Tim. 3:13).

Vaughan's sense of an impending apocalypse developed gradually, with important poetic consequences for *Silex* as a whole, and it naturally sought different forms of expression from the millenarian zeal that inspired many Puritans. His was shaped by an acute recognition of political oppression rather than of liberation; he was now the victimized martyr waiting to be rescued, while Antichrist—the tyrant of the Last Days—was the current "regime" producing "forgeries, which impious wit / And power force on Holy Writ" ("The day of Judgement," p. 531, ll. 35-36). Moreover, in direct opposition to many of the "saints" who were anticipating a thousand-year reign, Vaughan's plea in this poem, repeated elsewhere in *Silex*, for God to "Descend, descend" cuts through any notion of an exalted rule here on earth by a few.⁶ But if the Welsh author's belief in the imminent End formed one response to Puritan domination, it was not limited to a few calculated instances of doom-saying. Vaughan was, or came to be, like his master, a "seer" of darkness—a poet of "The Night" and not just of nocturnal meditations. He concentrated less on the fate of his enemies than on his own relationship to time, and with his deepening awareness of the Last Days, he gave the "story" of his regeneration a figural interpretation—one that emphasized the historicity of his struggle with darkness in relation to the larger, determining perspective supplied by Christian eschatology.

Viewed in its entirety, *Silex*, like the Bible, moves from Genesis to Revelation, beginning to end, light to darkness. "Regeneration" (a morning poem) stands in clear opposition to "The Night" (an evening poem), and as Vaughan's two finest poetic achievements, they help both to map the "progress" of the collection and to indicate the temporal poles in the two parts around which the devotional imagination gathers. Indeed, the pattern of worship in the volume is only an enlarged version of the daily pattern of worship Vaughan prescribes for every person in "Rules *and* Lessons" (pp. 436-39). In that poem, the speaker begins with his "regeneration" each morning, and he proceeds to an intensified recognition of the obedience demanded by God as morning approaches "High-noon" ("Ascension-day"); at this point, "all but preludes thy End" (l. 107), and with the sun in decline and night approaching, he prepares for his (eventual) death and also for the next day. Like the Bible and *Silex* as a whole, the progress of time is both linear and cyclical since the day looks forward

---

⁶ Norman Cohn has pointed out how Origen and, later, Augustine domesticated radical millenarianism by spiritualizing its conquests: the Kingdom of God was "an event which would take place not in space or time but only in the souls of believers," (*The Pursuit of the Millennium* [1957; rev. ed. New York: Oxford Univ. Press, 1970], p. 29). As Ross Garner, *Henry Vaughan: Experience and The Tradition* (Chicago: Univ. of Chicago Press, 1959), p. 101, indicates, Vaughan was in substantial agreement with Augustine on this issue.

to an end that is also a new beginning; and like both of these works, it admits to an increasing recognition of darkness: "Man is a *Summers day*; whose *youth*, and *fire* / Cool to a glorious Evening, and Expire" (ll. 113-14). The passing of the day, of man's life, and of the life of man—all neatly overlap in this "*sic vita*" view of time, and in each case the expiration can be made "glorious" only by the intervention of God.

To suggest that the two parts of *Silex* reflect two different views of time is not to imply that the first focuses exclusively on beginnings and the second only on endings. Certainly *Silex 1650* has its poems on the Last Things and its share of night pieces, just as the second part includes several "morning" poems like "Cock-crowing" and "Palm-Sunday"; but it does seem to me that Vaughan responds to these similar experiences in fundamentally different ways, and the distinctions have much to do with his increasing recognition of the imminent End, of the "darkness" that is to precede it, and of the radical nature of the transformations accompanying the Apocalypse. In Part I, Vaughan subscribes to conventional seventeenth-century notions of decay. There is little sense of the poet creating or responding to a "myth of Transition"—Frank Kermode's term for the period of time "which does not properly belong either to the End or to the *saeculum* preceding it."[7] The world into which the speaker has been regenerated is, like Donne's in "The First Anniversary," lethargic, crippled, and languishing. "Tyme now / Is old, and slow, / His wings are dull, and sickly," the poet reports in "Buriall" (p. 428, ll. 33-35), but otherwise he gives little indication either in this verse or elsewhere in the volume that a cataclysmic change is imminent. The crack caused by the fall in the past and recorded in "Corruption" has nearly paralyzed time, and the first words the reader encounters after "Regeneration," with its extraordinary movement, is the soul's remark to the body in "Death: *A Dialogue*" that " 'Tis a sad Land, that in one day / Hath dull'd thee thus" (p. 399, ll. 1-2). Outside of the

[7] Kermode, *The Sense of an Ending: Studies in the Theory of Fiction* (London: Oxford Univ. Press, 1966), p. 12.

regenerative experience, time seems barely in motion: the body is left to a land of darkness in which "nothing moves without a shroud," and the soul looks forward to the day of redemption that, at this point, appears only to "creep."

Vaughan's perception of the End in *Silex* 1650 is of a distant prospect. It is a point of focus neither imminent in time nor always immediate to the imagination, and in the early stages of his pilgrimage the poet uses it as a means to inspire piety and devotion in this world: the corrupt self, like the reader of *Man in Darkness*, must sometimes be intimidated into the proper attitude of reverence. As a result, Vaughan's most straightforward treatments of apocalyptic themes in Part I are not meditations on the impending End but dramatized fictions whose purpose is either to help inaugurate the religious life or to sustain it on its correct course. "Day of Judgement," for example, the fourth poem in Part I, follows immediately after "Resurrection and Immortality," a poem whose closing inscription from the Book of Daniel—that favorite millenarian text—works to defuse any notion in this volume of an imminent Apocalypse or of the poet's desire to indulge in any attempts at predictions: "*But goe thou thy way untill the end be, for thou shalt rest, and stand up in thy lot, at the end of the dayes*" (12:13). Vaughan would have found congenial Sir Thomas Browne's touchily stated but blamelessly orthodox remark that "to determine the day and yeare of this inevitable time, is not only convincible and statute madnesse, but also manifest impiety";[8] he would also have agreed with Bishop Joseph Hall's more sober reminder, uttered in 1650, "that we do neither out of a credulous security put the day of the last judgement far off from us, nor out of a mis-grounded presumption passe our punctual predeterminations of it."[9]

Be bold, but not too bold in imagining the day: this attitude of cautious restraint shapes "Day of Judgement." The poem is a dress rehearsal, not a call, for the Apocalypse:

---

[8] Browne, *Religio Medici*, Part I, Section 46 in *Sir Thomas Browne: Selected Writings*, ed. Geoffrey Keynes (London: Faber and Faber, 1968), p. 52.
[9] Hall, *The Revelation Unrevealed* (London, 1650), p. 223.

> When through the North a fire shall rush
>   And rowle into the East,
> And like a firie torrent brush
>   And sweepe up *South*, and *West* . . .
>   (p. 402, ll. 1-4)

The first six stanzas form a tissue of echoes from Revelation; each, with its identical use of anaphora, proceeds with the formulaic regularity of the opening of the Seven Seals, but instead of giving us a seventh (whose seal immediately precedes the trumpet call to Judgment), the poem swerves away from a catastrophic ending and the weight of the clauses falls onto the problem of repentance, which is to mark the beginning of the proper devotional attitude in this life:

> Prepare, prepare me then, O God!
>   And let me now begin
> To feele my loving fathers *Rod*
>   Killing the man of sinne!   (ll. 29-32)

Furthermore, even though the poem closes with a quotation from 1 Peter 4:7 that "*the end of all things is at hand*," the Biblical context, retained by Vaughan in the stanzas leading up to the inscription, shows the line to be part of an exordium that underscores the importance of "a living F A I T H":

> Lord, God! I beg nor friends, nor wealth
>   But pray against them both;
> Three things I'de have, my soules chief health!
>   And one of these seme loath,
>
> A living F A I T H, a H E A R T of flesh,
>   The W O R L D an Enemie,
> This last will keepe the first two fresh,
>   And bring me, where I'de be.   (ll. 37-44)

In "Day of Judgement," historical time plays no part in the poem's structure; meditating on the End is a means for beginning the pilgrimage on the right foot. In "The Dawning," the other poem in Part I devoted explicitly to the Last Things, Vaughan's salute to the Second Coming is placed near the middle of the collection and its purpose is to keep the pilgrim on his spiritual toes. Like "Day of Judgement," the lyric is a self-contained drama showing little awareness of the Apocalypse as an immediate, historical reality. Vaughan is concerned with determining the hour of the day, not the day itself, of Christ's arrival, and the poem begins with a brilliant flurry of questions:

> Ah! what time wilt thou come? when shall that crie
>   The *Bridegroome's Comming*! fil the sky?
> Shall it in the Evening run
> When our words and works are done?
> Or wil thy all-surprizing light
>   Break at midnight?   (p. 451, ll. 1-6)

The poet's shadowboxing with God ensures that he will not lie like a "puddle" in "a Corrupt securitie" (l. 30)—a phrase that calls to mind Joseph Hall's stricture against a "credulous security." Led to renew his pledge to Christ, he concludes with a splendidly brisk account of spiritual readiness that does not presume to pass any "punctual predeterminations" on the day of His arrival:

> So when that day, and hour shal come
> In which thy self wil be the Sun,
> Thou'lt find me drest and on my way,
> Watching the Break of thy great day.   (ll. 45-48)

"The Dawning" is one of Vaughan's most spirited performances in Part I, and the poem helps illustrate how in this volume the Silurist's imagination was more deeply stirred by beginnings, even if they are conceived for the ostensible purpose of preparing for the End, than with the End itself. Not only is the Second Coming interpreted as a "dawning" (in contrast to Herbert's view of it as accompanying the invading darkness), but the poet is clearly betting on Christ arriving during the "early, fragrant hours" of the day. Notwithstanding both Matthew's choice of the midnight hour and the poet's own admission, made later in the verse, that the time must remain "unknown to us" (l. 26), the speaker in "The Dawning" lobbies heavily for morning as the only really suitable hour for heaven's arrival:

> Indeed, it is the only time
> That with thy glory doth best chime,
> All now are stirring, ev'ry field
>   Ful hymns doth yield,
> The whole Creation shakes off night.   (ll. 13-17)

In Vaughan's view of regenerative time (as opposed to degenerative history), the waking each day is figurally identical to the morning of Christ's waking on earth, an occasion the poet celebrates in a similar style elsewhere when he describes how "The Sun doth shake / Light from his locks, and all the way / Breathing Perfumes, doth spice the day" ("Christs Nativity," p. 442, ll. 3-6). In each case, the early hour is sacred—an intimation of eternity—and for both events the poet writes "hymns" that are partial anticipations of the "Ful hymns" which will be sung on the morning of the Second Coming.

"The Dawning" is the better half of a pair of poems given to morning and evening themes. A distant but distinct companion piece, "The Lampe" (pp. 410-11) is firmly connected to it by the Biblical text taken from Mark, repeated by Matthew, quoted at the end of the poem, and interpolated into the beginning of "The Dawning": "Watch ye therefore: for ye know not when the master of the house cometh, at even, or at midnight, or at the cockcrowing, or in the morning" (Mark's version). The first poem works toward the passage, the second develops out of it, but the different caliber of their performances is as clear as day is from evening. "The Lampe" is a studious late night preparation for the End, a meditation clothed in a little gothic dress and possessing some of the automatic instruction available in the emblem poem tradition. A flame is inspected for its moral application to man: each has its hour of life, but the lamp, which can outdo the speaker in "all acts of piety," is unable to store up oil for the future, while the person who spends his evening hours soberly contemplating the "message" in the flame will receive later treasures. There is nothing in this idea inherently any more hostile to poetry than gravestones were to Herbert in "Church-monuments," but the cramped form of the poem and the lack of any imaginative awareness of the End as an event that occurs in time keeps this meditation locked in its own nocturnal cell. Unlike "The Dawning," the hour of day stimulates no special response from the poet.

Placed side by side, "The Morning-watch" and "The Evening-watch" (pp. 424-25), make Vaughan's temporal preferences seem more like prejudices. The first, in praise not just of nature but nature in its early hour, is the most enthusiastic lyric utterance in all of *Silex*—sure proof that morning is "the only time / That with thy glory doth best chime"; the second is not a lyric at all but another dialogue between body and soul. Both poems are patterned very broadly after the order for morning and evening worship in *The Book of Common Prayer*, dual offices retained in Herbert's "Mattens" and "Evensong"; but Vaughan alters one element from the original in his pair: the first verse is his imaginative recreation of a Psalm, his personal offering of a hymn to be sung during the service, while the second is more in the pedantic mode of the Collect with its question-and-answer format. To anyone reading these two poems together, it is difficult to escape the impression that the desire to be reborn each morning and issue, with prompt eloquence, an Adamic hymn is closer to the poet's heart than the wish to go to bed and meditate on "The last gasp of time" ("The Evening-watch" l. 15). Indeed, the lyric experience of the first seems almost willfully squeezed out of the second when, in the later poem, the body is told not to think about tomorrow: after the previous performance, who can blame him for asking "How many hours do'st think 'till day?" (l. 10).

Given Vaughan's enthusasm for beginnings in *Silex* 1650, it seems only natural that "Regeneration," the first poem in the volume, should contain perhaps the most astonishing celebration of the early moments of faith in all the religious poetry. Spiritual awakening and the waking of the primitive

Church become mutually sacred experiences, with the description of the one intensifying the description of the other and both increasing our delight in the process of regeneration itself. Halfway through the poem, Vaughan's wayward and still unregenerate pilgrim turns toward the East—the source of all beginnings—and he prepares to enter a natural, albeit carefully formed, grove of trees:

> Here, I repos'd; but scarse well set,
>   A grove descryed
> Of stately height, whose branches met
>   And mixt on every side;
>   I entred, and once in
>   (Amaz'd to see't,)
> Found all was chang'd, and a new spring
>   Did all my senses greet;
>
> The unthrift Sunne shot vitall gold
>   A thousand peeces,
> And heaven its azure did unfold
>   Checqur'd with snowie fleeces,
>   The aire was all in spice
>   And every bush
> A garland wore; Thus fed my Eyes
>   But all the Eare lay hush.   (p. 398, ll. 33-48)

Ruth Preston Lehmann has argued how this place of primitive worship is "not a grove that resembles a church, but a church interpreted as a grove"[10]—a distinction that seems at once fine and yet not quite fine enough. Taken together, the two stanzas do give us the two views Lehmann has put forth and in the order of her argument but without her qualifying negative: a grove that "resembles" a church in stanza five becomes a church "interpreted" as a grove in stanza six. The one, in fact, seems to grow out of the other, and for good reason. Writing about the British Church in its early days, Thomas Fuller describes how the Church had converted pagan temples to its own use, "not out of covetousness . . . but out

---

[10] Quoted by Garner, *Henry Vaughan*, p. 59.

of Christian thrift; conceiving this imitation an invitation to make heathens come over more cheerfully to the Christian faith."[11]

Vaughan's pilgrim has something of Fuller's heathen in him and the poet some of the strategy Fuller recounts. Both speaker and reader are lured cheerfully to church by a grove in nature, and both undergo a conversion in which "a new spring / Did all [the] senses greet." Like the pilgrim, we move from outside to inside, from an account of stately beauty to an unmediated vision of divine presence in nature, and at the moment in which "all [is] chang'd," Vaughan intensifies the ritualistic overtones (suggestions of stained-glass windows and incense appear) to make the parallel between grove and church seem more than accidental and the resemblances more of an identity. But Vaughan's temple in nature, even at the end of stanza six, is hardly a modernized Anglican church in disguise;[12] or if it is, it is inseparable from the primitive associations that nurtured it. Precisely because the poet is dedicated to evoking the religious experience in its primal phase of wonder and amazement, this place of worship is yet without a fully articulated structure. At the center of the poem, Vaughan returns us—as he will do later in "The Night"—to the origins of devotional mystery: in this case, it is to the moment when the speaker's self and the early Church have just been swept clean—a time when "thy glory doth best chime."

If in *Silex 1650* time seems to creep and the poet returns freely to the early hours of faith, *Silex 1655* reflects a decided increase in the tempo of history and the poet a clear recognition of worldly time as winding down with startling speed. Judgment Day is no longer to be contemplated from afar. The speaker of "Abels blood" impatiently demands to know "*How long*" it will be until Christ's arrival, while "The Stone" dramatizes how even the most stealthy of sinners cannot hope to evade the penetrating eye of God: in a moment of "revelation"

---

[11] Fuller, *The Church History of Britain*, 6 vols. (Oxford: Oxford Univ. Press, 1845), 1:36.
[12] Claude J. Summers and Ted-Larry Pebworth, "Vaughan's Temple in Nature and the Context of 'Regeneration,' " *JEGP* 74 (1975): 351-60.

anticipating the final Revelation, the speaker throws off his disguise to describe how at Judgment God's previously silent witnesses will "into loud discoveries break" (p. 515, l. 24). Underscoring this attitude of expectation, Vaughan's second Judgment Day poem, placed near the end of Part II, concentrates on ushering in the actual day itself. In a prayer that both asks God to "make haste, / Sin every day commits more waste" and that also serves as a final countdown ("And thy old enemy, which knows / His time is short, more raging grows"), the poet, echoing Isaiah (51:9), calls on God with a touch of Old Testament boldness:

> Yet, when thy mercy nothing wins
> But meer disdain, let not man say
> *Thy arm doth sleep*; but write this day
> Thy judging one: Descend, descend!
> Make all things new! and without end!   (p. 531, ll. 42-46)

Always a poet of darkness, Vaughan becomes a poet of the invading darkness in Part II. He responds vigorously to the possibilities of the coming End and, while shying away from prophecy in a poem like "White Sunday," he does not altogether eschew the opportunity to underline his own chosen status in these final days:

> And yet, as in nights gloomy page
> One silent star may interline:
> So in this last and lewdest age,
> Thy antient love on some may shine.   (p. 486, ll. 37-40)

Indeed, in its rhetorical side-stepping, "White Sunday" is singular in showing the poet sorting through the problems of how to proclaim his apostleship in Christ—the sense of election those chosen by God were to feel in the Last Days (Acts 2:17-18)—when it was equally likely that he might be taken for one of the "false Christs" also scheduled to appear at this hour (Matt. 24:24) and readily visible to Vaughan: "Can these new lights be like to those, / These lights of Serpents like the Dove?" (ll. 9-10). Vaughan's answer, of course, is no, but the "fire" these "new lights" boast necessarily usurps some of the poet's. An utterance that might easily have been in imitation of "Those flames which on the Apostles rush'd" (l. 5) turns into something of a witty tightrope walk in which the author argues how, at this late hour, a partial or "lesser commerce" (l. 22) with the light can be the only sign of salvation. Those claiming a full exposure to the sun are, in fact, betraying their own blindness. However knotty the poem is in places (and it is), Vaughan manages to clear a space for himself; and even though he does not go so far as to single himself out as an actual member of the elect, his careful side-stepping is all part of a not so delicate scramble in these final days for a place in heaven:

> O come! refine us with thy fire!
> Refine us! we are at a loss.
> Let not thy stars for *Balaams* hire
> Dissolve into the common dross! (ll. 61-64)

With the End near, Vaughan wrote in Part II on subjects that even the most untutored in apocalyptic prophecies would recognize as appropriate to the hour. His poem "The Jews" (for which there is no counterpart in *Silex* 1650) responds to the traditional millenarian belief in the conversion of the Jews as a signal of the Second Coming. Updating Herbert's poem with the same title, Vaughan stresses not the typological affinities between the wandering Israelites and all Christians exiled from their homeland, but a typological view of history in which a homecoming is about to be completed. The "fast and foul decays" associated with the occasion of Christ's first coming have reappeared, and deliverance seems imminent:

> So by all signs
> Our fulness too is now come in,
> And the same Sun which here declines
> And sets, will few hours hence begin
> To rise on you again, and look
> Towards old *Mamre* and *Eshcols* brook. (p. 499, ll. 26-31)

Historically, things have come almost full circle; so, too, has Vaughan's imagination, which responds to the increasing darkness not by celebrating beginnings but by looking toward the End itself, which anticipates a beginning that will have no end. "Cock-crowing," for instance, in which the speaker awaits expectantly for "Thy appearing hour," assumes greater apocalyptic resonances than does "The Dawning," and "Palm-Sunday," out of place in the liturgical scheme of feast days in *Silex*, celebrates Christ's entrance into Jerusalem in a manner that simultaneously suggests the arrival of the New Jerusalem. Furthermore, at the point in the latter poem when Vaughan might have been stimulated into giving a morning hymn—an occasion to which he responded with such originality in Part I—he delivers instead a singularly lame performance, heavily indebted to Herbert's exquisite lyric at the end of "Easter." With the sun in decline historically, the poet of Part II seems no longer so willing to get up with the sun each morning. He was, however, more attuned to writing about evening than at any other point in his career.

"The Night" is Vaughan's "myth of Transition." Long in the works (at least one phrase can be traced as far back as "Priorie Grove"), the poem is in a direct line with "Midnight" and "The Constellation," the two best nocturnal meditations in *Silex* 1650, but it differs from them in both its "degree" of vision and its view of time. Basically a "twilight" poem, it equates, in the most pervasive of the many puns in the poem, the late hour of the day with the last days of time and pulls together the various apocalyptic strains in Part II to form a supreme meditation on a moment of change, historically perceived and individually experienced. Elective affinities, light and darkness, the conversion of one Jew, a land of "blinde eyes" where Christ first appeared, and the poet's recognition of his "late and dusky" age—all of these concerns are present in "The Night" and identify the poem as a response to the invading darkness rather than an exercise in mystical ascent or an exploration into cabalistic or Hermetic texts.[13]

---

[13] Durr, *On The Mystical Poetry of Henry Vaughan* (Cambridge, Mass.: Harvard Univ. Press, 1962), pp. 112-22, Bain Tate Stewart, "Hermetic Symbolism in Henry Vaughan's 'The Night,'" *PQ* 29 (1950): 417-22; and

Vaughan signals the importance of time and vision in "The Night" by framing the poem around the relationship between the two. He opens with a statement about the clarity of perception in the past and closes with the recognition of its limited possibilities in a present, which prefigures the imminent End: "As men here / Say it is late and dusky, because they / See not all clear" (ll. 50-52). Within this dialectic, he unfolds and develops a complex parallel between the Pharisee Nicodemus and himself that both establishes their "kinred" (l. 36) connections and underscores their basic differences. He begins as if delivering a sermon and quotes the chapter and verse of his lesson. Better poet than preacher, Vaughan mistakenly reverses the chapter and verse number. His text is John 3:2, not 2:3, where in the figure of Nicodemus the poet discovers a surrogate worshipper-teacher who was also searching for the "sacred vail" of Christ, but during a moment in history exceptionally rich in devotional potential:

> Through that pure *Virgin-shrine*,
> That sacred vail drawn o'r thy glorious noon
> That men might look and live as Glo-worms shine,
>   And face the Moon:
> Wise *Nicodemus* saw such light
> As made him know his God by night.   (p. 522, ll. 1-6)

Vaughan's "preaching," though, continues to reveal certain peculiarities. After his reference to Christ as "*Virgin-shrine*" and his comparison of men to glowworms, allusions that have created considerable critical commentary, Vaughan unequivocally describes Nicodemus as "wise" in the closing couplet. Now Nicodemus was certainly "wise" to seek out Christ particularly, as we learn in the next stanza, since he lived in a "land of darkness and blinde eyes" (l. 8); he was also, as Augustine points out, the most influential teacher of the Jews and thus has a significant claim to intelligence.[14] But the one

---

A. W. Rudrum, "Vaughan's 'The Night': Some Hermetic Notes," *MLR* 64 (1969): 11-19.

[14] Augustine, Tractate 11 in *A Select Library of The Nicene and Post Nicene Fathers*, series 1, 14 vols., ed. Philip Schaff (New York: Charles Scribner's Sons, 1898-1909), 7 (1908): 74-77.

thing that Biblical exegetes agree on, surprisingly enough, is Nicodemus' lack of wisdom in any Christian sense. Augustine, Chrysostom, Luther, and Calvin all comment extensively on the Pharisee's inability to understand Christ's parables about putting on the New Man.[15]

It is possible that Vaughan was ignorant of this established view of Nicodemus, but it would then still be surprising that the poet of "Regeneration" would not have come to his own, similar understanding of Nicodemus' limited wisdom. The answer to this problem lies more likely in Vaughan's view of history, one that affects the structure of the poem: there has been a general dimming of the lights, and if Vaughan were to pause over the Pharisee's own problems of understanding, he would fail to establish at the outset a model of piety in the past that he can recollect in the succeeding stanzas in order to measure the present spiritual degeneration.

The next stanza clarifies further our notions of Vaughan's strategy as the poet eschews in the first line any possible questions about the quality of the Pharisee's faith; alliteration and exclamation tell us of Vaughan's awe over Nicodemus' being able to "speak with the Sun":

> Most blest believer he!
> Who in that land of darkness and blinde eyes
> Thy long expected healing wings could see,
>   When thou didst rise,
>   And what can never more be done,
>   Did at mid-night speak with the Sun!   (ll. 7-12)

The dialectic between past and present now becomes explicit, as does Vaughan's identification with Nicodemus: both the teaching Pharisee and the instructing poet live in a "land of

---

[15] The commentaries on John 3:1-5 are collected respectively in *Homilies of Saint John Chrysostom* in *A Library of Fathers of the Holy Catholic Church* (Oxford: John Henry Parker, 1847), 20:199-214; *Luther's Works*, 55 vols., ed. Jaroslav Pelikan, vols. 1-30 and Helmut T. Lehmann, vols. 31-55 (St. Louis: Concordia Publishing House, and Philadelphia: Muhlenberg Press, 1955-1976), 22 (1957): 275-87; and Jean Calvin, *Commentary on the Gospel According to John*, trans. Rev. William Pringle in *Works of Jean Calvin*, 52 vols. (Edinburgh: Calvin Translation Society, 1844-56), 34:103-14.

darkness and blinde eyes," and both have had to thwart the "established" religion and seek Christ under the cover of darkness. Yet just when Vaughan's excitement seems to verge on recapturing the vestiges of the original experience, the couplet suddenly measures the distance between Nicodemus and Vaughan and outlines the latter's apparent severance from Christ: "And what can never more be done, / Did at midnight speak with the Sun!" The poet recognizes his spiritual kinship with Nicodemus but also admits to their different situations; the journey to Christ must be rediscovered anew and within the current historical context.

The next two stanzas unfold some of the difficulties that now beset such a pilgrimage. Christ has apparently fled the land in the wake of the Puritan triumph, as Vaughan asserted earlier in "The Brittish Church," and He has left no clearly visible signs by which to track him:

> O who will tell me, where
> He found thee at that dead and silent hour!
> What hallow'd solitary ground did bear
>   So rare a flower,
>   Within whose sacred leafs did lie
>   The fulness of the Deity.   (ll. 13-18)

While Nicodemus actually saw the rare flower of Christ, Vaughan seems not even to have any guides to direct him. Curiously, however, his lament is exclamatory, not interrogative; and we see that the stanza simultaneously confirms the direction of the quest in its pun on the "sacred leafs" of Scripture at the same moment that it describes the anxiety of possible spiritual exile. Within the Bible, one can perhaps discover "the fulness of the Deity," a phrase that seems less likely to refer to Behmen's original bisexual man than to be an expression of hope that follows naturally from a poet who has so far had only a partial glimpse of Christ.[16] Over the next three stanzas Vaughan's task is to identify further the meaning of "fulness."

[16] Rudrum, "Vaughan's 'The Night,'" p. 17.

In reading John 3:2, the poet has been on the right path. Yet because of the time and the times, it is not easy to translate words into works; and he continues to envy Nicodemus' perspective:

> No mercy-seat of gold,
> No dead and dusty *Cherub*, nor carv'd stone,
> But his own living works did my Lord hold
>   And lodge alone;
> Where *trees* and *herbs* did watch and peep
> And wonder, while the *Jews* did sleep. (ll. 19-24)

Unable to establish for himself an external life with Christ, Vaughan thinks in stanzas five and six of defeating the world through the privacy of prayer:

> Dear night! this worlds defeat;
> The stop to busie fools; cares check and curb;
> The day of Spirits; my souls calm retreat
>   Which none disturb!
> *Christs* progress, and his prayer time;
> The hours to which high Heaven doth chime.
>
> Gods silent, searching flight:
> When my Lords head is fill'd with dew, and all
> His locks are wet with the clear drops of night;
>   His still, soft call;
> His knocking time; the souls dumb watch,
> When Spirits their fair kinred catch. (ll. 25-36)

The startling use of the vocative in the first line, the string of appositions, and the overall intimate and self-contained quality of this section separate it dramatically from the previous four and subsequent three stanzas of the poem. Here, Vaughan's decision to write in Welsh *dyfalu* form has important consequences for the meaning of the entire work. First, the appositional phrases recollect deliberately the syntactic structure of Herbert's "Prayer [I]" and indicate how Vaughan is exchanging spiritual guides as he attempts to bring the devotional experience into his own historical context: Nicodemus has offered Vaughan an analogue in the past for the poet's coming to Christ at night, but it is Herbert to whom Vaughan must turn in order to discover the proper form in which he can effect his mediation with Christ. It is as if this transition reenacts in miniature Vaughan's sudden and dramatic growth as a religious poet where his knowledge of the Bible had infused him with the desire to speak with God, but until his reading of Herbert, he did not know the way.

Second, the appositional phrases allow Vaughan to create a still point in the center of the poem in which the static quality of each description works to arrest the motion of the verse and to determine the verbal quiet necessary for a unitary vision. By building phrase upon phrase and including in the sixth stanza two dependent clauses that hang unresolved, the poet moves toward fusing the temporal with the timeless and thus breaks with the dialectical rhythms of the poem, which have so far revealed him only measuring present confusion against a more opportune past. Vaughan has realized that it is by making the timeless rediscovery of Christ in the immediate life that he can join Nicodemus in the past. As the devotional high point of "The Night," these stanzas remain suspended eternally; and the occasional repetition of ideas which has caused some readers dismay argues only more strongly for Vaughan's success at escaping time by undermining a strictly logical progression of thought. Night is "*Christs progress*" time; he makes his spiritual inroads by calling to the entire person, not by appealing just to his reason.

There is also a strategy in the placement of the two stanzas. The first one describes the more general spiritual values Vaughan attributes to night and their effects on both him and others. The second attempts more daringly and through particular detail to approximate the wonder he shows over Christ's sudden appearance. In this stanza the poet signals his communion with Christ by allowing his auditory imagination full range. As he depends heavily on the language of the Song of Songs in which the beloved comes to the lover, he repeatedly chooses words in the first three lines rich in *l*'s, *r*'s and *w*'s to swallow up and mute any sharp sounds that might accumulate from the *d*'s and *t*'s. "All the Eare lay hush," (l. 48) Vaughan says in "Regeneration" at another moment of intense devotional excitement, but this time both poet and reader listen to "His still, soft call; / His knocking time."

The intimacy Vaughan establishes with Christ is simple, sensuous, and stunning, and by suggesting the wonders of devotion, he is able finally to trace out imaginatively "the fulness of the Deity" (l. 18). The last line of the stanza offers itself as a beautifully inclusive summation of the poem to this point: meditation at night has allowed Vaughan to "catch" the "kinred" spirits of Nicodemus and Herbert who together have helped him toward a vision of Christ. Thus, the Welsh poet accomplishes what he has said earlier "can never more be done" (l. 11), for he does "at mid-night speak with the Sun!" (l. 12).

Despite the achievement of a timeless vision, no poem of Vaughan's shows better his reluctance to dissolve into rapture. The union of individual with Christ, which resolves all differences and allows for the metaphoric fusion of the most disparate images of light and darkness, can only be a temporary experience in this life. Brought up to the present at last, Vaughan turns to lament the immediate realities of his late age, a world of chaos and noise in which his spiritual guides, Nicodemus and Herbert, have no place. The poet's sudden emphasis on the clatter of contemporary confusion underscores, all the more, the value he places on the motionless quiet in the previous two stanzas:

> Were all my loud, evil days
> Calm and unhaunted as is thy dark Tent,
> Whose peace but by some *Angels* wing or voice
>   Is seldom rent;
> Then I in Heaven all the long year
> Would keep, and never wander here.   (ll. 37-42)

But with the recollection of "loud, evil days," both poet and poem begin to move anxiously forward as Vaughan interprets his version of a world turned upside down in the apparent context of the confusion that is to precede the Apocalypse. Daylight floods into the poem for the first time, chasing out the remaining shadows of night; the still point of stanzas five and six gives way to Vaughan's "wandering" in stanza seven, which in turn becomes a more frenetic running "To ev'ry myre" (l. 46) in stanza eight; and sight made possible by "this worlds ill-guiding light" (l. 47) discovers now only perpetual error and illusion:

> But living where the Sun
> Doth all things wake, and where all mix and tyre
> Themselves and others, I consent and run
> To ev'ry myre,
> And by this worlds ill-guiding light,
> Erre more then I can do by night. (ll. 43-48)

Although most readers equate "Sun" in the first line with the "ill-guiding light" of the world, it is also possible that we are meant to retain the figurative meaning of "Sun" as Christ which he has used in the second stanza. This section of the poem indicates that the "Sun" (Christ) has become the central issue around which all things "mix and tyre" and that Vaughan, like others who now have only "this worlds ill-guiding light," also contributes to the manifold chaos by consenting to run to "ev'ry myre." In this late age it is as difficult to sustain spiritual steadiness as it was earlier to recover the authentic vision of Christ which Nicodemus had experienced.

"The Night" succeeds precisely where some of his other poems fall down, for it refuses to make any easy divisions between the poet and his corrupt times. In this late poem, Vaughan recognizes unhappily that he abets, through his pointless wanderings, the chaos in the very world from which he wishes to escape. Acutely aware of his limitations, he looks to God in a *deus ex machina* last stanza that describes how faint light will be purged of its "duskiness" so that a "dazling darkness" (l. 50) can extend forever; it is perhaps the most astonishing performance in all of Vaughan:

> There is in God (some say)
> A deep, but dazling darkness; As men here
> Say it is late and dusky, because they
> See not all clear;
> O for that night! where I in him
> Might live invisible and dim. (ll. 49-54)

The voice resembles none of the others we have heard in the poem so far. Both remote and extremely present, detached yet "possessed," it seems to shuttle between two realms—two worlds with their separate views of time—without relinquishing touch with either. Beginning with the quietly startling appearance of the indefinite relative pronoun, the only time one is used in the poem, Vaughan measures a frame distant, slightly austere, and beautiful in which he can place all the flurry of the preceding stanzas. But he denies the vision its full power with the sudden transition to the simile whose very intrusion as well as its subject matter indicates that a momentous change is, in fact, in the process of occurring. Lateness, the approaching end of time, is the conclusion men around Vaughan have been reaching "because they / See not all clear." The remote is becoming immediate, and the closing apostrophe is the poet's prayer to help bring in the resplendent darkness of eternity that is already apparent on the horizon.[17] Moreover, his strategy in the simile of introducing witnesses who, though unidentified, share a number of characteristics with the poet, also becomes clear: they allow Vaughan a surrogate means to depict a vision of the coming End without his running the risk of seeming to commit the "manifest impiety" of predicting God's will. For the moment he is report-

---

[17] For a brief but valuable comparison of Vaughan's structural use of time to that of other seventeenth-century poets, see Lowry Nelson, Jr., *Baroque Lyric Poetry* (New Haven: Yale Univ. Press, 1961), pp. 36-37. Vaughan had good authority in Isaiah 29:14-17 for associating blurring vision with the end of history and for thinking, as he also does in "White Sunday," of partial vision in the Last Days as a sign of salvation. I have treated this point in more detail in "Vaughan's 'The Night' and his 'late and dusky' Age," *SEL* 19 (1979): 129.

ing, and it is in the context of this report that he gives his powerful closing prayer.

Finally, even though Dionysius the Aeropagite is probably in the background of Vaughan's thoughts here on divine darkness, I would offer a more contemporary gloss that accounts for the relationship of this stanza to the rest of the poem and for the tension Vaughan has maintained throughout in the central opposition between light and darkness. Donne, in a sermon written to be preached at Paul's Cross in 1622, traces out the conditions of conflict in this life through the irreconcilable images of light and darkness:

> It is an opposition against God, by any colourable Modifications, to reconcile opinions diametrally [sic] contrary to one another, in fundamentall things. *Day* and *Night* may joyne and meet, *In Diluculis* and *in Crepusculis*. The drawing of the day, in the Morning, and the shutting in of the day in the Evening, make day and night so much one, as sometimes you cannot tell which to call them: but *Lux & tenebrae*, light and darknes, *Midnight* and *Noone* never met, never joynd.[18]

To Donne, dawn and dusk can appear to the eye easily interchangeable so that we often fuse, or confuse, the beginning of the day with its end. But he also indicates that if this illusion is real, it is also temporary; we are ultimately able to recognize the separation of day from night, noon from midnight, and the beginning from the end.

Vaughan's poem is a complex restatement of these observations that describes, on one level, the possible fusion of day and night; but it admits, on another level, the irreconcilability of the two. Vaughan sees that he and Nicodemus live at nearly opposite ends of Christian history, the one at its dawning, the other at its dusk; but despite this vast separation in time, when Vaughan recapitulates Nicodemus' experience of coming to Christ at night, he also manages symbolically to fuse the end

---

[18] *The Sermons of John Donne*, ed. George R. Potter and Evelyn M. Simpson, 10 vols. (Berkeley: Univ. of California Press, 1953-1962), 4 (1959): 193.

(dusk) with the beginning (dawn) and makes them "so much one, as sometimes you cannot tell which to call them."

Nevertheless, from a slightly different perspective we see that this still point in the center of the poem which marks the intersection of light and darkness, beginning and end, poet and Christ, can only be a momentary fusion, since the world to which Vaughan returns in stanzas seven and eight is unmistakably divided and distinguished. A holistic vision that contains simultaneously light and darkness, noon and midnight, is available in this life but only to the poetic imagination, which can yoke together these contraries through pun and metaphor. The best Vaughan can do at present in uniting noon and midnight is through his metaphoric communion with the "Sun" (Christ) at night; but it is finally impossible, as he laments in the subsequent stanzas, to translate symbolic language into realistic values and resolve permanently in this world such apparent opposites.

Though Vaughan would doubtlessly have agreed with Donne that "*Midnight* and *Noone* never met, never joynd," his last stanza goes one step further by pointing to how these contraries will become reconciled in the divine. In God's "dazling darkness" the fusion of noon and midnight will be made complete and permanent; there, all of the anxious movement the poet associates with the light of these last days will be tempered by the order he knows exists in darkness. The dusk that Vaughan sees settling around him suggests that God's hand is already at work bringing about the End; but before the Apocalypse actually occurs the poet reveals how, with the aid of Nicodemus and Herbert, he is able for a moment to experience the still point of eternal communion with God that will be his future.

CHAPTER EIGHT

Thalia Rediviva: Looking Backward and Forward

> I turned aside to see if [Thalia] was still asleep but she was gone, and this did not a little trouble me. I expected her return till the day was quite spent, but she did not appear. At last, fixing my eyes on that place where she sometimes rested, I discovered certain pieces of gold which she had left behind her, and hard by a paper folded like a letter.
>
> —Thomas Vaughan, *Lumen de Lumine*

IN A LETTER of June 15, 1673, written to his cousin, John Aubrey, Vaughan mentioned in his summary of accomplishments, "Thalia Rediviva, a peece now ready for the presse, with the Remaines of my brothers Latine Poems" (p. 688). Aubrey had been inquiring into the details of Henry's and Thomas's lives for Anthony à Wood's projected history of Oxford which appeared the following year and later elicited the poet's gratitude "that my dear brothers name (& mine) are revived, & shine in the Historie of the Universitie" (p. 692). For reasons that are impossible now to determine, *Thalia Rediviva* did not appear in print until 1678. Five years had elapsed since it had been first mentioned and more than twenty since Vaughan had completed his last major work, the second part of *Silex*, published in 1655. None of his literary ventures had brought him much fame. Neither *Poems* nor *Olor* were reprinted in his lifetime and, despite its claim to being a "second edition," *Silex* 1655 included along with the new verse only a reissue of the unsold leaves of Part I. If the Welsh poet had hoped to displace Christopher Harvey as Herbert's favorite son, it can only be said that he failed miserably: bound along with *The Temple* for much of the seventeenth century, Harvey's *Synagogue* crept into the public eye more times in a decade than *Silex* did in a century. Vaughan's reputation, the preface to *Thalia* wisely observes, was "*better built in the sentiment of several judicious Persons, who know him very well able to give himself a lasting Monument, by undertaking any Argument of note in the whole Circle of Learning*" (p. 616).[1]

Modern criticism has subsequently vindicated Vaughan and come to agree with I. W.—the author of the note to the reader—but it has been hard pressed to find much merit in the volume for which the note was written. The reasons are not difficult to discover. Appearing considerably after *Silex* but containing some material written even earlier than the religious verse, *Thalia* has earned the reputation for being simply a repository for Vaughan's literary flotsam: "little escaped his own salvaging" is the dry report of one specialist.[2] Amid the wreckage,

---

[1] Besides the notice in Wood's *Historia et Antiquitates Universitatis Oxoniensis* (1674), Vaughan received partial recognition in Edward Phillips's *Theatrum Poetarum* (London, 1675), p. 70 ("The Modern Poets"), where he is described loosely as "the Author of certain *English* poems, which came forth *anno.* 1658 under the Title of *Olor Iscanus*" (p. 70). Eighteen lines of "The Resolve" were reprinted in *Witts Recreations* (1650, 1654, 1663, and 1667), with the note "I would commend to thy sharpest view and serious consideration; The Sweet Caelestiall sacred Poems by Mr. *Henry Vaughan*, intituled *Silex Scintillans*." But the only contemporary author who shows signs of having read the religious poetry with any profit was Nathaniel Wanley, whose *Scintillulae Sacrae* remained in manuscript until 1928. See *The Poems of Nathaniel Wanley*, ed. L. C. Martin (Oxford: Clarendon Press, 1928), esp. the introduction and commentary.

[2] Harold R. Walley, "The Strange Case of *Olor Iscanus*," *RES* 18 (1942): 29. Other than a brief chapter in F. E. Hutchinson, *Henry Vaughan: A Life and Interpretation* (Oxford: Clarendon Press, 1947), pp. 212-23, devoted mainly to bibliographical problems, *Thalia* has never been the focus of any sustained attempt at interpretation. This fact is only slightly remarkable considering Vaughan's reputation as a nature poet. Comments on the secular verse are interspersed throughout James D. Simmonds, *Masques of God: Form and Theme in the Poetry of Henry Vaughan* (Pittsburgh: Univ. of Pittsburgh Press, 1922), who finds more merit than most in the "Etesia" poems, while Barbara K. Lewalski, *Protestant Poetics and the Seventeenth-Century Religious Lyric* (Princeton: Princeton Univ. Press, 1979), pp. 350-51, gives a short, cogent overview of the religious verse. In spite of appropriating the subtitle of *Thalia* into his own title, Peter Bement's "Henry Vaughan's 'Countrey Muse,'" *Poetry Wales* 11 (1975): 116-31 is disappointingly brief on the collection. Poems receiving extensive individual at-

moreover, there is only one poem, "Daphnis: An Elegiac *Eclogue*," that can legitimately claim to represent a generic departure from the earlier works, and this pastoral lament has been almost universally criticized as one of the poet's most recognizably tattered pieces. Otherwise, stylistically and thematically, there is little that is new about *Thalia*. Most of the verse is in couplets and in modes already familiar to his readers; few, if any, of the lyrics command the attention of Vaughan's finest poems, nor does the collection achieve much cumulative power from its organization. A miscellany of "Choice Poems on Several Occasions," the volume distinguishes the secular verse from the "Pious thoughts and Ejaculations" by placing several translations from Boethius and Claudian between them; but other than that, the very lack of an imaginative ordering design in *Thalia* is strong counterevidence for its significant presence in *Poems*, *Olor*, and *Silex*.

It is also almost impossible not to be aware of a sense of spent energy in the religious verse. In the aftermath of *Silex*, with its powerful commitment to an eschatological view of history and concern over personal salvation, the devotional poems often seem written in a vacuum, pulling out previous themes but without having a firm context in which to place them. "*To Christian Religion*," for instance, summarizes, while greatly simplifying, the vision of the westward migration of the Church which helped earlier to shape Vaughan's role as a religious poet; but detached from the poetry it inspired, the idea seems deprived of its original meaning, as if the poet is now working with only some loose ends of *Silex* and little of the substance that went into its making. To a large degree,

---

tention include: "*To his Learned Friend and Loyal Fellow-Prisoner*, Thomas Powel *of* Cant. Doctor *of Divinity*," which is examined by Marilla, *SPHV*, pp. 334-37; by A. U. Chapman, "Henry Vaughan and Magnetic Philosophy," *Southern Review* 4 (1970-71): 215-26; and by Rudrum, "Some Remarks on Vaughan's Secular Poetry," *Poetry Wales* 11 (1975): 36-54; "Daphnis: An Elegiac Eclogue" by Robert Wilcher, *DUJ* 36 (1974): 25-40, who discusses the possible political allusions in this poem; and Vaughan's two celebrations of Christmas ("*The Nativity*" and "*The true Christmas*") by A. B. Chambers in "Christmas: The Liturgy of the Church and English Verse of the Renaissance," *Literary Monographs*, vol. 6, ed. Eric Rothstein and J. A. Wittreich, Jr. (Madison: Univ. of Wisconsin Press, 1975), pp. 109-51.

the verse bears out this suspicion. The most obvious gap is the most important: Herbert's absence is duly noted in "*The Ecclipse*" when the Welsh author opens with the most audible echo of his master in *Thalia*, "Whither, O whither did'st thou fly"—a line taken almost verbatim from "The Search"; and even though Vaughan's other master—Christ—is occasionally present, there is little sense of the poet's attempting a vigorous imitation of Him. Missing, too, from *Thalia* is a strong commitment to a political vision. Instead of presenting himself as a representative Anglican suffering captivity, a role that generated a variety of rhetorical possibilities, the poet's response to history has narrowed to a few local skirmishes that entrap rather than liberate his energies. His celebration of Christ's birth in "*The Nativity*," for instance, is caught in a web of complaints, one of which involves a dispute over taxes, and the poem is never really able to get started. Although still conscious of the dangers of verbal contamination (see "*The Request*," p. 667, l. 10), Vaughan's position as a defender of the faith has shrunk noticeably; so too have the creative tensions coming from his attempt to combine Juvenal with Herbert.

Given the delimited focus of *Thalia*, it should hardly be surprising that the religious verse divides thematically between looking backwards and seeking retreat. Both represent forms of envelopment rather than development; both attempt to conserve a vision of the past. The one blends an attitude of personal innocence with a time of poetic creativity and the other seeks to preserve the author in a state of possible sanctification achieved partially by the composition of "good works" in *Silex*. The opening lines of "*Looking back*," for example, seem doubly committed to recollecting Vaughan's poetic "youth" in *Silex* as well as his "first happy age":

Fair, shining *Mountains* of my pilgrimage,
    And flow'ry *Vales*, whose flow'rs were stars:
The *days* and *nights* of my first, happy age;
    An age without distast and warrs:
When I by thoughts ascend your *Sunny heads*,

>   And mind those sacred, *midnight* Lights:
> By which I walk'd, when curtain'd Rooms and Beds
>   Confin'd, or seal'd up others sights. (p. 660, ll. 1-8)

"Fair, shining *Mountains* of my pilgrimage" revises the stormy assault of "Regeneration"—"a monstrous, mountain'd thing"—into a vision of the pastoral ideal, a time "When I by thoughts ascend your *Sunny heads*, / And mind those sacred, *midnight* Lights." Although the Welsh poet removes these activities to "An age without distast and warrs" and hence destroys any sense of absolute historical accuracy to his reflections, it is still impossible to escape the suggestion that the ambiance he particularly admires and wishes to recollect also points to the distinctive poetic achievements of *Silex*. Minding "those sacred, *midnight* Lights" returns us to "Midnight," "The Constellation," and "The Night," to name only the most obvious nocturnal moments in which the verbal and the devotional senses are firmly united. Furthermore, the transfigured thoughts—those that "ascend your *Sunny heads*"—seem also an attempt to repossess in miniature the heightened experiences of "Mount of Olives [II]" and the Ascension poetry of *Silex*, Part II: the overall vision of innocence is the vision at the end of the religious verse as well as of childhood.

But the double perspective, or depth of field, presented in "*Looking back*" also produces a blur in focus, and I do not mean the one that produced the infamous slip about "How brave a prospect is a bright *Back-side*" (l. 15). Rather, the images demand attention more for their own sake than for their contribution to the "argument." They deny us both a sense of a sharply realized past and the immediacy of a speaking voice in the dramatic present. Unlike "The Retreate," for instance, in which a speaker looks back from the outset, "*Looking back*," as the present participle suggests, places us within the act of reflection itself but without first giving us a firm sense of who is doing the reflecting and for precisely what reasons. It is hardly surprising, therefore, to find Vaughan's sudden description of being refreshed to be formulaic and unconvincing (ll. 9-14) since the referents meant to carry these remembrances are themselves unclear. Despite the speaker's claims of being rejuvenated, the poem itself seems heavily burdened by its own literary past.

The religious verse is most successful when the poet is most willing to accept the limited status of his muse and, instead of attempting to "re-collect" some of the more heightened imaginative moments of *Silex*, is content simply to "revive" a single one of its motifs. As if to demonstrate this point, the lyric immediately following "*Looking back*," "*The Shower* [II]," narrowly defines its context by developing one symbol—dew—that is prevalent throughout the religious verse but which receives specific shaping at the end of its namesake in *Silex*, Part I:

> Yet, if as thou doest melt, and with thy traine
> Of drops make soft the Earth, my eyes could weep
> O're my hard heart, that's bound up, and asleep,
>   Perhaps at last
>   (Some such showres past,)
> My God would give a Sun-shine after raine. (p. 413, ll. 13-18)

The later poem answers to the first in the form of heaven responding to the suppliant. The heart, once bound up and asleep, has now been wakened into giving a brief but exquisite hymn of praise, one that serves to represent and not re-present a greater sunshine than that which happens in nature alone:

> Waters above! eternal Springs!
> The dew, that silvers the *Doves* wings!
> O welcom, welcom to the sad:
> Give dry dust drink; drink that makes glad!
> Many fair *Ev'nings*, many *Flowr's*
> Sweeten'd with rich and gentle showers
> Have I enjoy'd, and down have run
> Many a fine and shining *Sun*;
> But never till this happy hour
> Was blest with such an *Evening-shower*! (p. 661)

What is striking here is how the double perspective of "*Looking back*" has been translated and miniaturized into a doubling of language itself: the echoing is no longer diffuse and spectral but central to the life of the poem. Welcome-welcome, drink-drink, many-many, and then the further repetition of "Many fair *Ev'nings*" and "Many a fine and shining *Sun*"—all work together to sharpen our response to the singular experience expressed in the final couplet. Quietly understated ("But never"), it frames the exception to all that has come before; it also firmly locates the poem and the speaker in an immediate temporal context ("this happy hour").

The verbal doubling in "*The Shower* [II]" helps to make up for the lack of rhetorical possibilities in a volume of verse in which the poet is no longer attempting to double as Herbert. The chime and symphony of *Silex* has been reduced to a series of grace notes in *Thalia*, whose poetic models are essentially those which the author has already created. "*Discipline*" and "*Affliction* [II]," for instance, continue in the manner of "*The Shower* [II]" to give a miniaturized view of earlier, "grander" experiences now recollected with an eye toward their further refinement. Neither shows Vaughan challenging his enemies or calling directly to God; in both poems, the neat octosyllables restrict the likelihood of any real verbal uprising. The sixteen lines of "*Discipline*" replay the rebellion of man, with its original and contemporary overtones, and sculpt out the poet's now tame position in his response to human unruliness:

> Fair prince of life, lights living well!
> Who hast the keys of death and hell!
> If the m[u]le man despise thy day,
> Put chains of darkness in his way.
> Teach him how deep, how various are
> The Councels of thy love and care.
> When Acts of grace and a long peace
> Breed but rebellion and displease;
> Then give him his own way and will,
> Where lawless he may run until
> His own choice hurts him, and the sting
> Of his foul sins full sorrows bring.   (p. 661, ll. 1-12)

Vengeance is Thine: even the poet's desire to correct, let alone to combat, human folly has been distilled out of this definition of discipline. A similar reduction of energy happens in "Affliction [II]," a fourteen-line poem praising all of the pleasures and none of the pains of being crossed by God. "Man *blossoms* at thy touch" (p. 662, l. 3) summarizes the substance of the poem and much of the doctrine of *Silex*, Part I, including that expressed in "Affliction [I]," but it also allows now for little sense of the human struggle to surface. Glossed rapidly and at times with smoothing nonchalance, affliction becomes a synonym for a healall: "The fall is fair ev'n to desire" (l. 11).

These poems are thematic doubles of earlier attitudes. Vaughan's celebration of his country retreat, "*Retirement* [II]," uses a twin rhetorical structure ("I ask not why . . . I ask not why") to emphasize the centripetal vision of a mind given largely to repeating the exemplary actions of rustic behavior found in the Bible; in doing so the verbal repetitions only inscribe more deeply the attitude of meekness established at the end of "Retirement [I]" in *Silex*. Unlike Vaughan's other celebrations of "*rural shades*," this one seems a genuine contribution to the *beatus ille* tradition as it developed in the seventeenth century. As Maren-Sofie Røstvig says, with some surprise, this poem "displays a positive delight in retirement."[3] Like Mildmay Fane and Charles Cotton, who both composed verses on this same topic, Vaughan achieves that note of inward satisfaction so central to the mode:

> Fresh *fields* and *woods*! the Earth's fair *face*,
> God's *foot-stool*, and mans *dwelling-place*.
> I ask not why the first *Believer*
> Did love to be a Country liver?
> Who to secure pious content
> Did pitch by *groves* and *wells* his tent;
> Where he might view the boundless *skie*,
> And all those glorious *lights* on high:
> With flying *meteors*, *mists* and *show'rs*,

[3] Røstvig, *The Happy Man: Studies in the Metamorphoses of a Classical Ideal*, 2 vols., 2nd ed. (Trondheim: Norwegian Universities Press, 1962), 1: 205.

> Subjected *hills, trees, meads* and *Flow'rs*:
> And ev'ry minute bless the King
> And wise Creatour of each thing. (p. 662, ll. 1-12)

Nothing is going to upset this poet. The psalmist who used to give songs in the night has become a country lover; Abraham no longer appears as one of the named heroes of the old faith ("Religion") but simply as an anonymous "Country liver." Reduced in scale, the one delivers and the other figures in a landscape which is not so much a startling presentation of God as a neatly arranged brochure that outlines the advantages of rural retreat. Corruption—"the dismal *Sinks*" of the city—is visible only as a foil and not as a threat to retirement, just as bits of Vaughan's earlier poem "Corruption" reappear but now without being framed by the fall; and though it might be only a coincidence if we hear in the contented dogtrot rhythms of the final lines the echoing sound of Marvell's complacent mower who is sure that "the Gods themselves with us do dwell," the slightly self-satisfied note of closure nonetheless completes the easeful mood of a muse that, in the words of Virgil attached to the title page of *Thalia*, "blushed not to dwell in the woods." The Silurist has shut up shop.

Vaughan's most vigorous devotional performance in *Thalia* takes the idea of verbal doubling as far as it can go as a stylistic resource. "*The Recovery*," unlike "*The Shower* [II]," "*Affliction* [II]," and "*Retirement* [II]," has no obvious corresponding type in *Silex*. Indeed, its subject, the supremacy of God over nature, represents a departure from the poet's more usual practice of showing God present in the phenomenal world:

> Fair *Vessell* of our daily light, whose proud
> And previous *glories* gild that blushing Cloud:
> Whose lively *fires* in swift projections glance
> From hill to hill, and by refracted chance
> Burnish some neighbour-*rock*, or tree, and then
> Fly off in coy and winged *flams* agen:
>   If thou this day

>   Hold on thy way,
> Know, I have got a greater *light* than thine;
> A light, whose *shade* and *back-parts* make thee shine.
>   Then get thee down: then get thee down;
>   I have a *Sun* now of my own.   (pp. 664-65, ll. 1-12)

The rhetorical doubling is at once the most thoroughly observed and sophisticated in all of Vaughan's poetry, barely noticeable except as it is perfectly integrated into the theme. Semantically, the repetition of "light" emphasizes unobtrusively the "greater" dimension of God's light, while the syntactic doubling earlier in the stanza ("whose proud... whose lively") has already raised by several powers the sun's illumination. Only in the refrain ("Then get thee down"), the most obvious form of doubling in the poem, does the double meaning of the sun/son pun fully emerge, now with the purpose of driving home the poet's "recovery" of Christ.

But the second stanza, in its almost identical duplication of the first, points out the narrow line that separates repetition from exhaustion, imitation from emptiness. It lays bare the rhetorical construction of the poem, particularly as the opening few lines turn in on themselves through a series of self-evident acts of verbal doubling:

> Those nicer livers, who without thy Rays
> Stirr not abroad, those may thy lustre praise:
> And wanting light (*light*, which no *wants* doth know!)
> To thee (weak *shiner!*) like blind *Persians* bow.   (ll. 13-16)

Paradox, ambiguity, rhetorical duplication (both antistasis and epizeuxis) and periphrasis—all work to tighten the verse until repetition borders on verbal exhaustion. Only when Vaughan reinstates the hierarchy of meanings contained in the pun does the poem untangle itself, but not before the earlier "original" statement has come to seem a predictable solution. Duplication is now a dead end, and the stanza appears as a tissue of verbal seams rather than a scene in which divinity has been recovered. Word and word have been visibly separated.

The verbal inwardness of *Thalia*, perhaps at its extreme in

"*The Recovery*," matches in kind the inward thematic focus of Vaughan's country muse, and in each case what is a poetic virtue at one moment can easily become a liability at the next. In "*The World* [II]," it is possible to witness something approaching a final narrowing or collapse of the religious poet's vision. Vaughan's response to anything beyond the self in retirement has become minimal, and the extraordinary withdrawal in this poem reduces even further the rhetorical possibilities of language. "Can any tell me what it is" (l. 1) has now replaced the vast sweep of the opening line of its namesake in *Silex* I: the world has become a place of illusion rather than a target for correction. Accompanying this change in perspective, one that denies the poet any public role whatsoever, is also a change in the poet's attitude toward his medium, or rather an intensification of an attitude held in *Silex* but that never fully dominated his art. Vaughan's suspicions about the "fallen" nature of speech clearly surfaces and with greater poetic consequences: "But since of all, all may be said, / And *likelines* doth but upbraid, / And mock the *Truth*, which still is lost / In fine *Conceits*, like streams in a sharp frost" (ll. 11-14). The phrase does not inaugurate a rhetoric of silence or a condition of verbal despair; it does, however, lead the poet to sever his verbal ties with any reality beyond retreat ("Here I renounce thee, and resign / Whatever thou can'st say, is thine") and to begin a series of attenuated descriptions of the world, the purpose of which is to maintain the poet in his distance from his subject while he undergoes a kind of preparation for the "pure thoughts and peaceful hours" of retirement:

> Thou art not *Truth*; for he that tries
> Shall find thee all deceit and lyes.
> Thou art not *friendship*; for in thee
> 'Tis but the *bait* of policy.
> Which, like a *Viper* lodg'd in *Flow'rs*,
> Its venom through that sweetness pours.
> . . . .

> Thou art not *Riches*; for that *Trash*
> Which one age hoords, the next doth wash . . .
>
> (p. 670, ll. 21-26, 33-34)

As "the world" disappears into a series of negatives (five in all), repetition or doubling literally embraces the *via negativa* as if to signal the exhaustion of a rhetorical mode that has sustained the creation of much of the verse in *Thalia*: retreat is both verbal and thematic and in each case nearly complete. Significantly, the poem following this one, "The Bee," is Vaughan's longest celebration of solitude in the collection: it is also his last. In the next verse he gives his farewell to Christian religion and asks "Who shall the happy *shepherds* be / To watch the next *Nativity*" (ll. 19-20). *Thalia* does not end with a vision of an imminent Apocalypse but with a recognition of the world continuing on, with its burden being only increased by time. The moment of an historical crisis has passed and with it the poet's sense of his place in it, but he does not, like Colin Clout, conclude his part by hanging up his pipe in despair: he simply measures its diminishing notes in a pastoral setting before he relinquishes it to another generation in another place further westward.

The sense of finality *Thalia* gives to Vaughan's career as a devotional poet happens also with the secular verse but in a different manner. These verses provide a synoptic account of the author in his different poetic phases that prepares us for his summary reckoning of the muse in the concluding elegy "Daphnis. An Elegiac *Eclogue*." Like the "brief lives" currently being composed by his cousin Aubrey, they "revive" Vaughan in his youth, maturity, and dotage where they combine to form a "*lasting Memory*" to substitute for the public recognition he failed to receive. And like a good antiquarian at least, nothing did escape his salvaging. Amoret reappears, this time as Etesia or Fida, the country beauty; the place of his youthful courtier days is revisited in "*To Lysimachus, the Author being with him in* London." Even his strong political attitudes are recollected in "The King Disguis'd. *Written about the same time that Mr. John Cleveland wrote his.*"Although there are good reasons to suppose that not all of these lyrics are, in fact, juvenilia,[4] they nonetheless serve to flesh out the poet's gay-spirited "early days" best summed in *"The Eagle,"* a vigorous imitation of youthful poetic furor in which the author's "*unfledg'd* witt" (l. 2) challenges the flight of the bird in its planetary odyssey.

Vaughan's middle years—those of his "maturity" so to speak—are equally well delineated. An "educated man," he displays his mastery of different subjects (magnetic lore, astrology, and the classics) in three studiously witty poems, *"To his Learned Friend and Loyal Fellow-Prisoner,* Thomas Powel *of* Cant. *Doctor of Divinity," "In Zodiacum Marcelli Palingenii,"* and *"On Sir* Thomas Bodley's *Library*; *The Author being then in* Oxford." All of the "wisdom" and self-possession found in these poems is gathered together to form the substance of his transcendent attitude in *"The importunate Fortune, written to Doctor Powel of Cantre."* Once more, even though this "group" evades exact dating, the assured and confident voice in the poems describes an author who has "arrived." Best epitomized in the elegy *"To the pious memorie of C. W.,"* it progresses rapidly and recognizably toward ripeness in the epithalamion honoring J. Morgan of Whitehall. In the first instance, it is easy to determine an approximate date of composition since the title observes that C. W. (Charles Walbeoffe) died on September 13, 1653, a time when Vaughan was clearly at his peak, and in the poem the author refers to himself, appropriately enough, as "The Just Recorder of thy death and worth" (l. 22). In the other verse, however, the

---

[4] Marilla, *SPHV*, p. 276 and pp. 294-95, argues tentatively for a date of composition after 1650 for *"The Eagle"* and a post-Restoration date for the composition of *"To Lysimachus."* Whether or not he is right on this score (and I think he probably is), the three dates a reader can readily discern ("The King Disguis'd," "To the pious memorie," and "To the Editor of the matchless Orinda") correspond to, and in fact help to pinpoint, the author in his different "phases."

poet's star is already in "decline":[5] admitting readily to his "neglected" status, he sees himself as outdated—as someone whose worth as a poet and promoter of traditional values of love will be recognized only by a later generation of readers. Finally, Vaughan's "dotage" seems duly recorded in three "late" occasional verses. "To Mr. M. L. *upon his reduction of the* Psalms *into Method*," "*Upon sudden news of the much lamented death of Judge* Trevers," and "*To the Editor of the matchless* Orinda" show the poet living on in a world well lost, gruff, crusty, and even embittered over his obscurity.

As might be expected, the most substantial of the secular poems are those belonging to his "middle years," and of this group the finest effort is certainly the elegy to Charles Walbeoffe, Vaughan's cousin and close acquaintance. Ambitious yet assured, the lament takes many of the features of the war elegies and reworks them in light of the introspective and intimate vision developed in *Silex*. The result is a poem that achieves moments of sublimity on both a public and private level. The conventional apology, for instance, that often initiates the lament in Vaughan and in other elegies of the period touches a dignified, personal note that cuts between formality and self-indulgence:

> Now, that the publick Sorrow doth subside,
> And those slight tears which *Custom* Springs, are dried;
> While all the rich & *out-side-Mourners* pass
> Home from thy *Dust* to empty their own *Glass*:
> I (who the throng affect not, nor their state:)
> Steal to thy grave undress'd, to meditate
> On our sad loss, accompanied by none,
> An obscure mourner that would weep alone.   (p. 629, ll. 1-7)

---

[5] I use the word purposefully, echoing "N. W." in his commendatory poem, "*To the ingenious Author of* Thalia Rediviva" (l. 21). Hutchinson, *Life*, p. 215, seems a little oversensitive that Vaughan, only fifty-seven when *Thalia* was published, should be described by "N. W." as already in his "declining years." There is plenty of evidence in *Thalia* to suggest that "The Uscan Swan"—the poet and not necessarily the person—has crested.

With measured certainty, Vaughan defines his duty: to revitalize the forms of grief whose ritual offices have been already spent. A latecomer, as he was in the elegy to R. W., he is not too late to regard himself as Walbeoffe's "Just Recorder," and for openers his one long sentence, with its pauses, hesitations, and gradual linguistic descent, has the effect of methodically paring away all customary pretense. The self, "undress'd," is down to its solitary essentials by the final line, the only one of the last four that spans the meter without a break in the speaking voice: "An obscure mourner that would weep alone." In its concern with the sorrows of solitude, the line also quietly delivers the most important criterion for an elegist.

The control manifested in the beginning of the poem is manifested throughout as Vaughan structures his lament to describe first Walbeoffe's outer features—his loyalty and integrity—and then his inner, "Man's secret region and his noblest part" (l. 58). Besides the marked balance, the central part of this elegy (ll. 25-74) is distinguished from those of "*R. W.*" and "*R. Hall*" by the intense sympathy that exists between the poet and his subject, one that is developed in the course of the poem until it achieves a kind of cosmic intimacy at the end. Vaughan and Walbeoffe are not just kin but "kinred" spirits. Both survived the rebellion only to suffer "The tedious Reign of our Calamity" (l. 24); both lived "When Warr and open'd Hell / Licens'd all Artes and Sects, and made it free / To thrive by fraud and blood and blasphemy" (ll. 50-52). But neither man compromised his soul—"Such clean, pure hands had'st thou!" (l. 57). Each made, in fact, a virtue out of necessity and won his separate peace. Concluding the middle portion of the poem is a moving description of Walbeoffe's inner regions to which the poet is "privy," and, with meticulous scrutiny, Vaughan recounts a spiritual victory in language that could easily serve as a gloss on his own victory in *Silex*:

> Of that faire Room, where thy bright Spirit lay:
> I must affirm, it did as much surpass

> Most I have known, as the clear Sky doth glass.
> Constant and kind, and plain and meek and Mild
> It was, and with no new Conceits defil'd.
> Busie, but sacred thoughts (like *Bees*) did still
> Within it stirr, and strive unto that Hill,
> Where redeem'd Spirits evermore alive
> After their Work is done, ascend and *Hive*.
> No outward tumults reach'd this inward place,
> 'Twas holy ground: where peace, and love and grace
> Kept house: where the immortal restles life
> In a most dutiful and pious strife
> Like a fix'd *watch*, mov'd all in order, still;
> The *Will* serv'd God, and ev'ry *Sense* the Will!   (ll. 60-74)

"In a most dutiful and pious strife" defines the difference between God's ways and those of the world in which "strife" possesses neither duty nor piety. The inner room—the space apart from the "Artes and Sects"—, however, is a match for God's creation: still yet moving, "the immortal restles life" is an image of the universe and of the generative principle of *discordia concors* that governs the heavens and is shared by the divine and the divinely appointed. "In this safe state death mett thee. Death which is / But a kind Usher of the good to bliss" (ll. 75-76). Like the end for which the poet of *Silex* has been preparing, this one is represented as a moment of sublime relaxation; and if within the doubling of death and the hesitation, the slight pause of the enjambment, we sense a ripple of tension reminiscent in miniature of the larger gap discovered in *Olor* between pastoral and elegy, the potential vertigo of going over the edge yields quickly to the comfortable figure of death as "But a kind Usher of the good to bliss." Reversing the imagery of "The Night" but retaining its sense of an imminent ending, Vaughan prepares to meet Walbeoffe in the next world: "Some bid their Dead *good night!* but I will say / *Good morrow to dear Charles!* for it is day" (ll. 91-92).

No one wrote Vaughan's epitaph or memorialized his career in the heroic vein that the Welsh poet fashioned for Walbeoffe. Although *Thalia* came laden with tributes, including one "Pindaric" in imitation of Cowley, the commendatory verses have little merit—most are predictably effusive—and none subscribes to any more than a partial view of the poet's career: Katherine Philips's poem is in belated praise of *Poems* and *Silex* 1650; Thomas Powell's commemorates what is probably the ur-collection of *Olor*; and N. W. and I. W. commend the present volume. The patchwork effect is also not helped by the fact that the verses by Powell and I. W. describe poems that have never appeared in print. But Vaughan, who was in the habit of constantly summarizing his "progress" near the end of each volume ("Priorie Grove," "*Ad fluvium Iscam*," and "To the Holy Bible"), provides something of a concluding vision to his career that more than compensates for the limited accounts given of the author at the beginning of *Thalia*. Several "late" poems that Vaughan wrote serve as epitaphs of a kind not to himself but to the age in which he wrote, one that has already come to appear to him in a distant and remote light, whose imaginative experiences can be reflected upon but cannot be translated into the present historical context of post-Restoration England.

"*To the Editor of the matchless* Orinda," which Hutchinson has termed "the latest poem in *Thalia*,"[6] revisits the past by way of commending the editor for "reviving" her works, and Vaughan begins by reflecting on an earlier, grander period of art that, by implication, also includes his own:

> Long since great witts have left the Stage
> Unto the *Drollers* of the age,
> And noble numbers with good sense
> Are like good works, grown an offence.
> While much of verse (worse than old story,)
> Speaks but *Jack-Pudding*, or *John-Dory*.   (p. 641, ll. 1-6)

The allusion to *Silex* is obvious in the third line, and though Vaughan was not one of the "great witts" of the stage, his parallel syntax suggests that his "noble numbers" belong to that time "Long since." Like Dryden in his more famous de-

---

[6] *Life*, p. 218.

scription of a race of giant poets living before the flood ("To Congreve"),[7] Vaughan shadows a pygmy present with a more heroic past where, once again, the Civil War serves as the watershed:

> And wit, as well as piety
> Doth thrive best in adversity;
> For since the thunder left our air
> Their *Laurels* look not half so fair. (ll. 15-18)

Orinda also belongs to that earlier age. A figure in *Olor* for all that was excellent about poetry, she is now viewed as one of the last representatives of that great age whose works "when we did a Famine fear, / Hast blest us with a fruitful year" (ll. 23-24). But within the recollective vision of the verse, Katherine Philips is more than just a point of elegant reminiscence for an aging warhorse. As someone who transforms nature through her revitalizing powers, she embodies or signifies the idea of *Thalia Rediviva* itself, a pastoral muse revived and celebrated and pictured by Vaughan at the end of the poem as hovering between myth and reality, a miracle whose luminous presence is glimpsed in its fullest potentiality in the past and perhaps unable to be altogether realized in the present:[8]

---

[7] See W. Jackson Bate, *The Burden of the Past and the English Poet* (1970; rpt. New York: W. W. Norton & Co., 1972), esp. pp. 26-27, and also I. W.'s remark to the reader that amplifies the sense of belatedness present in both "*Upon sudden news*" and "*To the Editor*": "*Howsoever the price as now quarrell'd for among the Poets themselves is no such rich bargain: 'tis only a vanishing interest in the Lees and Dreggs of Time, in the Rear of those Fathers and Worthies in the Art, who if they know anything of the heats and fury of their Successors must extreamly pity them*" (p. 616).

[8] Writing of Thomas Vaughan's depiction of Thalia in *Lumen de Lumine*, Alan Rudrum argues that "while it is obvious that Thomas Vaughan's Thalia importantly has to do with the phenomenal world, the world of appearances, it is also the case, I believe, that her function does not stop there; to suggest her function accurately we must also speak of the *potential* (that which is not yet phenomenal) and of that which is phenomenal only to a cleansed vision," *Literature and the Occult: Essays in Comparative Literature*, ed. Luanne Frank (Texas: The Univ. of Texas at Arlington, 1977), p. 238. The connection between Henry's and Thomas's attitudes toward Thalia (if Orinda is indeed given this status) is striking and suggestive; but equally significant

> But if among those sweet things, we
> A miracle like that could see
> Which nature brought but once to pass:
> A *Muse*, such as *Orinda* was,
> *Phoebus* himself won by these charms
> Would give her up into thy arms;
> And recondemn'd to kiss his *Tree*,
> Yield the young *Goddess* unto thee. (ll. 34-40)

Despite being a poem in praise of the publication of her works, the ending suggests that the key to apprehending Orinda's more than ordinary stature—her mythical being in fact—is not an editorial but an epistemological problem: if "we / A miracle like that could see," then Apollo would yield her up as a young goddess to be worshipped by others. But the passage also retains a strong sense that she will remain only a memory—"A *Muse*, such as *Orinda* was"—locked in Apollo's arms and unavailable to a less imaginative age even though her poems have now been brought out into the public. Thalia is not so much revived as remembered.

The final poem in *Thalia*, at least to Vaughan's share in it, is, like the volume itself, a memorial to a luminous past now fully mythologized and completely severed from a dismal present. "Daphnis. An Elegiac *Eclogue*" (pp. 676-80) extends the poet's suspicions about the revival of a muse such as Orinda's was into a formalized dirge lamenting the death of a single "fictional" poet who is valued not so much for his possible underlying biographical significance as for his symbolic meaning. Almost universally criticized for its "confused" attitude toward its subject, the elegy seems willfully indifferent toward the idea that Daphnis must represent a specific historical figure. Sometimes said to be one or the other of the poet's brothers—William or Thomas—or possibly even Charles I,[9] the

---

is how the overlapping serves to help define further the differences between a writer who is known essentially for his excursions into terra incognita and his twin brother, whose interests were primarily in poetry. In this instance, the occult is literally mediated by the muse.

[9] Hutchinson, *Life*, pp. 220-21 and Wilcher, " 'Daphnis: An Elegiac Eclogue' by Henry Vaughan."

identity of the dead person did not sufficiently interest Vaughan beyond scattering a few clues in the text that have served only to tantalize critics into reading the poem on a local level. But on a broader plane, the confusion or the diffusion of focus also guarantees that no single person—historical or otherwise—can fully satisfy the pastoral design of the poem. Indeed, what distinguishes Vaughan's lament from the tradition of pastoral elegy in general is how the mourning of the dead person has little effect in significantly altering either the emotions of the speakers or the mythopoeic elements of the poem. Damon and Menalcas begin in sorrow and end only a little short of despair; grief is not effectively purged in the course of the poem, nor is nature restored to a more innocent, beneficent, and fruitful state. Joy might be predicted for the next day, but the clouds mentioned at the outset of the poem have, by the conclusion, only darkened into night, leaving neither swain looking especially forward to fresh woods and pastures new. In brief, the cyclical features associated with the genre of pastoral elegy are short-circuited. Renewal, continuity, the transmission of poetic authority from the dead to the living and from one generation to the next: all the elements of repetition visible even in Vaughan's immediate source—Virgil's Fifth Eclogue—have only a vestigial significance in "Daphnis."

What remains is a residue of potent memories deprived of their nourishing powers in the present; they keep threatening a return but are invariably cut off by the narrative structure of the poem. When Damon embarks on the longest reflective passage in the elegy, one devoted to giving a splendid vision of the Usk, Vaughan is obviously as intent on mythologizing his innocent days and homeland as he is on having Damon give the conventional pastoral account of the dead poet in his youth. His native region is another Mount Acidale replete with swains, maidens, garlands, and roundelays:

Here many Garlands won at Roundel-lays
Old shepheards hung up in those happy days,
With knots and girdles, the dear spoils and dress

> Of such bright maids, as did true lovers bless.
> And many times had old *Amphion* made
> His beauteous Flock acquainted with this shade;
> A Flock, whose fleeces were as smooth and white
> As those, the wellkin shews in Moonshine night. (ll. 51-58)

Undisturbed, its innocence seems protected by the tranquility of the meditation, itself a narrative insert set apart from the more immediate world of the poem at large. But the moment is also filled with prophetic import:

> Here, when the careless world did sleep, have I
> In dark records and numbers noblie high
> The visions of our black, but brightest Bard
> From old *Amphion's* mouth full often heard;
> With all those plagues poor shepheards since have known,
> And Ridles more, which future times must own. (ll. 59-64)

Idealized, yet suffused with autobiographical possibilities, the scene identifies a triple transmission of vision from "our black, but brightest Bard"—sometimes thought to be Merlin—to "old *Amphion*"—usually interpreted as Vaughan's tutor Matthew Herbert—to the "I" in the passage, Damon, perhaps a surrogate for the poet himself. The substance of the vision, however, is only of darkness: "those plagues poor shepheards since have known." In the middle of this earthly paradise is someone singing of its destruction, and with the death of Daphnis the seeds begin to sprout. Although Damon describes how Daphnis was mourned by "undone Swains in sad songs" (l. 71), his account of a wound healed in the past has little effect on the structure of the narrative frame. Menalcas continues the rupture by adding in choric fashion, "So thrives afflicted Truth! and so the light, / When put out, gains a value from the Night" (ll. 79-80).

Daphnis does receive his due by the two interlocuters, but it is at best partial and subdued and certainly not conclusive since it appears near the middle of the poem and is followed by a lengthy dirge on "Heaven's just displeasure & our unjust ways," (l. 143). Daphnis's fall has destroyed the lines of innocence, the connections to a lost paradise, and it is not regained on an imaginative level within the structure of the poem. If any link with the past is forged, it involves, rather, the repetition and amplification of the "dark records"—the dismal prophecies—of the black but brightest bard. In contrast to being "regenerated" in the image of a youthful Daphnis, Damon and Menalcas have assumed the burden of knowledge which Merlin was reputed to have borne:[10]

> Menalcas: Ah happy *Daphnis*! who, while yet the streams
> Ran clear & warm (though but with setting beams,)
> Got through: and saw by that declining light
> His toil's and journey's end before the Night.
> (ll. 151-54)
> . . . .
> Damon: What future storms our present sins do hatch
> Some in the dark discern, and others watch;
> Though foresight makes no Hurricane prove mild;
> Fury that's long fermenting, is most wild.
> (ll. 159-62)

As the last poem in Vaughan's last volume of verse, the elegy plays hauntingly with the poet's own career, which also involved a deeper reckoning of Merlin's vision. The "hoarse bird of Night" in *Poems* developed into the more immediately menacing threats to the pastoral in *Olor*, until being absorbed in *Silex* into the voice of an underground Anglican—a "pious *Convert*" to Herbert's poetry—defending himself in a world of darkness. And yet in none of these volumes does Merlin's vision altogether dominate. Vaughan has his "*Philomel*" in *Poems*, his pastoral dreams in *Olor*, and the "still, soft call" of Christ—the shepherd of the Christian pastoral—in *Silex*; and with each volume the experience of innocence is increas-

[10] Of the many accounts of Merlin in the Renaissance, the most pertinent is probably Thomas Heywood's *The Life of Merlin Sirnamed Ambrosius* (London, 1641). The engraving on the frontispiece, moreover, shows Merlin in a pastoral setting not, of course, playing on a pipe but writing; the scene is glossed: "*Merlin* well verst in many an hidden *spell* / His Countries *Omen* did long since foretell, / Grac'd in his *Time* by sundry *Kings* he was, / And all that *he* predicted came to passe."

ingly internalized although in no instance is it completely inviolable: indeed, in the religious verse, it achieves a new level of vulnerability (and value) as the poet's own "hawkish" utterances threaten to displace the sounds of the "dove" in his poetry. But in "Daphnis. An Elegiac *Eclogue*," the voice of innocence is obliterated; it is overridden by a vision of darkness and not recovered:

> I heard last *May* (and *May* is still high Spring,)
> The pleasant *Philomel* her Vespers sing.
> The green wood glitter'd with the golden Sun
> And all the West like Silver shin'd; not one
> Black cloud, no rags, nor spots did stain
> The Welkins beauty: nothing frown'd like rain;
> But e're night came, that Scene of fine sights turn'd
> To fierce dark showrs; the Air with lightnings burn'd;
> The woods sweet Syren rudely thus opprest,
> Gave to the Storm her weak and weary Breast.
> I saw her next day on her last cold bed;
> And *Daphnis* so, just so is *Daphnis* dead!   (ll. 13-24)

Furthermore, at the end of the poem, Vaughan includes an incident that seems deliberately to play with and then foil our expectations of a recovery, of a *"thalia rediviva."* With the dirge apparently concluded on a downward note, Menalcas suddenly responds to the presence of an intervening call: "What voice from yonder Lawn tends hither? heark"; but the cry he and the reader hear only signifies loss and a shepherd's realization of having stayed too late into the evening:

> 'Tis *Thyrsis* calls, I hear *Lycanthe* bark.
> His Flocks left out so late, and weary grown
> Are to the Thickets gone, and there laid down.   (ll. 170-72)

Poetic regeneration in this collection is finally only a series of echoes and a tale of potentiality set in the past. In Vaughan's last surviving correspondence, his letter to Aubrey in 1694, the experience itself becomes material for a fable: the hawk that once "gott into his mouth & inward parts" recedes altogether into a dream and into the mouth of another poet.

Index of Vaughan's Works

POETRY

Poems (1646), xviii, 3-24, 25, 26, 30, 34, 46, 58, 76, 79, 80, 83, 99, 212, 214, 228, 233; "Amyntas *goe, thou art undone,*" 10; "A Rhapsodie," 15, 19; "A Song to *Amoret,*" 10-11; "Juvenal's Tenth Satyre Translated," 8, 19-24, 25, 58; "Les Amours," 7; "To all Ingenious Lovers of POESIE" (Preface), 7-8, 12, 23; "To Amoret gone from him," 10, 12, 13; "To Amoret, *of the difference 'twixt him, and other Lovers, and what true Love is,*" 11; "To Amoret. The Sigh," 10, 14; "To Amoret, Walking in a Starry Evening," 10; "To Amoret Weeping," 19; "To his Friend Being in Love," 10, 88n; "To my Ingenuous Friend, R. W.," 10, 15, 77, 94; "Upon the Priorie Grove, His usuall Retyrement," 17-19, 25, 201, 228

Olor Iscanus (1651), xviii, xix, 24-69, 75-76, 78-80, 83, 89, 99, 106-108, 123, 212, 214, 228, 233; "*Ad fluvium Iscam,*" 43-44, 228; "*Ad Posteros,*" 42-43; "An Elegie on the death of Mr. R. Hall," 38-40, 109, 112, 114, 226; "An Elegie on the death of Mr. R. W.," 35-38, 104, 109, 112, 114, 226; "An Epitaph upon the Lady *Elizabeth,*" 40-43, 109, 155; "*In Amicum foeneratorem,*" 48-49; "*Monsieur Gombauld,*" 7, 35-36; "The Charnel-house," 28, 30, 33-34, 48, 52, 174; "The Publisher to the Reader," 26-29; "To his fellow-Poets at *Rome,*" 60; "To his friend," 46, 50-51; "To his friends (after his many sollicitations)," 60; "To his Inconstant friend," 60-61; "To his retired friend, an Invitation to *Brecknock,*" 51-56, 80, 99; "To his Wife at *Rome,*" 60; "To my worthy friend Master T. *Lewes,*" 56-57; "To the best, most accomplish'd Couple——," 38-39, 79, 89; "To the most Excellently accomplish'd, Mrs. *K. Philips,*" 40-41; "To the River *Isca,*" 27-28, 30-32, 34, 41-42, 48, 53, 56; "Upon a Cloke lent him by Mr. *J. Ridsley,*" 45, 47-48, 62, 83; "Upon Mr. *Fletchers* Playes, published, 1647," 66-69; "Upon the *Poems* and *Playes* of the ever memorable Mr. *William Cartwright,*" 62-66

Silex Scintillans (1655), xvii-xxii, 27, 44, 62n, 70-211, 214, 233; *Silex*, Part I, 107-108, 123, 143-45, 147, 151, 155, 228; *Silex*, Part II, 85, 98, 107-108, 142-43, 145-56; "Abels blood," 168-77, 198; "Admission," 158; "Affliction," 98, 143, 219; "Anguish," 98; "Ascension-day," 98, 117, 145-46, 151, 162n, 190; "Ascension-Hymn," 85-87, 98, 148; "As time one day by me did pass," 108; "Authoris (de se) Emblema," 78; "Buriall," 191; "Childehood," 155, 188; "Christs Nativity," 91, 143, 195; "Cock-crowing," 91-92, 148-49, 191, 201; "Come, come what doe I here?" 88-

Silex Scintillans (1655) (cont.)
90; "Corruption," 99-103, 147, 191, 220; "Day of Judgement," 143, 192-94; "Death," 152; "Death. *A Dialogue*," 191-92; "Dedication," 172; "Disorder *and* frailty," 80; "Distraction," 173, 176-78; "Dressing," 143; "Easter-day," 143; "Easter Hymn," 143; Epigram to *Silex Scintillans*, 172; "Fair and yong light!" 108, 111; "H. Scriptures," 178; "*Isaacs* Marriage," 79-80, 164-65; "I walkt the other day," 83-85, 108, 110; "Jesus weeping" [I and II], 131; "Joy," 180-81; "Joy of my life!" 108; "L'Envoy," 124, 154; "Love-sick," 80; "Man," 94-97; "Midnight," 201, 216; "Misery," 98; "Mount of Olives" [II], 143-45, 216; "Palm-Sunday," 191, 201; "Peace," 165; Preface, 72-77, 82, 116-17, 149, 152, 156; "Psalm 65," 90-91, 152; "Psalm 104," 90-91; "Psalm 121," 90-91; "Quickness," 153; "Regeneration," 82-83, 85, 89-94, 117, 154, 161, 163, 178, 190, 191, 196-98, 203, 207, 216; "Religion," 104, 147, 164-65; "Resurrection and Immortality," 192; "Retirement," 107, 219; "Rules *and* Lessons," 90, 103, 118, 163-64, 182, 190; "Silence, and stealth of dayes!" 108, 110-15; "St. Mary Magdalene," 151; "Sure, there's a tye of Bodyes!" 107; "The Ass," 151; "The Brittish Church," 87-88, 132, 178, 204; "The Burial of an Infant," 77; "The Call," 106-107; "The Check," 173-76; "The Constellation," 166-68, 201, 216; "The Daughter of *Herodias*," 151; "The Dawning," 193-96, 201; "The day of Judgement," 152, 189, 199; "The Evening-watch," 196; "The Feast," 152; "The Garland," 150-51; "The Holy Communion," 143; "The Jews," 200-201; "The Lampe," 195-96; "The Match," 80, 117-21, 134, 143, 149; "The Men of War," 131-34, 163; "The Morning-watch," 98, 161, 196; "The Mutinie," 178-81; "The Night," xx, 91-92, 163, 165-67, 186-211, 216, 227; "The Palm-tree," 149-50; "The Passion,"·143; "The Proffer," 91-92, 148, 181-85; "The Resolve," 118; "The Retreate," 77, 79, 155, 161-62; "The Search," 162n; "The Showre," 217; "The Starre," 148; "The Stone," 198-99; "The Tempest," 78-79; "The Throne," 152; "The Timber," 151; "The Water-fall," 153-54; "The World," 129-30, 178, 222; "The Wreath," 80, 152; "They are all gone into the world of light!" 107-110, 148; "To the Holy Bible," 154-56, 228; "Unprofitablenes," 98; "White Sunday," 148-49, 189, 199-200, 209n

Thalia Rediviva (1678), xviii, xix, 27, 212-235; "Affliction [II]," 218-20; "Daphnis. An Elegiac *Eclogue*," 214, 223, 230-34; "Discipline," 218-19; "*In Zodiacum Marcelli Palingenii*," 224; "Looking back," 215-17; "On *Sir* Thomas Bodley's *Library*, 224; "Retirement [II]," 219-20; "The Bee" 223; "The Eagle," 224; "The Ecclipse," 215; "The King Disguis'd," 224; "*The importunate Fortune, written to Doctor* Powel *of* Cantre," 224; "The Nativity," 215; "The Recovery," 220-22; "The Request," 215; "The Shower [II]," 217-18, 220; "The World [II]," 222-23; "To Christian Religion," 214, 223; "*To his Learned Friend and Loyal Fellow-Prisoner*," 224; "To Lysimachus," 223; "To Mr. M. L. *upon his reduction of the* Psalms *into Method*," 225; "*To the Editor of the matchless* Orinda," 225; "To the *pious memorie of C. W. Esquire,*" xix, 224-27; "*Upon sudden news of the much lamented death of Judge* Trevers," 225

PROSE

Flores Solitudinis, 134-42; *Of Life and Death,* 136-37, 142; *Of Temperance and Patience,* 136-37, 142; *The Life of Holy Paulinus,* 136-42, 150, 188; *The World Contemned,* 137-38, 160-61; "To the Reader," 136, 173
Man in Darkness, 105, 111, 128-29, 186, 188, 192
Letters, xv, 234
Of the Benefit Wee may get by our Enemies, 59-60
The Mount of Olives, 122, 125-28, 143, 145, 151

General Index

Adolphus, Gustavus, 6
Alexander the Great, 20
Alighieri, Dante, 110, 155, 162, 167, 185n
Allott, Keneth, 5n
Ambrose, St. 141
Andrewes, Lancelot, 78-79, 121, 157, 159n, 163, 171n, 185
Anselm, 124
Ascham, Roger, 75-76
Aubrey, John, xv, 58, 99, 212, 223, 234
Augustine, St., 123, 141, 160, 202-203
Ausonius, 140

Bacon, Francis, 61-62, 90-91n, 94-95, 97
Bate, W. Jackson, 229n
Baxter, Richard, 118n, 131n, 133
Beaumont, Francis, 67, 68n
Beeching, H. C., xviii, 28, 81n
Bement, Peter, 213n
Bembo, Pietro, 76n
Bennett, Joan, xvin, 81n
Bernard, Richard, 138
Boethius, 214
Book of Common Prayer, 98, 117, 118n, 125-27, 146, 196
Booty, John F., 126
Bradbury, Malcolm, 9n, 46n, 77n, 146n
Browne, Thomas, 26, 192
Browne, William, 9, 79
Bunyan, John, 73, 160
Burton, Robert, 49-50, 57
Bush, Douglas, 137
Bush, Edward, 135n

Calhoun, Thomas O., xviiin, 30n, 81n
Calvin, Jean, 160n, 203
Camden, William, 124
Capp, B. S., 122n, 130-31n, 187n
Carew, Thomas, 3, 6, 8, 10, 14, 24, 90
Cartwright, William, 4, 7, 23-24, 46, 62-66, 74-75
Causabon, Isaac, 20
Chambers, A. B., 214n
Chambers, E. K., xviii, 28n, 81n
Chambers, Leland B., 129n
Chapman, A. U., 214n
Charles I, 4, 6, 23-26, 29, 65, 186-88, 230
Charles II, 131n
Chrysostom, St. John, 126, 203
Claudian, 214
Cohn, Norman, 190
Colie, Rosalie, 11n
Constantine the Great, 135-36
Cornaro, Luigi, 137
Cotton, Charles, 219
Cowley, Abraham, 43, 228
Cradock, Walter, 122-23, 125
Crashaw, Eluned, xviin

Davenant, William, 4, 46, 62
De Man, Paul, 45, 49
Dick, Oliver Lawson, 58n
Digby, Kenelm, 3
Digby, Kildare, 26-27
Digby, Venetia, 3
Dionysius the Aeropagite, 210
Dodd, A. H., 7n
Donne, John, 5, 9, 11-12, 58, 63,

INDEX

78-79, 116, 162, 171n, 183-84, 191, 210-11
Dryden, John, 228-29
Dunlap, Rhodes, 6n, 91n
Durr, R. A., xviii, 70-71, 81n, 181n, 183n, 201n
Dyce, Alexander, 8n

Eliot, T. S., 28
Elizabeth (daughter of Charles I), 41-42, 155
Ellis, Robert, 62n
Ellrodt, Robert, 85n
Erbery, William, 122n, 123, 125, 130, 132, 139, 187-88
Eucherius, Bishop of Lyons, 135-38, 150, 160-61

Fane, Mildmay, 219
Felltham, Owen, 79
Ferrar, Nicholas, 117n
Feuillerat, Albert, 73n, 172n
Ficino, Marsilio, 148
Fish, Stanley, 174n, 186n
Fletcher, J. B., 4n
Fletcher, John, 46, 62, 65, 66-69, 74-75
Fogle, French, 7n
Foxe, John, 124
Frank, Luanne, 229n
Freud, Sigmund, 49
Friedenreich, Kenneth, 52n, 53-54n, 71n
Frost, Robert, 25
Fuller, Thomas, 197-98

Gardner, Helen, 14
Garner, Ross, xviii, 190n, 197n
Gibson, Edmund, 124n
Goodman, Godfrey, 163n
Gollanz, Israel, 119n
Graham, James, Marquis of Montrose, 10
Grant, Patrick, 160n

Grierson, Sir Herbert, 12
Griffith, Alexander, 139
Grosart, Alexander B., xviii, 159-60
Guevara, Don Antonio de, 59
Guiney, Louise, 22n

Habington, William, 5, 8, 10, 14, 18, 79
Hall, Joseph, 139, 172-73n, 192
Hamlet, 49-50
Harbage, Alfred, 4n
Harding, Davis P., 60
Hartman, Geoffrey H., 29n, 32n
Harvey, Christopher, 106, 111, 116, 212
Hastings, Sir George, xxi
Hatley, Griffith, 122
Hayter, R., 131n
Hazlitt, W. Carew, 5n
Hazlitt, William, 8-9
Heath, Douglas, 62n
Heltzel, Virgil B., 3
Henrietta, Maria, 4, 6
Herbert, Edward, 5
Herbert, George, 69, 172, 174, 177, 181, 184, 194, 200, 206, 207, 211, 215, 218, 233. See also imitation, literary, under Vaughan, Henry. Works cited: *A Priest to the Temple, or The County Parson*, 116; *A Treatise of Temperance and Sobriety*, 137; *Outlandish Proverbs*, 186; *The Temple*, 44, 72, 77-78, 81-82, 85, 98, 99, 105, 111, 116, 119, 145, 186, 212. Poems: "Affliction I," 143-44; "Church-monuments," 105, 174; "Church-musick," 186-87; "Church-rents and schisms," 122, 186-87; "Conscience," 157-58; "Decay," 99-104; "Deniall," 80, 177; "Dulnesse," 78n;

Herbert, George (*cont.*)
"Easter," 201; "Easter-wings," 85; "Even-song," 196; "H. Scriptures," 98; "Lent," 107; "Life," 105-115; "Love I," 149; "Love II," 149; "Love III," 152; "Love Unknown," 150; "Man," 94-96; "Mattens," 196; "Mortification," 105; "Obedience," 117-21, 150, 157; "Peace," 84; "Prayer I," 156, 205; "The Altar," 85; "The Call," 106; "The Church Militant," 87, 125, 186-87, 189; "The Church-porch," 118, 184; "The Collar," 161, 162n, 177-78; "The Dedication," 145; "The Familie," 158; "The Glance," 144, 148; "The Jews," 200; "The Pearl," 115; "The Pilgrimage," 93; "The Search," 255; "The Temper," 78; "Time," 105; "Vertue," 85, 105
Herbert, Matthew, 122, 232
Herford, C. H., 55n, 76n
Hermeticism, 201, 204, 229n
Herrick, Robert, 15-16, 65, 106
Heywood, Thomas, 233n
Hill, Christopher, 7n, 122n, 131n, 135n, 187
Hill, G. B., 11n
Holmes, Elizabeth, xvin
Homer, 3, 8, 16
Horace, 22
Howe, P. P., 9n
Howell, James, 4
Hughes, Merritt, Y., 29n
Hutchinson, F. E., xviii, 7n, 18n, 22, 26n, 27n, 30n, 54, 122n, 129n, 135n, 136, 140, 181n, 213n, 225n, 228, 230n (biographer of Vaughan); 78, 81, 116n, 117n, 142n (editor of Herbert)

Itrat-Husain, 160n

James I, 3
Jerome, St., 123, 140-41
John of Patmos, 133-34
Johnson, Samuel, 11, 20-21, 43
Jones, Jenkins, 130n, 135n
Jones, Theophilis, 122n
Jonson, Ben, xxi, 3, 4, 9, 14-17, 22n, 23, 31, 46, 54-56, 58, 61, 69, 75-79, 157
Juvenal, 21-23, 58, 159, 162. *See also* "Juvenals Tenth Satyre Translated" and "hoarse bird of Night" under Vaughan, Henry

Kermode, Frank, xxii, 71, 191
Kernan, Alvin, 185
Keynes, Geoffrey, 192n
Knevet, Ralph, 106

Lamont, William, 130n, 131n
Lehmann, Helmut T., 203n
Lehmann, Ruth Preston, 197
Lewalski, Barbara K., xxi, 81n, 152n, 160n, 172n, 213n
Lewes, Thomas, 122
Lloyd, Howell A., 7n
Llwyd, Morgan, 122
Lord, Humphrey, 118
Lovelace, Richard, 10, 24, 55, 57
Low, Anthony, 90
Lucan, 6
Lucius, King, 124
Luke, 134
Luther, Martin, 160n, 203
Lynch, Kathleen M., 4n
Lyte, H. F., xviii, 70

Madsen, William G., 160n
Maclean, Hugh, xviin
Mahood, M. M., xvin
Marcus, Leah, 125
Margoliouth, H. M., 29n
Marilla, E. L., xviii, 15n, 17, 18n,

INDEX 241

27n, 28, 30n, 65, 66n, 68n, 71n, 88n, 114n, 127, 174, 214n, 224n
Martin, L. C., 22n, 178, 182, 213n
Martin, St., 141
Martz, Louis L., 9n, 77, 82n, 142n, 146n
Marvell, Andrew, xviii-xix, 11, 29, 38, 220
Matthias, Roland, 30n
Massinger, Philip, 22n
McCarthy, William, 18n
Medine, Peter E., 20n
Merlin, 232
Milton, John, xviii-xix, 18, 29, 36n, 44, 53, 57, 136n, 158-59, 161-62, 168
Miner, Earl, xxi, 54n, 55n, 58n, 60n, 62n, 129n
Montague, Walter, 6
Morgan, Gwenllian, 22n
Morgan, J., 224
Mosely, Humphrey, 28

Nelson, Lowry, Jr., 209n
Nicholson, Marjorie, 12
Nieremberg, Juan Eusebius, 135-37, 142, 150, 171n
Noot, Jan Van der, 45
Novarr, David, 141
Nuttall, Geoffrey, 122n, 123n

Oley, Barnabas, 125n
Ong, Walter, 178
Orgel, Stephen, 6
Orinda, see Philips, Katherine
Ovid, 58, 60-61

Palmer, David, 9n, 46-47, 63n, 76n, 146n
Parker, Samuel, 158-59
Parker, William R., 27
Parkinson, J. P., 79n, 159
Parry, John J., 5n
Partridge, Loren, 76n

Patrick, J. Max, 16n
Patterson, Annabel M., 16n, 158
Paul, St., 160, 189
Paulinus, Bishop of Nola, 135-42
Peacham, Henry, 3, 24
Pebworth, Ted-Larry, 198n
Pelikan, Jaroslav, 203n
Pettet, E. C., xvin, 71, 75, 81n, 98n, 105, 160n
Philips, Katherine, 40-41, 58, 61, 72, 225, 228-30
Phillips, Edward, 213n
Pico, Gianfrancesco, 76n
Plutarch, 59-60
Pompey, 20
Potter, George R., 116n, 162n, 210n
Powell, Thomas, 27-28, 122, 135, 224, 228
Powell, Vavasor, 122-23, 125, 127, 130, 132, 139
Pringle, William, 203n
Puritanism in Wales, 121-42, 187-90

Ramsay, G. G., 22n
Randolph, Thomas, 5, 10, 15, 24, 62n
Rees, Sir Frederick, 30n
Reeves, Marjorie, 142
Richards, Thomas, 121n, 122n, 126n
Rickey, Mary Ellen, 80, 82n
Ricks, Christopher, 85n
Riland, John, 118
Rogers, Thomas 116
Røstvig, Maren-Sofie, 43, 219
Rothstein, Eric, 214n
Rudrum, Alan, 15n, 18n, 22, 27n, 47, 114n, 146, 201-202n, 204n, 214n, 229n

Sandler, Florence, 160n
Sandys, George, 90

Sarbiewski, Casimir, 58
Schaff, Philip, 202n
Scott, Izora, 76n
Seidel, Michael, 20
Sejanus, 20, 22-23
Sherry, Beverly, 163n
Shilleto, A. R., 57n
Shirley, James, 4, 8
Sidney, Philip, 14, 73, 75, 171-72
Simmonds, James D., xvin, 14, 28, 33, 53n, 54n, 71-72, 111, 127, 129n, 142n, 163n, 181, 182n, 213n
Simpson, Evelyn, 55n, 76n, 116n, 162n, 210n
Simpson, Percy, 55n, 76n
Sinclair, John D., 185n
Singleton, Charles, 45n
Smith, A. J., 9n, 19, 24n, 129n
Smith, Sir Thomas, 7n
Somerset, Thomas, 136
Sparrow, Anthony, 147
Spedding, James, 62n, 91n
Spenser, Edmund, 9-10, 44, 223
Stapleton, Robert, 20-21
Starn, Randolph, 76n
Stein, Arnold, 82n, 105
Stevenson, Burton, 185n
Stewart, Bain Tate, 201n
Strafford, Earl of, 22-23
Suckling, John, 3-6, 10, 24
Summers, Claude, 198n
Summers, Joseph H., 82, 93n, 107n, 109n, 129, 174n, 177n

Tasso, Torquato, 6
Taylor, Jeremy, 137-38
Thomas, Patrick, 58n
Thorn-Drury, G., 5n
Townshend, Aurelian, 6, 8

Valerian, 135, 137
Valéry, Paul, 70

Vaughan, Henry:
—Anglican apologist, xviii-xxii, 87-88, 116-56, 215; concern with sanctification, 134-56; continuing feast days, 98; distaste for zeal, 103, 122, 127, 129-33, 139-40, 164-65, 167-68, 181-85; imitating Christ, 117-21, 126-56, 163-85, 205-206, 215; in captivity, 124, 126; matching Herbert, 93-94, 116-21, 144-51; monastic behavior, 134-42; providing communion, 126-27, 143-56; regenerated, 152-56; rewriting *The Book of Common Prayer*, 117-18, 125-27; self-confirmed minister, 117-25; view of the true church, 123-25, 197-98
—Bible, use of, xxi, 98, 104, 115, 128, 154-56, 178, 190, 204, 206. Books: Daniel, 192; Ecclesiastes, 188; Genesis, 169; Isaiah, 199; Job, 172-73; John, 129-30, 131-34, 146, 202; 1 Kings, 164; 2 Kings, 138-39; Luke, 131-34; Mark, 146, 195; Matthew, 195; Revelation, 74, 168, 180; Song of Songs, 206. Epistles: James, 146, 148; Peter, 193. Persons: Daniel, 126; David, 126, 138, 172; Elijah, 138-39, 141-42, 164; Elisha, 138, 141-42; Jacob, 138; Job, 172-73; Jonathan, 138; Joseph, 138; Judith, 126; Nicodemus, xx, 201-211
—birds: "hoarse bird of Night," 19, 24, 30, 159, 233; Philomel, 18, 25, 30, 159, 233
—Caroline court poetry, influence of, 3-19, 23-24
—civil war, response to, xvii-xxii, 22-24, 25, *passim*
—conversion, xv-xix, 69, 70-115

—death, attitudes toward (elegies), 33-43, 88-89, 104-115, 225-27, 230-34
—"Gent.," 7, 17, 30, 123
—imitation, literary: courtly modes of, 8-11, 62-69; of George Herbert, xv-xxii, 70-77 (general), 77-97 (formalistic), 97-115 (thematic), 116-56 (figural), 156-62 (rhetorical), 186-88 (prophetic); dangers of imitating Herbert, 111; Vaughan imitating himself, 215-23.
—literary ambition, xviii-xix, 8, 15, 18, 29-30, 42-44, 46, 50, 55, 62-69, 73-75, 117
—love poetry, 9-19, 213n
—pastoral, versions of, 16-18, 25-26, 30-43, 48, 52-53, 56, 69, 74, 164-65, 212-35
—poet, versions of the, xv-xvi, xviii, 9, 15-16, 30-31, 43-44, 46, 47, 68-69, 73, 75-76, 115-16, 123-25, 157-59, 172-73, 185, 190, 220, 223-34
—satire (irony), 8, 19-24, 46, 48-51, 57-58, 127, 129, 157-85
—Silurist, 123-25
—structure of collections: 16-20, 23-24 (*Poems*); 29-44, 58-61 (*Olor*); 107-108, 116-17, 142-56, 189-201 (*Silex*); 223-30 (*Thalia*)
—time, use of: in secular poetry, 98-99; in religious verse, 98-115, 214; temporal structure of *Silex*, 190-201; Vaughan's sense of the End, 186-211
—verse, epistle, use of, 45-69, 78, 83

—voices, conflict of, xx, 19-20, 23-24, 30-44, 45, 157-85, 215, 233
Vaughan, Thomas, 121-22, 212, 229n, 230
Vaughan, William (brother to Henry and Thomas), 230
Vendler, Helen, 93
Virgil, 6, 36, 40, 43-44, 99, 134, 135n, 220, 231

Walbeoffe, Charles, 224-27
Walker, David, 135n
Walker, John, 122n
Walley, Harold R., 26, 27n, 213n
Waller, Edmund, 9, 24
Walton, Isaac, xxi, 119
Wanley, Nathaniel, 213n
Wedgewood, C. V., 6n
Weemse, John, 184-85n
Westminster Directory for Public Worship, 117-18
Whittier, John Greenleaf, 54
Wilcher, Robert, 214n, 230n
W., I. (?Williams, John), 213, 228, 229n
W., N. (?Williams, Nathaniel), 228
Wimsatt, William K., 174
Wittreich, Joseph Anthony, Jr., 128, 214n
Wolfe, Don M., 36n, 136n
Wood, Anthony, 26, 212-13n
Woodhouse, A.S.P., 130n
Woolf, Rosemary, 105n
Wordsworth, William, 28, 153, 159n
Wotton, Henry, 63n

Young, Thomas, 36n

Zagorin, Perez, 7n, 23n

Jonathan F. S. Post is an Associate Professor at the University of California, Los Angeles. He has published articles in such journals as *Studies in English Literature*, *Philological Quarterly*, and *English Literary Renaissance*.

LIBRARY OF CONGRESS CATALOGING IN PUBLICATION DATA

Post, Jonathan F. S., 1947-
Henry Vaughan: the unfolding vision.
Includes index.
1. Vaughan, Henry, 1622-1695—Criticism and interpretation.   I. Title.
PR3744.P67   1982   821'.4   82-47609
ISBN 0-691-06527-6   AACR2

Printed by Libri Plureos GmbH in Hamburg, Germany